THE ASTROLOGICAL REVOLUTION

THE ASTROLOGICAL REVOLUTION

UNVEILING THE SCIENCE OF THE STARS
AS A SCIENCE OF REINCARNATION AND KARMA

ROBERT POWELL
&
KEVIN DANN

LINDISFARNE BOOKS
2010

2010

LINDISFARNE BOOKS
an imprint of Anthroposophic Press/SteinerBooks
610 Main St., Great Barrington, MA 01230
www.steinerbooks.org

Cover and book design: William Jens Jensen

LIBRARY OF CONGRESS CATALOGING-IN-PUBLICATION DATA

Powell, Robert, 1947–
  The astrological revolution : unveiling the science of the stars as a science of reincarnation and karma / Robert Powell and Kevin Dann.
    p. cm.
  Includes bibliographical references.
  ISBN 978-1-58420-083-3
  1. Astrology. 2. Reincarnation. 3. Karma. I. Dann, Kevin T., 1956– II. Title.

BF1711.P743 2010
133.5—dc22

2010013254

Printed in the United States of America

Contents

Chapers 1 to 4 by Robert Powell and Kevin Dann;
chapter 5 and Appendices by Robert Powell

Acknowledgments

In gratitude to the editorial board of the *Journal for Star Wisdom*—William Bento, Brian Gray, and Robert Schiappacasse—for their dedication in continuing research into the mysteries of star wisdom (Astrosophy), and also with many thanks to David Tresemer for his creation of the StarHouse in Boulder, Colorado, which has housed many star wisdom gatherings since it was constructed in 1990.

The editing was taken up by Kevin Dann, who in the process became coauthor of the book, and to whom I am deeply grateful for his beautiful crafting and enrichment of the text.

The grant also helped with the typing of the original manuscript—and here, warm thanks are extended to Dianna Marsden, who typed the first draft, which gestated for many years after that time.

My heartfelt gratitude also goes to Lacquanna Paul for her unfailing encouragement.

An immense debt of gratitude is owed to Rudolf Steiner, Elisabeth Vreede, and Willi Sucher (see bibliography) for pioneering the new star wisdom of Astrosophy.

I would also like to thank publishers Chris Bamford and Gene Gollogly of Lindisfarne Books for taking on the manuscript and enabling this book to become available, and William Jens Jensen for his meticulous work in shepherding this book into print.

There are many others who have helped in one way or another to whom my gratitude and appreciation are extended, without naming everyone explicitly.

Robert Powell
April 30, 2010
Cosmic Festival of the Resurrection

As an indication for readers of this book: the introduction and the first five chapters outline the story of the astrological revolution. The appendices describe some fundamentals of the astrological revolution, which may be read even before delving into the story of this revolution. However, it is clear to the authors that, in telling the story of something as vast and grand as the astrological revolution, here we can give only an outline of this revolution. It will be up to others to expand on what we have been able to provide in this volume.

INTRODUCTION: SETH'S PILLARS

BY KEVIN DANN

On a fine spring day in April 1914, a detective from the New York City Police Department walked into a luxury suite in the Carnegie Hall Building at 7th Avenue and 56th Street and arrested Miss Evangeline Adams for fortune-telling. The dozen or so fashionably dressed men and women waiting in the reception room may have included Enrico Caruso, Mary Pickford, or Charlie Chaplin, for these and other New York notables were among her clients. Ever since her arrival in Manhattan in March 1899, Evangeline Adams had been a crafty self-promoter who invented Boston Brahmin roots (she claimed untruthfully that she was descended from John Adams) to lend respectability to her profession of astrology. Nonetheless, astrology has failed to achieved such dignity, even though film stars, judges, presidents, and millions of ordinary people have found it helpful in understanding the puzzle of their own biographies: Caruso swore that he never crossed the Atlantic without first seeking from Miss Adams the most propitious day for sailing; Miss Adams's client J. P. Morgan is often quoted as saying "Millionaires don't use astrology; billionaires do!" (a quote invented by Evangeline Adams); half a million CBS Radio listeners eagerly sent in their birth information with a box top from Forhan toothpaste in hopes of having Evangeline Adams cast their horoscope on the air; and Judge John J. Freschi reputedly declared upon acquitting Adams (again, the only source is Adams herself) of illegal fortune-telling ("The defendant raises astrology to the dignity of an exact science.").

At nearly the same moment as Evangeline Adams was being arrested, a much younger science—Assyriology, the linguistic, historical, and archaeological study of ancient Mesopotamia and neighboring cultures—was bringing discoveries that would eventually lead to a much clearer understanding of astrology's ancient roots in the Near

East. Between 1910 and 1930, *The New York Times* regularly carried sensational reports of archaeological finds from Babylon, Nineveh, Nippur, and other ancient cities. Some of the vast number of cuneiform clay tablets that held the long-lost secrets of Babylonian star lore made their way to American museums, including the Metropolitan Museum and J. P. Morgan's private library on Madison Avenue. In 1910, Morgan gave Yale University $100,000 in US Steel stock to establish a professorship in Assyriology. Cuneiform-pondering linguists and Indiana Jones–style tablet hunters became popular figures in novels, film, and plays. The word *decipher* showed up frequently in headlines and advertising copy, and the quest to penetrate the mysteries of Babylonian culture seized the national imagination in a way unseen since Champollion's translation of the Rosetta Stone in the 1820s. Americans' enormous interest in the Near East reflected a widespread desire for affirmation of Old Testament stories in the face of the brash new religion of Darwinism. The clay tablets told epic stories of the gods—Ea, Marduk, Nabu, Inanna—of a primeval flood, and of planetary movements against the backdrop of the stars. For the fast and fleeting flapper generation, there was the reassurance of cosmic permanence in the simple triangular marks in clay.

Near the end of the first century, in his *Antiquities of the Jews,* the Roman historian Josephus wrote of how Adam, the first human being, instructed his son Seth to erect two pillars—one of brick and another of stone—to depict knowledge of the starry heavens. Adam's plan was that, even if the brick pillar would be destroyed in the Flood, the stone pillar would survive to teach humanity what was written on it. Josephus could not have known at the time just how often that brick pillar would become lost, damaged, misread, scoffed at, ignored, and condemned over the twenty centuries that followed. Like knowledge of the fairy world (which has ever and always been "going away," vanishing from human sight, while simultaneously coming into view in new forms), the knowledge held by Seth's descendants, astrology, has perished perennially in a flood of rationalism, materialism, and scientism, not to mention charlatanry, which has deluged and drowned this ancient arena of human experience. In 1914, that moment in Manhattan was just another of countless paradoxical simultaneities through the centuries during which astrology seemed always to suffer its death throes at the very moment of its rebirth.

At nearly the same moment as the tarnished brick pillar of Evangeline Adams's 7th Avenue astrology and the clay tablets from Nineveh or Nippur were so widely celebrated, the stone pillar was reappearing, though few took notice then or now. About a year before Miss Adams's arrest in Strasbourg, France, Rudolf Steiner gave the last in a series of lectures titled "The Life of the Soul Between Death and Rebirth." He delivered those lectures over seven months in nearly a dozen cities, Milan, Hanover, Vienna, Bern, Linz, Tübingen, Frankfurt, Munich, Breslau, Düsseldorf, and Strasbourg. In them was a palpable quality of "research in progress." Humorous asides and small anecdotes alternate with vast, esoteric panoramas that portray the mysterious voyage of the human soul after death, as well as the ways human acts and decisions of the previous life play into the next through records inscribed into the starry world. Given the sweeping scope of these lectures, one might easily pass over a small passage such as this:

> When individuals pass through the gate of death, they die under a certain configuration of stars. Such a configuration is significant for an individual's further life of soul, since it remains as an imprint. The endeavor to enter the same configuration at a new birth remains in one's soul to do justice once again to the forces received at the moment of death. It is an interesting point that, if one works out the configuration at death and compares it with the configuration of the later birth, one finds that it closely coincides with the configuration at the previous death.[1]

Through his remarks just before this passage, Steiner clearly indicates that this was a very recent discovery for him: "The fact...came to me in an extraordinary way during the investigations of the last few months." He refrained from stating that this discovery about the relationship between death and rebirth is "a general law." As with so much of the remarkable knowledge that he brought into the world, Steiner left a tremendous amount unsaid about his discovery, leaving open the possibility of future research to clarify and extend the findings of his own spiritual research.

For Robert Powell, this single paragraph from a 1912 lecture became a Rosetta Stone (or, in the sense of Josephus's parable, a "pillar

---

1 Steiner, *Life between Death and Rebirth*, p. 97, November 28, 1912, in Munich (translation revised).

of stone") for research into the mysteries of karma and reincarnation as revealed by a study of the stars. The scientific principles outlined here are themselves stone pillars—ones that humanity can take up with confidence at this time, no matter how many brick pillars have been lost, eroded, or corrupted over the intervening centuries since Babylonian astrologers looked up into the night sky.

CHAPTER ONE

STAR WISDOM LOST AND FOUND

When in the heights, Heaven was not named,
And the Earth beneath did not yet bear a name,
And the primeval Apsû, who begat them,
And chaos, Tiamat, the mother of them both,—
Their waters were mingled together,
And no field was formed, no marsh was to be seen;
When of the gods none had been called into being,
And none bore a name, and no destinies [were ordained];
Then were created the gods in the midst of [Heaven].
    —ENUMA ELISH, Babylonian creation myth[1]

THE PATH OF ENLIL

It is fitting that this Babylonian creation myth should begin by posit-ing a time before the naming of Heaven, since the Babylonian tem-ple astronomers were such gifted observers and namers of Heaven and its resident gods. The *tupsar Enuma Anu Enlil* (literally, "scribes of the stars Anu and Enlil") brought forth in their native Sumerian language, a rich vocabulary of the starry world. Along with the dark night hours, the vast steppes of the Syrian Desert afforded these sky-watchers long vespertinal (dawn) and crepuscular (dusk) opportuni-ties for celestial observation. Two hours before sunrise, the temple astronomers caught sight of a faint halo of light in the east. More than an hour later, the brightest of the fixed stars still burned against a backdrop of the shimmering, shifting rainbow-hued sky, until the first light of day finally caught the top of a nearby mountain, her-alded by the song of desert larks, wheatears, and swallows. A planet such as *Ishtar* (Venus) or *Nebo* (Mercury) augured good or ill for the

---

1 King, *The Seven Tablets of Creation*, p. 87.

day when rising into the Sun's aura, depending on what constellation stood behind them.

Lunar and solar eclipses; planetary conjunctions and oppositions—all manner of celestial phenomena served as signs of impending events, which could be influenced by magical ritual; hence, the skywatchers were critical negotiators of the Heaven–Earth interface. The kings, and thus their public, depended on the *tupsar Enuma Anu Enlil* to help maintain cosmic harmony between the gods and humanity. Along with divining astral omens, these same men read the future from the evanescent patterns of pungent sacrificial smoke or from the entrails of slaughtered animals. They kept meticulous track of approaching trouble, advised royal authorities on sacrificial protocol, and they often cured with incantations and exorcism. At the dying of each day, the *tupsar Enuma Anu Enlil* watched *Nergal* (Mars), *Marduk* (Jupiter), and *Ninib* (Saturn) against the fading crimson solar nimbus, and, even before the sky turned from red to blue and then black to show off the entire heavens, they knew the names of the stars about to show themselves.

Mul Shu Gi, "the Old Man" (Perseus); *Mul Mash Tab Ba Gal Gal,* "the Great Twins"; *Mul Al Lul,* "the Crab"; and *Mul Ur Gu La,* "the Lion" were constellations known to the Babylonian astronomers and belonged to "The Thirty-three Stars on the Path of Enlil" listed on the first tablet of *Mul Apin* ("The Plow Star"). *Mul* is the Sumerian–Akkadian word for "star" (and, by extension, "constellation"). The list of the Thirty-three Stars begins with Perseus, Gemini, Cancer, and Leo, and then sweeps up through Boötes to cross through the Lyre, the Swan, Cassiopeia, and back to Perseus.

In the mid-nineteenth century, British Museum archaeologists Austen Henry Layard and Hormuzd Rassam unearthed from ancient Nineveh, the capital of Assyria in northern Mesopotamia, the *Mul Apin,* two clay tablets, named from the first line of the text, describing these stars. The tablets contained just one of some 10,000 cuneiform texts collected during the seventh century B.C. by Ashurbanipal, the last great king of ancient Assyria, for the world's first known library. The *Enuma Elish* creation account, reaching back to the dawn of time, also came from the excavations in the long undisturbed mounds on the eastern bank of the river Tigris, near the modern city of Mosul. In these broken, worn clay bricks fashioned twenty-five centuries ago, there were extraordinary tales of gods and goddesses, and of stars and planets. Indeed, as in ancient Egypt, Greece, and Rome, the Babylonian gods were always associated with the stars, including the "wandering stars," or planets (Greek *planetai*). The cuneiform tablets showed clearly that the Babylonian astronomers noticed five stars that moved in relation to the background of the fixed stars.[2] They connected these five stars with the five gods belonging to the Babylonian pantheon: *Ninib, Marduk, Nergal, Nebo,* and *Ishtar.*

From Babylonian cuneiform texts, we know the characteristics of these five gods:[3] *Ninib* the god of justice; *Marduk* the lord of wisdom; *Nergal* the god of war; *Nebo* the divine scribe; and *Ishtar* the goddess of love. In addition to the five wandering stars visible to the naked eye, the movements of the Sun (*Shamash*) and Moon (*Sin*) were also observed against the background of the fixed stars (in the case of the Sun, this movement was deduced), making a total of seven planets.

CHARACTERISTICS	BABYLONIAN	GREEK	ROMAN
"god of justice"	Ninib	Chronos	Saturn
"lord of wisdom"	Marduk	Zeus	Jupiter
"god of war"	Nergal	Ares	Mars
"divine scribe"	Nebo	Hermes	Mercury
"goddess of love"	Ishtar	Aphrodite	Venus

The *Mul Apin* tablets showed that the Babylonian astronomers observed that these seven planets always move within a belt through the same groupings of fixed stars, and that there were seventeen such groupings (constellations). Twelve of those constellations make up what we know today as the *zodiac,* or "circle of animals":[4]

---

2 The term *fixed stars* was used because they believed these stars never change their position in relation to one another, therefore appearing to be fixed upon the globe of the heavens. Modern astronomy has shown that the fixed stars are subject to minute shifts in position over tens of thousands of years. But this movement is so slight that during the course of the last five thousand years there has been very little change from the patterns of the constellations as they were at the time of the Babylonians.

3 Powell, *History of the Planets.*

4 The convention in reproducing the cuneiform character translation from the

MUL APIN TEXT NAME	TRANSLATION	GREEK ZODIAC NAME
Mul Lu Hung Ga	"Hired Man"	Aries (the Ram)
Mul Gud An Na	"Bull of Heaven"	Taurus (the Bull)
Mul Mash Tab Ba Gal Gal	"Great Twins"	Gemini (the Twins)
Mul Al Lul	"Crab"	Cancer (the Crab)
Mul Ur Gu La	"Lion"	Leo (the Lion)
Mul Ab Sin	"Furrow"	Virgo (the Virgin)
Mul Zi Ba Ni Tum	"Scales of Heaven"	Libra (the Scales)
Mul Gir Tab	"Scorpion"	Scorpio (the Scorpion)
Mul Pa Bil Sag	"Grandfather"	Sagittarius (the Archer)
Mul Suhur Mashŭ	"Goat Fish"	Capricorn (the Goat)
Mul Gu La	"Great One"	Aquarius (the Water Bearer)
Mul Sim Mah	"Swallow"	Pisces (the Fishes)

The *Mul Apin* text included two other star paths: the "path of *Anu*" and the "path of *Ea*." As *Anu* was the Babylonian "God of the Sky," *Ea* was the "God of the Ocean," and *Enlil* was "Lord of the Wind," the fixed stars (forming the paths of *Enlil, Anu,* and *Ea*) were first and foremost seen by the Babylonians as the abode of divine beings.[5] It is quite normal for the modern person to assume that—as with contemporaneous Egyptian, Australian, African, Oceanic, Asian, or later Greek and Roman mythology—the identification of the Babylonian pantheon with objects in the sky is a kind of innocent but erroneous imagination. This would be the gravest of errors, for both the mythic texts and the records of the Babylonian astronomers

---

ancient Akkadian is to use uppercase letters, separated by a period. The "Bull of Heaven" (Taurus), for example, is written *MUL.GUD.AN.NA*. For ease of reading, we have dropped the period notations, and italicized the letters: *Mul Gud An Na*.

5 Babylonian mythology largely derived from the older Sumerian mythology, and was written in Akkadian, a Semitic language using the cuneiform script.

are testaments to an entirely different mode of consciousness and perception. These texts were made by individuals who possessed clairvoyance for the spiritual world. Though faded and continuing to fade among their peers at the moment when the scribes created these cuneiform tablets, the ancient clairvoyance allowed Babylonian priest-astronomers (for indeed, the inseparability of the divine deeds from the doings of the stars meant that the *tupsar Enuma Anu Enlil* were simultaneously priests and astronomers) to see far beyond the physical realm, into the invisible world of the gods. Like the Orphic Hymns, the *Enuma Elish* is a cosmogony and cosmology, detailing the sequence of events involved in the creation of the cosmos—including the star path of the zodiac and the planetary wanderers upon that path.

Looking at the table opposite, it is striking to see how the ancient Babylonians gave almost exactly the same names to the zodiacal constellations as did the Greeks. One must not assume that the Babylonian priest-astronomers imposed these patterns and their associated myths upon the heavens. Although when we look to the night sky we see only the constellational patterns that we have learned from years of seeing connect-the-dots drawings, this in no way can be considered similar to the experience of ancient Babylonians. Their clairvoyance afforded them an actual suprasensory experience of the intrinsic essence or "beings" of the stars, with all of their variegated qualities, capacities, and "physiognomies."

Some twenty-five centuries ago, the *tupsar Enuma Anu Enlil* became the world's first real astronomers, owing to the fact that their stargazing had shifted from a strictly devotional activity to one whose systematic practice allowed them to make empirical descriptions—detailing the motion of the planets and the composition of the zodiacal path traveled by those planets—that would serve as the foundation for all subsequent astronomical science. The *Mul Apin* clay tablets from Ashurbanipal's great library of the seventh century B.C. were themselves simultaneously stone and brick, in Josephus's sense, being permanent records of a vast accumulation of astronomical knowledge from many centuries earlier. Moreover, in their transition to mathematical/empirical astronomy, they represented an unfolding "forgetting" of the stars and planets as actual "gods" or *beings*.

ERECTING A PILLAR OF STONE:
ZARATAS AND THE ZODIAC "PERTAINING TO THE STARS"

Within two centuries after King Ashurbanipal collected the *Enuma Elish, Enuma Anu Enlil, Mul Apin,* as well as other cuneiform texts into his great library, the Babylonian priest-astronomers had further refined their picture of the "Paths of the Gods." In two cuneiform texts dating from 475 B.C. and excavated from Babylon, the zodiacal constellations are divided into twelve 30° signs.[6] This is the original, or *sidereal,* zodiac (sidereal means "pertaining to the stars"). The sidereal zodiac places the star Aldebaran ("Bull's eye") at the center (15°) of the constellation of Taurus, and places the star Antares ("Scorpion's heart") at the heart of the constellation of Scorpio, at 15°.

These two stars constitute the fiducial axis, the defining axis of the sidereal zodiac given by the remarkable fact that Aldebaran and Antares lie diametrically opposite one another in the zodiac and are located at the center of their respective zodiacal signs. The stellar longitudes of other zodiacal fixed stars are determined in relation to this axis. For example, the beautiful star cluster in the neck of the Bull, the Pleiades, is at 5° Taurus; the two bright stars marking the heads of the twins, Castor and Pollux, are at 25 ½° and 28 ½° Gemini; the first magnitude star Regulus, marking the heart of the Lion, is at 5° Leo; the first magnitude star Spica, marking the tip of the sheath of wheat held by the Virgin, is at 29° Virgo, and so on. A Babylonian star catalog thought to date from the fourth century B.C. lists the bright zodiacal stars in terms of the twelve signs of the sidereal zodiac.

This refinement of the zodiac into twelve equal signs might seem at first glance to be a convenient and arbitrary scheme, but the sidereal zodiac that the Babylonians codified is anything but arbitrary. The 30° divisions reflect the clairvoyant perception of the exact extent of the influence of the spiritual beings underlying the twelve constellations of the zodiac. The *tupsar Enuma Anu Enlil* learned this arrangement not in abstract, geometrical terms, but as living pictures of the cosmic beings standing behind the stars. Those pictures were originally imparted to them by their teacher Zaratas. The Persian-born Zaratas,

---

6 The reader is referred to the foundational work by Powell, *History of the Zodiac* for all references to the history of the zodiac.

Star Wisdom Lost and Found

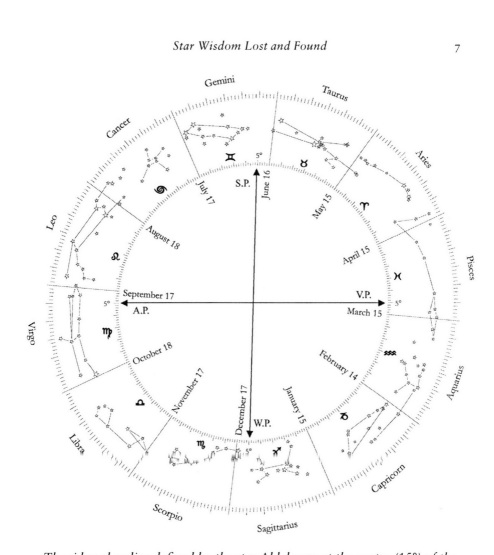

The sidereal zodiac defined by the star Aldebaran at the center (15°) of the
constellation of Taurus and by the star Antares at the center (15°)
of the constellation of Scorpio: Dates of the Sun's ingresses
into the twelve signs of the zodiac

known to the Greeks as Zoroaster, was a relative of King Cyrus the
Great (sixth century B.C.) and came to Babylon in the wake of Cyrus's
conquest of the city in 539 B.C.[7] He was soon acknowledged as a great

---

7 Zarathustra, who lived about 6000 B.C., is the name for the original founder
of the Ancient Persian culture. Zoroaster is the name for the reincarnated
Zarathustra during the sixth century B.C., when he was related to the Persian
king Cyrus the Great. Zoroaster traveled to Babylon following Cyrus's conquest
of Babylon, where he was recognized as a great initiate and introduced the first
definition of the zodiac. Zaratas is the name by which he was known to the
Babylonian priesthood.

teacher by the Babylonian priesthood. His fame was such that Pythagoras traveled to Babylon to receive initiation from him.[8]

Initiated by the sublime Being of the Sun, Ahura Mazda, so that his clairvoyance extended beyond the Sun to the mighty beings of the zodiac, Zaratas spoke of four "royal stars": *Aldeberan,* the Bull's Eye, the central star of *Mul Gud An Na,* the "Bull of Heaven"; *Regulus,* the Lion's Heart, shining from *Mul Ur Gu La,* the Lion; *Antares,* the glowing red ember of *Mul Gir Tab's* (Scorpio's) heart; and *Fomalhaut,* beneath the stream of water spilling from the urn of *Mul Gu La,* "The Great One" (Aquarius). To his clairvoyant perception, raised from the shifting seasonal zodiacal patterns as seen from the Earth, the four royal stars and their enveloping constellations marked for Zaratas the cosmic directions of space. Aldeberan he knew as the "watcher in the East"; Antares the "watcher in the West"; Regulus, the "watcher in the North"; and Fomalhaut was the "watcher in the South." Thus, Taurus—Scorpio marked the East–West (fiducial) axis, while Leo–Aquarius marked the North–South. Each of these Holy Beings was flanked on either side by other majestic spiritual beings, embodied in the zodiacal images of the Crab, the Twins, and so on. [9]

Zaratas's clairvoyance allowed him a panoramic vision of Time as well as Space, and he saw the imminent arrival of a period when humanity would no longer see these Holy Beings of the cosmos, nor even accept that such Beings existed. He understood that in this approaching period of spiritual darkness, humanity would need a science of the cosmos that would in veiled form express the cosmic mysteries, since the spiritual reality standing behind them would be lost. The mathematical exactitude that emerges from the astronomical texts of this period of ancient Babylon shows that Zaratas succeeded in this, the heart of his task as a teacher of the Babylonian *tupsar Enuma Anu Enlil.*

From the sacred Zoroastrian texts, particularly the *Zend Avesta,* one perceives some sense of the vastness of Zaratas's mission, which encompassed every sphere of human social, civic, and spiritual life as well as the teaching of astronomy and astrology. But the stars are

---

8 In his *Life of Pythagoras,* Porphyry says, "In Babylon he [Pythagoras] associated with the other Chaldeans, especially attaching himself to Zaratus…, by whom he was purified from the pollutions of his past life." (Guthrie, *The Pythagorean Sourcebook and Library,* p. 125).

9 Powell, *Christian Hermetic Astrology,* pp. 15–24.

never far from view. In the second part of the *Zend Avesta* there is an extraordinary collection of prayers to the Zoroastrian gods, including a whole paean to "the bright and glorious star *Tishtrya* (Sirius)," where one reads:

> I will sacrifice unto the stars *Haptoiringa*.... We sacrifice unto *Vanant,* the star made by Mazda...[to] the bright and glorious *Satavaesa* [who] rises up from the sea.... We sacrifice unto *Tishtrya,* the bright and glorious star, who from the shining east, moves along his long winding course, along the path made by the gods, along the way appointed for him, the watery way, at the will of Ahura Mazda.[10]

That *Tishtrya* is Sirius is certain; also that *Haptoiringa,* which means "with seven marks," is the group of seven stars making up the Big Dipper in the constellation of Ursa Major, the Great Bear. The identification of *Satavaesa* with Antares and *Vanant* with Fomalhaut is less certain. In this *Sîrozah* (hymn) from the *Zend Avesta,* Zaratas speaks also of the magical actions taught to counter the doings of demons, and these are frequently linked to particular stars: "I will sacrifice unto the stars *Haptoiringa,* to oppose the *Yâtus* [sorcerers] and *Pairikas* [seductive demonesses]." Zaratas taught the Babylonian astronomer priests that *Haptoiringa* were "entrusted with the gate and passage of hell, to keep back those of the nine, and ninety, and nine hundred, and nine thousand and nine myriad (99,999) demons, and demonesses, and fairies, and sorcerers who are in opposition to the *celestial* sphere and constellations."[11] To Zaratas's clairvoyant vision, there were as many demons—headed by the arch-destroyer of good, *Angra Mainyu* (Ahriman)—as gods, and so one's astral calculations needed to be accurate.

For many centuries before Zaratas's time, the Babylonian astronomers had concerned themselves with reading omens in the sky for the benefit of royalty. Inspired by his knowledge of the future unfolding of human history, into an age of increasing individualism and materialism, Zaratas introduced an entirely new art of prophecy, one that sought to describe the destiny of every individual human being. His clairvoyance permitted him to see the descent of the soul from cosmic

---

10 *Tishtar Yasht,* ("Hymn to Tishtrya"), *Zend Avesta II* (translated by James Darmesteter, *Sacred Books of the East,* vol. XXIII (1883), pp. 92–109.

11 West, *The Book of the Mainyo-i-khard,* p. 175.

heights, down through the planetary spheres, to Earth. Zaratas could also see that the planetary configurations at birth held the secret of the soul's destiny. Through a divinely inspired suite of initiation practices, he taught the *tupsar Enuma Anu Enlil* this faculty of seeing the soul's voyage into incarnation.

Especially significant for the Babylonian priest-astronomers was the passage of the Moon around the zodiac. They regarded the Moon as the gateway for the soul on its voyage into incarnation, and they could behold the "descent of the stork" at the moment of conception, when the archetype of the physical body (clairvoyantly beheld in the image of a stork) descends from the realm of the Moon to unite with the seed of the quickened embryo. By focusing their spiritual gaze on the Moon they could gain awareness of the moment of birth of the incarnating soul.[12] With this threefold knowledge of the sidereal zodiac of twelve equal signs, the moment of conception, and the planetary configurations at birth, the *tupsar Enuma Anu Enlil* could read the "omens" for an individual's birth. Thus originated the world's first horoscopes. The oldest known horoscope—preserved on another clay tablet dug up from Babylon by British archaeologists in the middle of the nineteenth century—has been dated to April 29, 410 B.C., and is cast in terms of the geocentric planetary positions in the sidereal zodiac.[13]

Zaratas impressed upon his disciples the importance of continuing this practice, not only because of the impending period of spiritual darkness, which would see humanity lose the brick pillar of star wisdom, but because of a particular event lying on humanity's horizon. Zaratas spoke of the coming *Saoshyant,* a great king who would be conceived in the womb of a virgin, and who would be born to redeem the world: "They will take him and crucify him upon a tree, and Heaven and Earth shall sit in mourning for his sake.... He will come [again] with the armies of light, and be borne aloft on white clouds.... He shall descend from my family, for I am he and he is I: he is in me and I am in him."[14] He told his disciples to guard this secret, until the time came when they would see from the stars that he was to

---

12 Powell, *Christian Hermetic Astrology*, pp. 22–23.

13 Abraham Sachs, "Babylonian Horoscopes," *Journal of Cuneiform Studies* 6, 1952, pp. 49–65.

14 The *Evangelium Infantiae,* from the *Codex Apocryphus Novi Testamenti* edited by Ioannes Carolus Tbilo (Leipzig, 1832), vol. I, p. 71.

be reborn, and then to follow the star, and bear gifts and offer worship to him. It is evident that the original science of astrology came down through Zaratas, known to the Greeks as Zoroaster, whose name means "Radiant Star." Its purpose was that humanity might welcome his own reincarnation as the *Saoshyant,* or Messiah, and through him come to recognize the Sun Being whom he called *Ahura Mazda,* the Source of the Good. Zoroaster inaugurated the tradition of the magi as stargazers dedicated to reading the heavens for signs of the coming of the Messiah. This tradition culminated with the three magi from the East; they were bearers of astrology as a living wisdom of the stars. The living star wisdom of the magi, based on the sidereal zodiac, was a true "pillar of stone" to endure through the coming time of darkness.

THE BRICK PILLAR LOST:
THE SIDEREAL ZODIAC AND THE ASTRONOMICAL ZODIAC

By the second century A.D., when the Greek astronomer Ptolemy drew up a star catalog (based partly on that of his predecessor Hipparchus of the second century B.C.) for his great astronomical work, the *Almagest,* the ancient clairvoyance for the heavens that had been preserved by the Chaldean and Babylonian magi had totally faded. Ptolemy's star catalog—with its unequal length zodiacal constellations based on sense perception alone—formed the basis for the definition of the unequal-length zodiacal constellations in modern astronomy. Less than seven centuries after an accurate picture of the sidereal zodiac had been codified, it was lost. The script on Seth's pillar of brick had been wiped clean.

If one compares the equal-division sidereal and the unequal-division astronomical zodiacs (see figure on the following page), it is clear that it is a matter of perspective as to which division certain stars belong. On the whole, the Babylonian sidereal signs are embedded in the zodiacal constellations of the same name. Most of the constellations of unequal-length divisions in the astronomical zodiac can be derived from the Babylonian equal-division signs simply by shifting the boundaries of the signs a few degrees—with the exception of the boundary between Virgo and Libra, where the astronomical constellation of Virgo extends almost halfway into the Babylonian sign of Libra. With this exception, it can be seen that the astronomical zodiac stemming from Ptolemy's star catalog could be

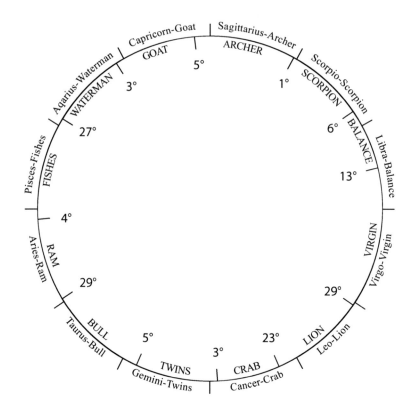

Sidereal Signs (outer) and Constellations (inner)

regarded theoretically as a modification of the division of the zodiacal belt by Babylonian astronomers into twelve 30° signs. Whether
or not we consider the prototype of the astronomical zodiac drawn
up by Ptolemy to be the Babylonian zodiac, the similarity between
the two is unmistakable.

A most striking example of Ptolemy's divergence from the ancient
clairvoyant perception is provided by the discrepancy between the
Babylonian portrayal of Virgo/Libra and that to be found in the
Almagest. The Babylonians saw Virgo and Libra as being equal
length, each 30° long. The bright star Spica is located toward the
end of the sign of Virgo at 29°. The Babylonians saw the Virgin as a
figure standing upright, holding the sheaf of wheat in her right hand,
the tip of the sheaf being marked by Spica. With her left hand she
reaches out toward the tail of the Lion. The Egyptians also portrayed

The Zodiac of Denderah (see enlargement of Virgo on page 174)

the Virgin as a standing figure holding the sheaf of wheat, as may be seen from the zodiac of Denderah at the Louvre Museum.[15]

Ptolemy's Virgin, on the other hand, is not upright but reclining. It can be said that Ptolemy thus "dethroned" the Virgin. As the Virgin represents the heavenly wisdom (Sophia), the dethroning of the Virgin signifies the loss of the divine wisdom that was accessible through the ancient clairvoyance. Moreover, Ptolemy's Virgin is not only lying down, but has her legs and feet extending halfway into the Babylonian sign of Libra. In this way Ptolemy displaced the figure of the Balance Holder from the heavens, who was seen holding the scales in his right hand,

Detail of the Balance Holder

---

15 Vetter, *Das Geburtshoroskop der Welt: Ägyptische Geburstskonstellation der Welt und die Kulturepochen*, pp. 38–39; see also Neugebauer and Parker, *Egyptian Astronomical Texts*, vol. 4, plate 35.

as depicted also in various Egyptian portrayals of the zodiac.[16] There is also a depiction of the Balance Holder in the Hebrew zodiac from the floor of the Beit Alpha synagogue in the Jordan Valley some twenty miles south of the Sea of Galilee.[17] In Christian iconography, St. Michael is the Balance Holder. With the loss of the ancient clairvoyance, not only was Divine Sophia (represented by Virgo) no longer accessible to human consciousness, but also "St. Michael" was banished from the zodiac, leaving only the Scales that he holds. This explains the peculiar situation that whereas the remaining zodiacal signs are all animal or human figures, only the Scales is a sign of something inanimate (mechanical). With the Babylonians and Egyptians the Scales was a sign to which a human figure belonged—that of "Michael" (known as Marduk to the Babylonians)—who was seen holding the Scales. In turning back to the Babylonian sidereal zodiac, the Balance Holder "Michael" is restored to his proper position in the heavens—alongside the Virgin (Divine Sophia), whom he protects.

THE SPIRITUAL REALITY UNDERLYING THE SIDEREAL ZODIAC

Though the clay tablets established the sidereal zodiac as the original and authentic zodiac from antiquity, archaeologists, linguists, historians, and other students of the ancient cultures of the Near East during the late nineteenth and early twentieth centuries almost universally discounted the possibility of the sidereal zodiac and the ancient horoscopes as empirical descriptions of reality. As much as they admired the observational skills and archival perseverance of the stellar scribes of Babylonia, modern students of the ancient world, like their contemporaries in all the historical sciences, were largely prisoners of a materialistic view that saw ancient magic, myth, and religion as the product of a primitive, pre-rational—and thus unscientific—consciousness. Museums throughout Europe and North

---

16 Cf. Neugebauer and Parker, *Egyptian Astronomical Texts*, vol. 4, plate 43 (Esna B).

17 The mosaic tile floor of the Beit Alpha synagogue (sixth century A.D.) shows the twelve zodiacal signs with their names written in Aramaic and Hebrew. The image on page 13 depicts a detail from that zodiac. It shows the sign of Libra, which depicts the Scales held by a figure, the Balance Holder. This detail conforms with Egyptian depictions of Libra, in which, however, the Balance Holder is sometimes shown in feminine form.

America competed for ownership of the enigmatic cuneiform tablets, and for primacy in deciphering them, but the scientific curiosity was inextricably linked with a naturalistic (i.e., wholly dependent on the physical senses) worldview. For the modern scientific community, astrology was the very height of pseudo-scientific quackery, the province of mystically misguided Theosophists and Spiritualists or, more commonly, of con artists and crooks.

Again, just as both pillars of ancient star wisdom seemed lost forever—this time in the haze of twentieth-century scientific materialism from one side, and opportunistic commercialism from the other—a great teacher appeared to recover and extend the ancient knowledge. Shortly after he began lecturing on esoteric subjects in 1900, the Austrian philosopher, educator, and spiritual teacher Rudolf Steiner (1861–1925) brought forth a true and complete picture of the evolution of human consciousness, one that includes a deep appreciation of both the nature of humanity's ancient clairvoyance for the starry world, and a magisterial command of how, when, and why that clairvoyance was eclipsed. He spoke of ancient peoples and their mythologies with authority imparted by his own hard-won clairvoyance, which saw that the zodiacal constellations indicate the outer aspect of spiritual beings. Steiner called those spiritual beings by their Hebrew names, "*Seraphim, Cherubim,* and *Thrones.*":

> Suppose you...wanted to point in the direction of certain Thrones, Cherubim, and Seraphim. Remember, these beings are by no means the same, like a group of twelve identical soldiers. They differ considerably from one another. Each bears its individual stamp so that, depending on where one's attention is directed, one sees quite different beings. So, to point out a particular group of Thrones, Cherubim, and Seraphim, one denotes them as a particular constellation. The constellations are like signposts. In one direction, over there, are the Thrones, Cherubim, and Seraphim known as Gemini, the Twins; over there, Leo, the Lion; and so on. They are, so to speak, guideposts that indicate the direction where particular beings may be found. So we conceive of the constellations as guideposts, or boundaries between these regions of beings. The constellations of the zodiac are more than mere signposts, but we must make

it clear that, as a first stage, when we speak of the zodiac, we are referring to spiritual beings.[18]

According to this description, the zodiacal constellations, seen as groupings of stars, present the outer, "physical aspect" of the spiritual beings called Seraphim, Cherubim, and Thrones. In this light, the word *zodiac* assumes new significance. This "animal circle" refers to the circle of *zoa,* from which the word *zodiac* is derived—a word John applied in the Book of Revelation to the "living creatures" around the throne of God.

> And round the throne, on each side of the throne, are four living creatures (*Zoa*), full of eyes in front and behind: the first living creature like a lion, the second living creature like an ox, the third living creature with the face of a man, and the fourth living creature like a flying eagle (Revelation 4:6–7)

John's vision of the living creatures is almost identical to Ezekiel's vision of the Cherubim. Ezekiel also calls the Cherubim "living creatures" (Hebrew: *hayoth,* corresponding exactly to the Greek *zoa*):

> And I looked, and behold, there were four wheels beside the Cherubim.... And every one had four faces: the first face was the face of a cherub, and the second face was the face of a man, and the third the face of a lion, and the fourth the face of an eagle. And the Cherubim mounted up. These were the living creatures that I saw. (Ezekiel 10:9, 14–15)

Elsewhere, Ezekiel refers to the living creatures in terms of "the face of a man," "the face of a lion," "the face of an ox," and "the face of an eagle" (Ezekiel 1:10). There can be no doubt that the visions of Ezekiel and John were essentially the same, and that both were referring to the same regions of the zodiac as Zaratas had seen when he imparted the teaching of the four royal stars. Rudolf Steiner, in his lectures on the spiritual hierarchies quoted from above, indicates that there are not merely four but actually twelve spiritual beings (at this point he refers to them as Cherubim, like Ezekiel) comprising the zodiac, the circle of living creatures:

---

18 Steiner, *The Spiritual Hierarchies and the Physical World*, p. 98.

You may have noticed that I have written out here only four names of the zodiac. They represent the four principal expressions of the Cherubim, but, in reality, each of these cherubic beings has, to the right and the left of it, a kind of follower or companion. Thus...we have twelve forces, or powers, in the Sun's periphery....But how are these powers belonging to the realm of the Cherubim related to the usual names of the zodiac?... One generally begins with the Ram (Aries), the Bull (Taurus), the Twins (Gemini), the Crab (Cancer), and the Lion (Leo); then comes the Virgin (Virgo) and the Scales (Libra). The Eagle has had to take the name *Scorpio* for a definite reason, due to a later transformation. Then come the two companion signs: the Archer (Sagittarius) and the Goat (Capricorn). The Human is called Waterman (Aquarius) for a particular reason we shall come to later. Finally, we have the Fishes (Pices).[19]

Here Steiner confirms the validity of the visions of John, Ezekiel, and Zaratas that the living creatures are Cherubim, the circle of whom comprise the spiritual reality underlying the twelve constellations of the zodiac. In the preceding quote, Steiner indicates that the spiritual beings identified in the direction of the twelve zodiacal constellations include not only Cherubim, but also Seraphim and Thrones.

ZODIACAL AGES AND CULTURAL EPOCHS

Given in 1909, Steiner's lectures on the spiritual hierarchies were heard by small audiences of a few hundred earnest spiritual seekers, at the same moment that millions were regularly reading newspaper articles about the sensational new deciphering of ancient Babylonian and Egyptian texts. None of the Assyriologists or Egyptologists proclaimed that their discoveries pointed to objective ancient understanding of the celestial beings behind the stars. Steiner's level of initiation enabled him—like Ezekiel, John, and Zaratas—to clairvoyantly behold the living creatures and determine their "sphere of influence" stemming from the zodiacal constellations. He recovered the stone pillar of star wisdom and offered it back to humanity.

---

19 Ibid., pp. 53–54.

Along with revealing for modern humanity the nature and activities of the holy living creatures of the zodiac, Rudolf Steiner also described a sequence of cultural ages arising as a consequence of the retrograde movement of the vernal point through the constellations of the zodiac (known as "precession of the equinoxes"). He indicated precise dates, implying that each age lasts for 2,160 years.

> We divide the post-Atlantean time into epochs of civilization, naming the first the old Indian, the second the old Persian, the third the Chaldean–Babylonian–Egyptian, the fourth the Greco–Roman, and then the fifth, in which we now live....A sixth will follow this, and so on. I have frequently shown how the fourth epoch began...about 747 B.C. and ceased...in A.D. 1413. That was the fourth; and now we are in the fifth."[20]

The time interval from 747 B.C. to A.D. 1413 is actually 2,159 years, since 747 B.C. = -746.[21] The date A.D. 1414 would indicate a period of exactly 2,160 years, one-twelfth of the "movement that manifests in the precession of the equinoxes—the movement of the point of sunrise and the spring equinox through the zodiac once in 25,920 years."[22] Since 25,920 years is the length of time taken for the vernal point (the location of the Sun at the moment of the spring equinox) to move retrograde through all twelve constellations of the zodiac, it follows that 2,160 years is the time required to retrograde through one constellation of the zodiac, since 12 x 2,160 = 25,920, assuming that the constellations are equal length (each 30° long). Steiner's dating of the cultural epochs implies that the constellations are equal in length; otherwise the cultural epochs would not uniformly last 2,160 years.

The question remains about whether the dates indicated by Steiner for the cultural epochs agree with the dates for the zodiacal ages derived by following the precession of the equinoxes in relation to the signs of the sidereal zodiac. The answer is "yes," provided we consider the difference between the zodiacal ages and the cultural

---

20 Steiner, *Mystery of the Universe*, p. 156.

21 Astronomers use a convention different from historians when writing B.C. dates. Historians write: 3 B.C., 2 B.C., 1 B.C., A.D. 1, A.D. 2, and so on, and astronomers write: -2, -1, 0, +1, +2. Thus, astronomers identify 1 B.C. as the year 0, 2 B.C. as the year -1, and so on.

22 Steiner, Ibid., p. 81.

epochs. This difference (a constant time-lag between the start of a zodiacal age and the beginning of the corresponding cultural epoch) amounts to 1,199 years (almost 1,200 years) as may be seen from the following consideration.

The star Aldebaran (the eye of the Bull) is at 15° of the sign of Taurus, making the present location of the vernal point approximately 5° Pisces.[23] The remaining 5° of Pisces to be covered in the future by the movement of the vernal point amounts to 1/6 of the sign of Pisces. Knowing that the vernal point takes 2,160 years to retrograde through one sign (30°) of the zodiac, we see that it takes 360 years to traverse 1/6 of a sign. This means that in approximately 360 years from now the vernal point will be at 0° Pisces = 30° Aquarius, and the zodiacal age of Aquarius will begin. The exact date of entry of the vernal point into Aquarius is A.D. 2375.[24] This signifies that the present Age of Pisces commenced in A.D. 215 and lasts 2,160 years until A.D. 2375. Similarly, the Age of Aries, which ended in A.D. 215, started 2,160 years earlier, in 1946 B.C. (= -1945 astronomically). The start of the Age of Aries coincided with the life of Abraham, the founder of the people of Israel, who introduced the sacrifice of the ram (Aries = Ram).

However, the start of the corresponding cultural epoch, according to Rudolf Steiner in the passage quoted, was in 747 B.C. According to Quintus Fabius, that was the year when the city of Rome was founded.[25] In Steiner's terminology, the cultural epoch corresponding to Aries, which started in 747 B.C. and lasted 2,160 years, was called the Greco–Roman epoch, the fourth cultural epoch since the Flood. The important point to note here is that the Aries cultural epoch (747 B.C.– A.D. 1414) commenced 1,199 years after the start of the zodiacal Age of Aries in 1946 B.C. It took 1,199 years for the new spiritual impulse that began in 1946 B.C., during the life of Abraham, to become a cultural impulse (the birth of Greek philosophy, the founding of Rome, and so on). The same applies to the fifth cultural epoch (European cultural age), corresponding to Pisces, since 1,199 years elapsed from the start of the Piscean Age in A.D. 215 (the birth of the prophet Mani)

---

23 Michelsen, *The American Sidereal Ephemeris, 2001–2025.*

24 Michelsen, *The American Sidereal Ephemeris,1976–2000*, p. 1 gives the date A.D. 2376.

25 Samuel, *Greek and Roman Chronology*, p. 249.

to the beginning of the fifth cultural epoch in A.D. 1414. So what does this time period of 1,199 years signify?

Over the course of his lifetime, Rudolf Steiner identified and elaborated a whole series of cosmic rhythms that play into the course of human history. Only once, however, did he note a six-hundred-year rhythm of culture, in a lecture where he referred to a period of six centuries from the Renaissance to our time:

> A certain renewal in the Renaissance.... Then again there is a period of six hundred years.... This brings us to the period in which we ourselves are living. We are living today at the beginning of a period of transition before the onset of the next 600-year wave of culture, when something entirely new is pressing in upon us.[26]

Here it is clear that 600 years, described by Steiner as a "wave of culture," is the *half-period* of the 1,199-year rhythm suggested by the time-lag between the beginning of a zodiacal age and its manifestation as a cultural period. Evidently two 600-year cultural waves elapse between the start of a zodiacal age and the start of the corresponding cultural epoch. Applied to the Piscean Age, the first cultural wave of 600 years was from 215 to 814, the year of the death of Charlemagne (Carolingian Renaissance), and the second cultural wave of 600 years was during the early Renaissance from 814 to 1414. Adding a further 600 years, we arrive at the year 2014 as the start of a new cultural wave. Though spoken in 1910, one can interpret Steiner's words "We are living today at the beginning of a period of transition before the onset of the next 600-year wave of culture," as pointing to this 2014 date. The 2014 date is suggestive in light of the highly anticipated end of the Maya calendar in December 2012.[27]

We could also look at the 600-year period measured from the Mystery of Golgotha (the crucifixion and resurrection of Jesus Christ) in A.D. 33. A.D. 633 (the year after the death of Mohammed) signified the beginning of the rise and spread of Islam. Another 600 years later, 1233 saw the rise of Scholasticism and the beginnings of mod-

---

26 Steiner, *Background to the Gospel of St. Mark*, pp. 152–153.

27 For astrological and other considerations of the 2012 date as a culmination of certain contemporary historical events, see Powell and Dann, *Christ & the Maya Calendar*.

ern science, outlined by figures such as the English philosopher Roger Bacon (ca. 1214–1294). Another 600 years, one year after the death of Goethe, 1833 denoted the end of an era in Germany. It was the year of death of the twenty-one-year-old Caspar Hauser, known as the "Child of Europe." A highly evolved being, his murder in 1833 was a sacrifice paralleling (in a lesser way) Christ's sacrifice on Golgotha.[28]

Considering the 600-year cultural waves measured from the start of a new zodiacal age, we see that two such cultural waves comprise the time interval of 1,199 years between the beginning of the new zodiacal age and that of the corresponding cultural epoch. The period of 1,199 years is the astronomical period of rotation of the "Venus pentagram" around the sidereal zodiac. During this period of 1,199 years, the spiritual influence connected with the new zodiacal age is "stepped down" and transformed into a cultural impulse. This transformation and "stepping down" of a spiritual impulse from the signs of the sidereal zodiac to become a cultural impulse is precisely the activity of the so-called Time Spirits (Greek *Archai*) connected with the sphere of Venus, the rotation of which is measured by the slow movement of the Venus pentagram backward through the signs of the sidereal zodiac. During two cultural waves of 600 years each (a total of 1,199 years), the Time Spirits work in bringing about a transformation of spiritual impulses from the zodiacal level to become active in the cultural life of humanity. This is the reason for the time-lag of 1,199 years between the start of a zodiacal age and the beginning of the corresponding cultural epoch.[29]

Against this background, when the time-lag of 1,199 years of the Venus pentagram is taken into account, there is an exact agreement between the Babylonian definition of the sidereal zodiac as twelve 30° signs (equal constellations) and Steiner's dating of the cultural epochs. In other words, the clairvoyance of the Babylonians (with regard to the extent of spiritual influence of the zodiacal constellations) agrees with Steiner's clairvoyance, which enabled him not only to describe the sequence of cultural epochs, but also to date them. This exact and

---

28 Steiner first pointed to the mystery of Caspar Hauser in a lecture in Karlsruhe, in 1911. See Peter Tradowsky, *Kaspar Hauser.*

29 See Powell, *Hermetic Astrology*, vol. 1, chapter 3, for an extensive description of the 1,199-year period of rotation of the Venus pentagram around the sidereal zodiac. The Venus pentagram is a five-pointed star traced by the conjunctions of Venus with the Sun during a period of eight years.

precise concordance of two kinds of clairvoyance, some 2,500 years apart, lends considerable support to the hypothesis that the sidereal zodiac is the authentic astrological zodiac.

RUDOLF STEINER AND THE "NEW AGE"

Rudolf Steiner was certainly not the first to link the precessional movement of the equinoxes to historical developments in human consciousness and culture. This ancient truth had been taught in the mystery schools but was lost. It emerged again in the late nineteenth century in the works of a wide range of authors. English evangelist H. Grattan Guinness (1835–1910)—whose book *The Approaching End of the Age: Viewed in the Light of History, Prophecy, and Science* ran to twelve editions between 1878 and 1896—displayed a state-of-the-art knowledge of precession, using it effectively in his reading of biblical prophecies.[30] Guinness, working largely from John Hymer's *Elements of the Theory of Astronomy* (1840), assigned a length of 25,800 years to the full precessional cycle around the zodiac. He noted how, in 12,000 years, the star Vega in the constellation Lyra would become the pole star. Guinness was no dilettante; his close observation of planetary cycles to effectively date the millennium yielded his discovery of the "Grattan Guinness Cycle," the shortest cycle that predicts lunar or solar eclipses with the same date in both the Gregorian calendar and the twelve-month lunar calendar.

While Christian millennialists anticipated an imminent end of an age, many people at the end of the nineteenth century were more excited about the "New Age" poised to commence. For many members of the Theosophical Society and other modern esoteric groups, equinoctial precession would be the cosmic mechanism that was about to precipitate a "New Age" shift in consciousness. Whatever legitimate astronomical basis it once had, the myth of the "New Age" quickly became a chameleon-like concept adapted to a wide range of apocalyptic expectations. There was a curious convergence that took place: after the formation of the Theosophical Society in 1875, the precession of the equinoxes began to be ascribed astrological significance, and many saw the Society itself (and its founder, Helena Petrovna Blavatsky) heralding the "New Age." Like so much of what

---

30 Guinness, *The Approaching End of the Age*, chapter 7.

is known today as "New Age," one can trace the origin of the modern myth to Blavatsky. In her *Secret Doctrine,* she discusses precession, but emphasized the Hindu concept of the *Kali Yuga,* whose advent, based on astronomical events, she held to be correctly dated 3102 B.C. She expected the end of Kali Yuga "about nine years hence," and declared, "We are at the very close of the cycle of 5,000 years of the present Aryan *Kaliyuga;* and between this time and 1897 there will be a large rent in the Veil of Nature, and materialistic science will receive a death blow."[31] Given its expected revolutionary impact on human history, it seemed important to know exactly *when* this New Age would begin. The turn-of-the-century millennialists, however, were largely imprecise in their calculations, just as the millennarian prophet William Miller had been half a century earlier.

Blavatsky never linked the end of Kali Yuga and the dark age of materialism to the migration of the vernal point into the sign of Aquarius; it seems this was first done in 1908 by Levi H. Dowling's *Aquarian Gospel of Jesus the Christ,* which was prefaced by an introduction describing the transfer of heavenly dominion from the Piscean Age to the Aquarian Age:

The human race is today standing upon the cusp of the Piscean–Aquarian Ages. Aquarius is an air sign and the New Age is already noted for remarkable inventions for the use of air, electricity, magnetism, etc. Men navigate the air as fish do the sea, and send their thoughts spinning around the world with the speed of lightning....

The Aquarian Age is preeminently a spiritual age, and the spiritual side of the great lessons that Jesus gave to the world may now be comprehended by multitudes of people, for the many are now coming into an advanced stage of spiritual consciousness; so with much propriety this book is called "The Aquarian (or Spiritual) Gospel of Jesus, the Christ."[32]

By the 1930s, the common expression "New Age" was joined by "The Age of Aquarius." In his *L'ère du Verseau: L'avènement de Ganimède* ("The Age of Aquarius: The Advent of Ganymede"), French occultist Paul Le Cour (1871–1954), who had an entirely dif-

31 Blavatsky, *The Secret Doctrine,* p. 612.

32 Dowling, *The Aquarian Gospel of Jesus the Christ,* p.6.

ferent vision and chronology of the new age to come, put the date for the beginning of the Age of Aquarius during the twentieth century, reflecting his expectation that a worldly "Christ the King" would appear in the year 2000.[33] Carl Jung may have done more than any other author to popularize the concept that the Aquarian Age had already begun in the twentieth century. In a 1940 letter to his friend and assistant Helton Godwin Baynes, Jung wrote, "1940 is the year when we approach the meridian of the first star in Aquarius. It is the premonitory earthquake of the New Age."[34] Jung's dating of the actual astronomical beginning of the age shifted over the years. In 1951, he stated that, because "the delimitation of the constellations is known to be somewhat arbitrary," it could be anywhere from 1997 to 2154 A.D. Again, the erroneous concept of unequal division of zodiacal constellations led to errors in calculating the advent of the next zodiacal age.[35]

Although Rudolf Steiner said much about future cultural ages and about expected changes in culture and consciousness in the approaching century, he never employed any of the "Aquarian" rhetoric of his contemporaries. By 1906, Steiner consistently referred to a zodiacal age as lasting 2,160 years, a Platonic Year as 25,920 years. That this figure was by no means the generally accepted norm at that time suggests that he arrived at it through his own spiritual-scientific research. In a remarkable 1917 lecture about the Platonic Year, Steiner links the macrocosmic rhythm of precession to two fundamental microcosmic rhythms. First is the number of breaths in a day = 25,920. Second, if one divides 25,920 by the number of days in a year (365.25) one gets 70.9, the average duration (from conception) of a human life.[36] These are further indications of the veracity of 25,920 as the actual value for

---

33 Le Cour, *L'Ére du Verseau, Avènement de Ganimède* (*Age of Aquarius: The Advent of Ganymede*), Atlantis, Paris, 1937. Le Cour's brand of apocalypticism, which had its roots in the anti-Masonic and anti-Semitic Jesuit-inspired occult group *Hiéron de Val d'Or*, is instructive for understanding the history of the so-called Priory of Sion made famous by the book *Holy Blood, Holy Grail*, and more recently, Dan Brown's novel *The DaVinci Code*.

34 Jung, *Letters, Volume I, 1906–1950*, p 285.

35 Jung, *Aion*, in *Collected Works, Volume 9, Part II*, p. 149. In *Flying Saucers*, Jung says "We are now nearing that great change which may be expected when the spring point enters Aquarius." (xii)

36 Steiner, *The Karma of Untruthfulness*, vol. 2, pp. 187ff.

the precessional rhythm, in that it is so perfectly consistent with the hermetic maxim "as above, so below."

If the New Age meant anything for Rudolf Steiner, it signaled the approaching second coming of Christ, which he called "the return of Christ in the etheric realm of the Earth," which his research at that time (1910) pinpointed would begin in 1933.[37] One of Steiner's principle tasks in preparing for this event was to teach about reincarnation and karma. As early as 1904, he taught about reincarnation as both an ancient doctrine and an eternal reality. He stressed that it was necessary for the teaching of reincarnation or repeated lives on Earth to have become lost for a time. This took place during the Age of Aries beginning in 1946 B.C. (or, more precisely, during the Greco–Roman cultural epoch [747 B.C.–A.D. 1414], corresponding to Aries), so that humanity could develop a free and independent sense of the individual self (or "I"). Although reincarnation and karma were constant themes throughout his years as an esoteric teacher, it was only at the end of his life, in a series of eighty-one lectures in 1924, that he devoted himself almost exclusively to a full exposition of this deepest of human mysteries. These lectures, entitled *Karmic Relationships* (published in eight volumes), examine the underlying laws of reincarnation and karma, and explore in detail the incarnations of an astonishing array of historical figures. Like all of Steiner's teachings, the lectures were a product of his fully conscious and exacting spiritual examination of the karmic history of these individuals. His revelations were especially stunning given the contemporary atmosphere of interest in reincarnation; the 1920s saw a continued and increased interest in "past lives" among Spiritualists and others who indiscriminately accepted the pronouncements of trance mediums. Indeed, combined with his many lectures warning of the dangers of hypnotism and other mediumistic practices, the *Karmic Relationships* series offered a veritable Ashurbanipal library of texts to shepherd modern science toward a healthy investigation of the laws of reincarnation and karma.[38]

In September 1924, just before his last public address, Steiner spoke in one of the karmic lectures about the difficulty of uniting star wisdom with reincarnation research in the modern era:

---

37 Steiner, *The Reappearance of Christ in the Etheric.* p. 16.

38 For samples of Steiner's lectures on spiritualism and mediumistic practices, see *Spiritualism, Madame Blavatsky, and Theosophy.*

We see here how great the difficulties are when one wishes to approach the wisdom of the stars rightly and righteously. Indeed the true approach to the wisdom of the stars, which we need to penetrate the facts of karma, is only possible in the light of a true insight.... It will show you once more, how through the whole reality of modern time there has come forth a certain stream of spiritual life that makes it very difficult to approach with an open mind the science of the stars, and the science, too, of karma.[39]

In his typically polite and understated way, Steiner was critiquing the rising tide of both pop astrology and modern spiritualism (and the mediumistic dimension of Theosophy). In 1924, Evangeline Adams was about to launch her career as a weekly radio personality. In Germany, the second national astrological congress had led to the formation of astrological organizations all over the nation. A year earlier (the year in which The American Astrological Society was founded), Paul Clancy had begun publishing *American Astrology* magazine, which promoted the practice of daily or weekly astrological horoscope columns. Within a decade, "Sun sign" astrological forecasts would appear in every major newspaper in Europe and North America. All of those astrologers worked with the tropical zodiac, and most were unaware of the sidereal zodiac. In the popular culture of 1924, *karma* was largely an exotic concept that remained in the hands of expatriated Hindu gurus or their Theosophical devotees, and reincarnation tales were becoming something of a fad, turning up in dime novels and film. Missing from all of the new expositions were the spiritual realities behind the original star wisdom.

When Zaratas prepared his disciples to receive his teachings, he held clairvoyant communication with the holy living creatures (Hebrew *Hayoth*; Greek *Zoa*). Twenty-five centuries later, almost exactly when the *Kali Yuga* (Dark Age) of the Hindu reckoning of human history was ending, Rudolf Steiner appeared as the teacher of a new star wisdom, and as a teacher of karma and reincarnation, and he stressed the spiritual beings of the stars—the Cherubim, Seraphim, and Thrones—as the true stewards of human destiny. Though

---

39 Steiner, *Karmic Relationships*, vol. 4, p. 111.

Kali Yuga may have ended, there were but a handful of individuals who were prepared to engage in the sort of strenuous, heart-filled cultivation of thinking for the path of spiritual science developed by Steiner. Indeed, the extent to which *Anthroposophy* (the name given by Steiner to the spiritual movement he founded) was about fostering relationships with spiritual beings, is embedded in the name itself, for Steiner taught that *Sophia* was a great spiritual being to whom he and his followers were dedicated.

HELIOCENTRIC (HERMETIC) ASTROLOGY

From antiquity down through the fifteenth century, it was generally believed that the Earth was at the center of the solar system and that the Moon, Sun, and all the planets orbited around the Earth. This Earth-centered, or *geocentric,* conception is based on the Greek word *Ge* (also *Gaea,* or *Gaia*) for the Earth and for the Earth goddess. In his *Almagest,* Ptolemy described a complex geocentric astronomical system with the Earth at the center and the Sun, Moon and planets revolving around the Earth. To account for the periodically recurring retrograde movement of the planets, Ptolemy described them as orbiting on small circles (epicycles) superimposed on larger cycles. Astonishingly, Ptolemy's geocentric astronomical system described the planetary movements to a high degree of accuracy. It therefore remained an unchallenged astronomical system throughout the Middle Ages.

Then, in 1543, the Polish astronomer Nicolaus Copernicus published his book *De revolutionibus orbium coelestium* ("On the Revolutions of the Heavenly Spheres"). He presented his view that the Sun is at the center of the solar system, and that, just as the Moon orbits around the Earth, so the Earth and all the planets orbit around the Sun. This is a *heliocentric* (Sun-centered) viewpoint, based on the Greek word *Helios* for the Sun. The German astronomer Kepler, using the astronomical observations of the Danish astronomer Tycho Brahe, refined Copernicus' heliocentric astronomical system.

It should be noted that Tycho Brahe presented his own astronomical system, which retains the heliocentric orbits of the planets around the Sun, but has the Sun itself (and the Moon) revolving around the Earth—that is, with the Sun and the Moon considered geocentrically. This heliocentric–geocentric system offers a basis for hermetic astrology.[40] Thus, *hermetic horoscopes* are based on Tycho Brahe's astronomical system. These are to be distinguished from the usual geocentric horoscopes cast by astrologers. In the hermetic horoscope, the positions of the Sun, Moon, Moon's Nodes, Ascendant, and Midheaven (plus other house cusps) are identical to those of the geocentric horoscope, but *the planetary positions are heliocentric* instead of geocentric. Unless otherwise stated, all horoscopes in this book are shown in terms of the sidereal zodiac, either in the form of geocentric horoscopes or as hermetic horoscopes with heliocentric planetary positions plus geocentric positions of the Sun, Moon, Ascendant, and so on.

In summary, there are two major differences between traditional Western-style horoscopes and those presented in this book. One difference is the use of the hermetic (heliocentric) horoscope. The second difference is the use of the sidereal zodiac in place of the tropical zodiac. Unless stated otherwise, all positions of the Sun, Moon, Moon's Nodes, planets (geocentric and heliocentric), Ascendant, Midheaven, and house cusps are given in degrees and minutes in the signs of the sidereal zodiac. Thus, all zodiacal positions mentioned in the text and in the horoscopes are in terms of the sidereal zodiac, to be distinguished from the tropical zodiac generally used in contemporary Western astrology.

THE ASTROLOGICAL REVOLUTION

Like all of the great spiritual teachers of history, Rudolf Steiner (though his wisdom touched on nearly all branches of human knowledge and activity) always knew much more than he said. Throughout his life as a teacher, he continually planted seeds for future students to take up and nurture toward new growth. In a lecture in Munich on November 26, 1912, Rudolf Steiner planted such a seed:

> When we pass through the gate of death, we die under a certain configuration of stars. This configuration is significant for one's further life of soul, because it remains there as an imprint. In one's soul, the endeavor to enter the same configuration at a new birth remains, to do justice once again to the forces received at the moment of death. It is an interesting point that, when

---

40 See Powell, *Hermetic Astrology*, vol. 1, chapter 2.

we work out the configuration at death and compare it with the configuration of our later birth, we find that it coincides strongly with the configuration at the former death.[41]

The seed was quite well hidden within the fertile earth of his other statements in this lecture. His indication about the symmetry of the starry patterns of succeeding incarnations came as an almost incidental example of how important it is that human beings draw from within what the cosmos has instilled. He immediately followed this with a shocking remark—that both Christ and Lucifer declare to humanity, "Ye shall be as Gods!" Steiner challenged both his listeners and all humanity to distinguish *which* spiritual being one should hear. Then, in a flash, he was musing about Homer's knowledge of the life beyond death as "unchangeable," before turning his attention to Michelangelo's sculptures for the Medici tombs in Florence, and how the four figures titled *Dusk, Night, Dawn,* and *Day* were sublimely accurate portraits in stone of clairvoyant images of the four levels of the human being, which he perceived clairvoyantly: the three human "bodies" (physical, etheric, astral) and the "I," or true self. He concluded with a brief story of how it was said that, when Michelangelo was alone with the *Night* figure, it arose and walked about.

With this seed statement (however unnoticed it was by his listeners), Rudolf Steiner laid the theoretical groundwork for the discovery of the astrological "laws" of reincarnation. His colleague Elisabeth Vreede (1879–1943) initially took up the task of developing a new star wisdom (*Astrosophy*) based on Steiner's indications. In her great work *Astronomy and Spiritual Science,* she elaborates on the possibility of reincarnation research, but without giving any actual examples.[42] Another of Steiner's colleagues, Günther Wachsmuth, later wrote his book *Kosmische Aspekte von Geburt und Tod* ("Cosmic Aspects of Birth and Death"), in which he presents reincarnation examples, though not very systematically.[43] Without having the Babylonian sidereal zodiac at his disposal, it was impossible for Wachsmuth to

---

41 Steiner, *Life between Death and Rebirth,* p. 97. This quotation was mentioned in the introduction. However, in view of its central importance for the astrological revolution, it is quoted again here.

42 Vreede, *Astronomy and Spiritual Science,* pp. 173–174, where she elaborates upon the foregoing quote by Rudolf Steiner.

43 Wachsmuth, *Kosmische Aspekte von Geburt und Tod,* pp. 128 ff.

make exact comparisons between death in one incarnation and birth in the next incarnation. For the same reason, Willi Sucher (1902–1985) was also hampered in his research into reincarnation. It was Elisabeth Vreede who had encouraged Sucher (with whom Robert Powell was privileged to work for several years) to take up this kind of research. Had he been equipped with the sidereal zodiac, he surely would have discovered some of the "laws" of astrological reincarnation long ago.

Although Rudolf Steiner quite clearly stated that "the zodiac was divided into twelve signs, which represent the constellations,"[44] Robert Powell's works on hermetic astrology are the first to utilize the sidereal zodiac (equal constellations/signs) rather than the astronomical zodiac (unequal constellations) used by Vreede, Wachsmuth, and Sucher. This clear reference to an equal-division sidereal zodiac ("twelve signs representing the constellations") has been ignored until now, as have the large number of other references by Steiner to the signs of the zodiac, which always (apart from a few isolated instances) referred to the equal-division signs of the sidereal zodiac. As mentioned, Steiner's dating of the cultural epochs, each 2,160 years in length, clearly implies the equal-division constellations of the sidereal zodiac. Utilization of the sidereal zodiac made possible the discovery of the astrological "laws" of reincarnation, and further research will undoubtedly discover new "laws."

In his *Hermetic Astrology*, volume 1, Robert Powell took the reincarnation examples given by Rudolf Steiner and analyzed them by comparing the birth horoscope with the death horoscope from the previous incarnation, where dates of birth and death are known. As a result of this work, the first two rules, or "laws," of astrological reincarnation were discovered.[45] The first rule of astrological reincarnation states that the angular relationship between the Sun and Saturn at death recurs (in the same way or in a metamorphosed way) at birth in the next incarnation.[46] According to Steiner, "In the human being, this relationship of Saturn to the Sun comes to expression in the "I" achieving an appropriate relationship to the astral body, and above all, in the proper incorpo-

44 Steiner, *The Spiritual Beings in the Heavenly Bodies*, p. 161.

45 "*Laws*" is written like this because it is not a matter of hard-and-fast laws, but rather "flexible" principles that do not hold in every case.

46 Powell, *Hermetic Astrology* (vol. 1, appendix III, pp. 332–356) elaborates on the first "law" of astrological reincarnation, with numerous examples.

ration of the astral body into the whole human organization."[47] There is nothing revolutionary about the first rule of astrological reincarnation. In contrast, the second rule of astrological reincarnation completely revolutionizes astrology. The second "law" states:

> The sidereal zodiacal position(s) of heliocentric Mercury and/or heliocentric Venus at birth in one incarnation tend(s) to align with the sidereal zodiacal position(s) of heliocentric Mercury and/or heliocentric Venus at death in the preceding incarnation.[48]

This second rule proves two things, of which traditional Western astrology is almost completely ignorant (with a few exceptions):

1. The sidereal zodiac—not the tropical zodiac of traditional Western astrology—is the authentic astrological zodiac. The sidereal zodiac is the original zodiac of the Babylonian, Egyptian, Greek, and Roman astrologers, and it—or a close variant—is used to the present day in Hindu astrology. This is in contrast to traditional Western astrology that utilizes the tropical astrology used by Arab astrologers, based on the tropical zodiac introduced to the West in the mid-twelfth century A.D., when Arabic astrological texts were translated into Latin. Whereas the sidereal zodiac divides the circle of zodiacal constellations into twelve equal stellar signs (equal-length constellations each 30° long), the tropical zodiac is defined to commence with the vernal point, where the Sun is located on March 21, and is thus of a calendrical nature, bearing no relationship to the zodiacal constellations.

2. The heliocentric (hermetic) horoscope is highly significant in addition to the traditional geocentric horoscope. Hindu astrology, for example, which represents a continuation of the ancient Babylonian astrology, considers only the geocentric sidereal horoscope at the moment of birth. The second "law" of astrological reincarnation points, moreover, to the fact that the heliocentric (hermetic)[49]

---

47 Steiner, *Materialism and the Task of Anthroposophy*, p. 246.

48 See Powell, *Hermetic Astrology*, vol. 1, p. 375.

49 *Hermetic* refers to an extension of the heliocentric horoscope in the sense of Tycho Brahe's astronomical system in which not only the heliocentric positions of the planets are referred to, but also the geocentric positions of the Sun, the Moon, the Moon's Node, etc., are included in the hermetic horoscope. See *Hermetic Astrology* for further details concerning the significance of the hermetic system.

horoscope of birth also needs to be taken into consideration, cast in terms of the sidereal zodiac.

These two findings of astrological reincarnation research—both implied necessarily by the second "law"—necessitate a completely new kind of astrology. At the present time, at the start of the new millennium, the two "laws" of astrological reincarnation research are virtually unknown, as are the consequences following from their discovery. Astrologers and astrologically interested people in the West thus continue to live in a belief system, which, in part, has no basis in reality. The only way out of this is to undertake a *complete reformation* of astrology, based on the "laws" of astrological reincarnation discovered so far; more will undoubtedly be discovered in the future. This book is intended to help facilitate the discovery of further "laws" and thus to further the astrological revolution leading to the reformation of astrology.

CHAPTER TWO

FROM LIFE TO LIFE
ASTROLOGICAL REINCARNATION RESEARCH

The Sun is its father, the Moon its mother,
The wind hath carried it in its belly, the Earth its nurse.
The father of all perfection in ye whole world is here.
> —"Emerald Table" of the *Corpus hermeticum,*
> (translated by Sir Isaac Newton, ca. 1680)

THE DESCENT OF THE STORK

Shortly before midnight—under a nearly full Moon on the tail of the Lion, which was opposite the Sun in the middle of Aquarius—on February 25, 1861, in the tiny Austro-Hungarian village of Kraljevec, attended by a midwife, Franziska Steiner gave birth to her first child. Two days later, on February 27, the baby boy was taken a couple of miles to the St. Michael Church in the neighboring village of Draskovec to be baptized. Perhaps Frau Steiner and her husband Johannes—a telegraph operator at the small, remote Kraljevec railroad station on the Puszta plain near today's border between Croatia and Hungary—along with giving thanks to St. Michael for their son's recovery (he had been bleeding at birth), also gave thanks to *Boldogasszony,* the "blessed lady" of Hungarian folk legend who helps women during childbirth. It is very likely that around the time of conception of their son Rudolf they had spoken of the "arrival of the stork"—referring to the widespread folk notion that the stork "brings" children to their parents. Such beliefs about the stork help to make sense of the mystery of birth and have their origins in an even deeper mystery—the mystery of conception.

In earlier times (for example, in ancient Egypt), there existed a subtle differentiation between two different conceptions: physical conception and conception of the *ka.* Translating the subtle knowledge of the ancient Egyptians into modern terms, we can affirm that

physical conception consists of the sperm fertilizing the egg, which is
then embedded in the wall of the womb. On the other hand, what was
the conception of the ka? The *ka* was perceived not only as the source
of a person's vital force, corresponding approximately to the Chinese
chi, the Hindu *prana,* and the alchemical *ether,* but also as an actual
"body" attached to the human being. In the language of alchemical
tradition, conception of the *ka* would be called "etheric conception,"
or manifestation of the etheric body (*ka*), thought of as a subtle body
of life energy, which surrounds and interpenetrates the physical body.
Clearly, the moment of the physical body's origin is physical conception. Similarly, the moment of origin of the *ka,* or etheric body, is
the etheric conception, which for the ancient Egyptians was identical
with *the descent of the stork.*

Ancient Egyptians, as we shall see, even had a cosmic rule that
specifies when the etheric conception takes place, a rule related to
the Moon, thus indicating that, whereas physical conception is an
earthly event, the event of etheric conception belongs to the Moon
sphere, thought of as the cosmic realm bounded by the orbit of the
Moon. Modern scientific knowledge is not accustomed to thinking of
the preexistence (prior to conception and birth) of the soul, but this
was almost universally accepted in antiquity, where the soul was said
to exist in cosmic realms—in the so-called planetary spheres—prior
to coming into earthly incarnation.

According to Professor B. L. van der Waerden, in his excellent
survey of the origins of horoscopic astrology, "The soul comes from
the heavens, where it partook of the circulation of the stars. It unites
itself with a body and forms with it a living being. This explains how
human character comes to be determined by the heavens."[1] This
notion underlying horoscopic astrology can be traced back to the
Babylonians and stems from the teachings of Zaratas:

> The notion that the soul, descending from Heaven, takes on
> the characteristics of the planetary spheres through which
> it passes, before it enters into corporeal existence, and that
> after death it makes its journey through the heavens in reverse
> direction and with opposite effect—this derives from the same
> religious circles as those in which the doctrine of the voyage

---

1 Van der Waerden, *Science Awakening,* vol. II, p. 147.

of the soul through the spheres had developed: the later Babylonian astral theology.[2]

According to the ancient Babylonian tradition of horoscopic astrology inaugurated by Zaratas, the Moon sphere was the last stage of the descent of the soul, the region where the incarnating human being dwells at the moment of conception, having descended there from the fixed-star realm through the seven planetary spheres. It is interesting to consider this tradition insofar as it helps us to understand the mystery of conception and, indeed, the whole cosmological background of astrology, which originated with the Babylonians. According to the teaching of this tradition, either simultaneously with or shortly after the occurrence of the physical conception, the soul released something known as a *spirit seed,* which then descended from above. The moment when the spirit seed descends from the Moon sphere to unite with the fertilized egg is the image that was clairvoyantly perceived in ancient times as the "descent of the stork"—frequently depicted in Egyptian hieroglyphs.

The modern folk belief about the stork bringing the child reveals a dim memory of the ancient clairvoyant image of the "spirit seed"— the spiritual archetype of the physical body that is built up in the highest cosmic realm, the zodiacal sphere, prior to the soul's descent through the seven planetary spheres. Approaching the end of its descent into incarnation, with the inspiration of the soul from its cosmic vantage point in the Moon sphere, etheric conception occurs close to the time of the physical conception. Modern astrological research into the Egypian cosmic rule for specifying the moment of etheric conception shows that it usually takes place shortly after fertilization. For the Egyptians, the appropriate cosmic moment of conception was specified by a principle known as the *hermetic rule.* Although ascribed to the great teacher of the ancient Egyptians, Hermes Trismegistus, the hermetic rule was known also to the Babylonians, as there are examples of Babylonian horoscopes in which the horoscope of conception is presented alongside the horoscope of birth. The conception horoscope belonged very much to the original astrology of the Egyptians and Babylonians, as an expression of the mystery of the soul's descent into incarnation.

2 Lewy, *Chaldean Oracles and Theurgy,* p. 146.

THE HERMETIC RULE

The hermetic rule or rule of Hermes is an ancient astrological law for determining the horoscope of conception retrogressively from the day and hour of birth. It stems from the ancient hermetic astrological corpus that was a sort of "bible" for Greek and Egyptian astrologers in the early centuries of their practice.[3]

Relating the moment of conception to the moment of birth, the hermetic rule holds the key, astrologically, to building up the physical body in the womb during the embryonic period. It states:

> *The zodiacal location of the Moon at the moment of conception is in line with the Ascendant–Descendant axis at the moment of birth.*

To grasp the astrological significance of the moment of conception, we shall take a look behind the scenes at events leading up to conception. This entails a leap of consciousness to grasp the esoteric reality underlying the incarnation of the human being that, of course,

---

3 Gundel, *Astrologumena*, p. 147. This corpus consisted of Greek astrological writings composed in Hellenistic Egypt, primarily in Alexandria, during the first two centuries B.C. Fragments of these writings were preserved and transmitted to later Greek astrologers. Common to the writings of the hermetic astrological corpus is that they are invariably attributed to the "ancient Egyptians," including Hermes and also Nechepso and Petosiris among these venerable founding fathers of astrology. The fragments attributed to Nechepso and Petosiris were written in the form of instructions from the priest Petosiris to the king Nechepso and contain references to the hermetic rule (see Powell, *Hermetic Astrology*, vol. 1, appendix 1 for an English translation). Why is the astrological rule for calculating the horoscope of conception called the *hermetic rule* and not the *rule of Petosiris*, the named authority for this rule in each of the fragments stating this ancient astrological tenet? Apparently, Nechepso and Petosiris were regarded simply as mediators of the teachings of Hermes. Thus, Hermes was recognized as the originator of this astrological rule, which then was entrusted to the "divine men" Nechepso and Petosiris. For example, Firmicus Maternus (fourth century A.D.) in his great work on astrology (the eight books of the mathesis) speaks of "most powerful Hermes" entrusting his secret to these "divine men." Similarly, a papyrus of A.D. 138 states that Nechepso and Petosiris "established" their teachings upon Hermes. Nechepso and Petosiris composed their astrological works in Egypt during the second century B.C., and fragments of these works— transmitted to later Greek astrologers—were collected by Ernst Riess. Rudolf Steiner's collaborator Elisabeth Vreede translated the hermetic rule from Greek into German. She encouraged Willi Sucher to apply this rule in his astrological research, and the application of the hermetic rule has become fundamental in hermetic astrology to finding the horoscope of conception.

was known to the Egyptians and Babylonians. The Egyptians, from whom the hermetic rule derives, had a highly developed esoteric cosmology in which subtle aspects of the human being were cognized beyond the level of the physical body. The Ascendant–Descendant axis is the position of orientation taken up by the human being in the middle of the period between earthly incarnations, while in the zodiacal sphere of fixed stars, during the formation of the "spirit seed," the spiritual archetype of the physical body. This archetype, or spirit seed, is formed by drawing forces from the twelve constellations—from Aries for the head, from Taurus for the throat and larynx, and so on, all the way down to the feet, the forces of which are drawn from the constellation of Pisces.

Then follows the descent of the human being from the zodiacal sphere through the seven planetary spheres, along with the spirit seed, diminishing in size from sphere to sphere from its initial expansion in the zodiacal realm of fixed stars. During this descent through the planetary spheres, a "vehicle of consciousness" for the individuality is built up. The Egyptians called this the *ba,* often depicted as a human-headed falcon. In the alchemical tradition, it is called the *astral body*. As the name indicates (*astral* = "of the stars"), this "body" is built up from the planetary spheres, the planets being considered as "moving stars" (Greek, *planetai*). Just as the spirit seed is formed in the zodiacal sphere as the archetype of the physical body from the circle of the twelve sidereal signs of the zodiac, so—in light of the Egyptian and Babylonian traditions—the astral body is shaped as a vehicle of consciousness appropriate for the incarnating individual from the seven planetary spheres in the descent through the planetary spheres.

From this brief survey of the ancient tradition, it is clear that the spirit seed and the astral body are two primary astrological realities or aspects of the human being. Both exist as spiritual archetypes, which become individualized in the process of incarnation. What individualizes the spirit seed is the choice of Ascendant, which then acts as a focal point for building up the spiritual archetype of the physical body according to the zodiacal signs. What individualizes the astral body is the choice of planetary positions for the horoscope at birth, by means of which a suitable vehicle is formed for the individuality to bring its talents and faculties to expression.

Here the composition of this vehicle (astral body) becomes differentiated by way of the background zodiacal influence of the Sun, Moon, and five planets.

During the process of incarnation, the spirit seed and the astral body work into the formation of the physical body and the vehicle of consciousness of the individuality. The whole descent into incarnation is made with a view to arriving on the Earth at the cosmic moment when the planetary configuration (hermetic and geocentric) of the chosen birth chart becomes actualized. The moment of birth is thus the goal of the incarnating human being. Essential to arriving at this goal is the moment of conception, occurring (on average) some nine months prior to the moment of birth.

Given the choice of zodiacal location of the Sun at the moment of birth, the period of embryonic development determines more or less when the moment of conception should take place. In the course of nine months the Sun, on its apparent path around the zodiac, moves through three-quarters of the zodiacal circle—that is, through nine of the twelve zodiacal signs. Thus, during an average gestation period of nine months, the zodiacal location of the Sun at the moment of birth is nine signs advanced from its position in the zodiac at the moment of conception. Once the Sun's position at birth is chosen, its approximate zodiacal location at the conception is specified, the element of variation being dependent on whether the embryonic period turns out to be longer or shorter than nine months.

The hermetic rule specifies the moment of conception more exactly. Going back from the moment of birth to the beginning of the embryonic period of development, the Moon's location in the zodiac at the moment of conception is the same either as that of the Ascendant chosen for the moment of birth, or as that of its opposite, the Descendant. Thus, given the choice of Ascendant for the moment of birth, chosen already long in advance in the zodiacal sphere of fixed stars, the zodiacal location of the Moon at conception is also specified in advance to be one of two possibilities. As we shall see in the next example of an application of the hermetic rule, karmic considerations can also play into the predetermination of the planetary configuration at the moment of conception, just as they play a role in the choice of planetary configuration at the moment of birth.

APPLICATION OF THE HERMETIC RULE

Because Rudolf Steiner always celebrated his birthday on February 27 (the date of his baptism), few people knew that his birthday was actually February 25.[4] Given that his baptism on February 27 was recorded in the church baptismal register, and given that his birth took place at about 11:15 or 11:30 p.m., clearly it is impossible that he was born on February 27. Moreover, there is a text in Steiner's handwriting that states, "My birth took place on February 25, 1861. I was baptized two days later."[5] Taking the stated time and date of his birth as 11:15 p.m. on February 25, 1861 at Kraljevec, the zodiacal longitude of the Ascendant and the Moon are computed to be 17° 25' Libra and 24° 43' Leo, respectively. Applying the hermetic rule, this means that the Moon's zodiacal longitude at etheric conception must have been about 17° or 18° Aries or Libra, with an Ascendant of 24° 43' Leo or Aquarius. Returning nine calendar months from February 25, 1861 leads back to May 25, 1860, and referring to an ephemeris for this time it is evident that the Moon was at about 18° Libra around midday on June 1, 1860. At first sight, this seems to be a possible date for the etheric conception as calculated by the hermetic rule, bearing in mind that his parents were married May 16, 1860. In fact, at 12:12 p.m. June 1, 1860, the Ascendant at Kraljevec was 24° 48' Leo and the Moon was at 19° 48' Libra in the sidereal zodiac.

Applying the hermetic rule, this fits well with the computed birth data, and could have been the moment of etheric conception. If indeed

---

4 A letter dated February 25, 1921, from Eugenie von Bredow, one of Rudolf Steiner's pupils in the Esoteric School, shows that she knew this: "My revered Master: Today, on the day that is actually the day of birth of your Individuality in this incarnation (while hitherto we always held it to be February 27), I would like to express to you in true commemoration my warmest good wishes for your well-being." The time of Rudolf Steiner's birth (11:15 p.m.) was communicated to the theosophical astrologer Alan Leo by Steiner himself. Leo utilized this time and the date February 27, 1861, generally acknowledged as Steiner's birthday, to cast a horoscope. We do not know whether Steiner communicated this time as being exact or stated it as "less than an hour before midnight" (if the latter, clearly Leo interpreted it to be 11:15 p.m. local time). In the original horoscope cast in 1909 by Alan Leo, the incorrect date of February 27 was reprinted repeatedly until 1980, when the Dutch astrologer Jan Kampherbeek published a correct horoscope, cast for February 25, 1861 at 11:15 p.m.

5 *Beiträge zu Rudolf Steiner Gesamtausgabe*, vol. 49/50 (Dornach, Switzerland: Rudolf Steiner Verlag, Easter, 1975), p. 6.

it was, then the birth time has to be corrected from 11:15 p.m., to 11:25 p.m., to yield for this moment (considered as the planned moment of birth) an Ascendant at 19° 34′ Libra and the Moon's position at 24° 48′ Leo in the sidereal zodiac, exactly fitting the hermetic rule. Nonetheless, how can we be certain that the correct date has been found, given the open-ended nature of the hermetic rule, by which several alternative dates of etheric conception are possible? In Steiner's case, the Moon was at 18° Aries two weeks earlier on May 19, and was again at 18° Aries June 15, 1860, two weeks after June 1.

There are several viewpoints to be considered. First, it can happen that there is some indication of the approximate length of the embryonic period. It is rare that parents know the exact date of the physical conception; but if it is known, the etheric conception as determined by the hermetic rule must lie close to it in time. Sometimes there is an approximate indication, such as "the child was born one week premature." Such indications, when stemming from medical sources, usually reckon with a pregnancy of about 270 days, which means (if one week premature) an embryonic period of approximately 263 days. Here again, the hermetic rule is given an approximate date around which the etheric conception must have taken place, in which case it is no longer a completely open-ended rule.

Second, failing any indication whatsoever as to the length of the embryonic period, there is the argument of probability—approximately 270 days being the mean duration of a human pregnancy. In the example under consideration, the interval from June 1 to February 25 amounts to 269 days, which is more probable than an interval of 255 days leading back to the date June 15 as a possible date of etheric conception. Likewise, 269 days is more probable than an interval of 283 days leading back to a possible date of etheric conception on May 19. Therefore, the intervals of 255 days and 283 days yield the two next most probable dates of etheric conception after the most probable date of June 1, given by the hermetic rule (in this particular example) as dates when the Moon was at 18° Aries in the sidereal zodiac. The probability diminishes still further for an interval of 242 days (27 days less than 269) or 296 days (27 days more than 269), where the Moon was again at 18° Libra in the sidereal zodiac as it was on June 1, 269 days before the birth date, since the Moon makes an orbit of the sidereal zodiac in 27.32 days. According to the argument

Comparison Chart

Outer - Geocentric	Inner - Geocentric
Death of Rudolf Steiner	Birth of Rudolf Steiner
At Dornach/Switzerland, Latitude 47N29', Longitude 7E37'	At Kraljavec/Yugoslavia, Latitude 46N22', Longitude 16E39'
Date: Monday, 30/MAR/1925, Gregorian	Date: Monday, 25/FEB/1861, Gregorian
Time: 9:45, Time Zone CET	Time: 23:25, Local Time
Sidereal Time 21:44:22, Vernal Point 6 ♓18'13"	Sidereal Time 9:47:41, Vernal Point 7 ♓11'52"

House System: Placidus, Zodiac: Sidereal SVP
Aspect set: Conjunction/Square/Opposition

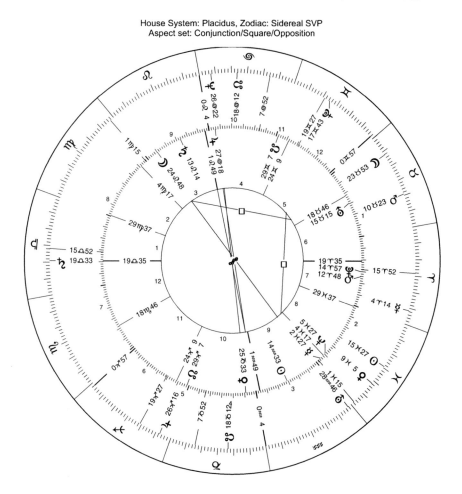

of probability then, June 1, 1860, was the most probable date for etheric conception in Rudolf Steiner's incarnation.

Probability is not the only consideration, however; premature and overdue births do occur. If other indications are not present, then the third consideration—in order to decide between several possible dates of etheric conception—is the astrological validity of the planetary configuration at the moment of etheric conception. Thus, the several possible planetary configurations at etheric conception

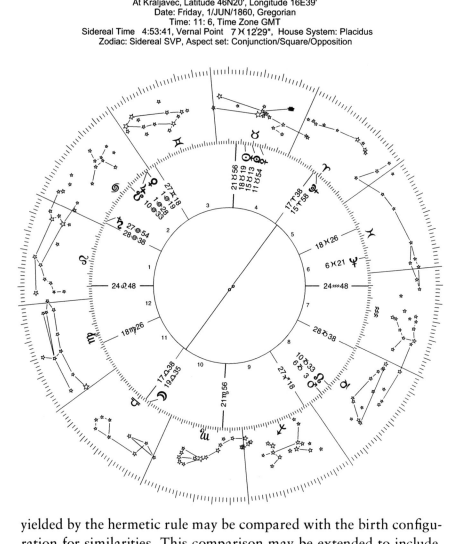

Conception of Rudolf Steiner (V. ^) - Geocentric
At Kraljavec, Latitude 46N20', Longitude 16E39'
Date: Friday, 1/JUN/1860, Gregorian
Time: 11: 6, Time Zone GMT
Sidereal Time 4:53:41, Vernal Point 7)(12'29", House System: Placidus
Zodiac: Sidereal SVP, Aspect set: Conjunction/Square/Opposition

yielded by the hermetic rule may be compared with the birth configuration for similarities. This comparison may be extended to include the death configuration in the case of the conception chart of a historical personality (assuming the date of death is known).

Finally, if the previous incarnation is known through karmic research, then just as the birth chart can be compared with the hermetic and geocentric birth/death charts of the previous incarnation, likewise the conception chart may be compared with them for similar aspects or planetary alignments in the sidereal zodiac.

As an example of these considerations, let us look at the conception chart (epoch) of Rudolf Steiner, computed for June 1, 1860, from the perspective of its astrological validity (see conception horoscope opposite). The word *epoch* denotes the horoscope for the moment of etheric conception. Most remarkable in the conception chart computed for June 1, 1860, is *the exact geocentric conjunction of Venus and Jupiter.* This striking relationship between Venus and Jupiter is taken up again in Steiner's geocentric birth chart, in which these two planets are more or less in exact opposition (see page 41, the geocentric birth horoscope, inner circle). This lends support to the astrological validity of the conception chart computed for June 1, 1860.

Moreover, if the conception chart computed for June 1, 1860, is correct, then the Ascendant at Rudolf Steiner's birth has to be corrected from 17° 25′ Libra (computed for the stated birth time of 11:15 p.m.) to 19° 35′ Libra (computed as the birth time of 11:25 p.m. according to the hermetic rule). Now, the geocentric sidereal longitude of Saturn at Rudolf Steiner's death was 19° 33′ Libra, so Saturn was exactly transiting the degree of the zodiac computed to be the Ascendant according to the hermetic rule. This lends considerable weight to the astrological validity of the Ascendant of 19° 35′ Libra, which is the authentic Ascendant according to the hermetic rule if June 1, 1860, was the date of conception. This confirmation of a birth time of 11:25 p.m. with an Ascendant of 19° 35′ Libra is based on the concept of a transit, i.e., that at the moment of Rudolf Steiner's death there was an exact transit of Saturn over the position of the Ascendant at his birth (see geocentric comparison death/birth horoscope on page 41).

The Horoscope of Conception
in the Light of Karmic Considerations

The spiritual science inaugurated by Rudolf Steiner and presented to the world was developed systematically for more than twenty years. It was only toward the end of this time, in 1924 (when a high degree of trust and confidence had been established in Steiner's work) that he gave the lecture series *Karmic Relationships.* The right foundation and atmosphere had been created to enable him to present the findings of his research on reincarnation and karma.

In the last of his first suite of *Karmic Relationships* lectures, Steiner stated that he chose well-known individuals to allow for proof and confirmation of his statements. He added that listeners had often come to him to ask: Where are the great initiates today, given that they existed in the past, and that they, too, must repeatedly reincarnate? Steiner spoke of how modern educational methods made it nearly impossible for the initiates of the past to incarnate "directly." As an example, he spoke of the nineteenth-century Italian patriot Giuseppe Garibaldi, whom he described as having previously been an initiate in the ninth century of the Hibernian Mysteries and led a colony from Ireland to Alsace.

In speaking of this, Steiner made a small, incidental comment about himself, which he rarely did. He noted how his own education benefited from the fact that he did not learn to write properly until he was twelve years old.[6] One imagines that the listeners at this and perhaps all of the eighty-one *Karmic Relationships* lectures of 1924 frequently went away wondering among themselves who Rudolf Steiner had been in his previous incarnation. Steiner was extraordinarily circumspect when it came to speaking of individual karmic histories; he almost never spoke of living individuals, and he certainly did not communicate publicly his own past incarnations. However, by the time of his death in 1925, it was widely accepted among anthroposophists that Steiner had been St. Thomas Aquinas, the foremost Catholic philosopher of the Middle Ages. In 1976, a privately printed book provided documentation of this,[7] and using the first two "laws" of reincarnation, it is possible to verify this statement.

The first "law" of reincarnation states that the angular relationship between the Sun and Saturn at death recurs in the same way or in a metamorphosed way at birth in the next incarnation. Comparing the horoscopes for Rudolf Steiner's birth with that of St. Thomas Aquinas's death, we find that the angular relationship between the Sun and Saturn at the death of St. Thomas Aquinas amounts to 176°, placing the Sun and Saturn in opposition. At the birth of Rudolf Steiner the Sun and Saturn were again in opposition, the angle between them being 179°. The first "law" of reincarnation thus offers confirmation of the statement that Rudolf Steiner was the reincarnation of St. Thomas Aquinas and implies, further, that there was no interven-

---

6 Steiner, *Karmic Relationships*, vol. I, lecture 12.

7 Kirchner-Bockholt, *Rudolf Steiner's Mission and Ita Wegman*, pp. 81–93.

Comparison Chart

Outer - Tychonic	Inner - Tychonic
Death of (St.) Thomas Aquinas (V. +)	Birth of Rudolf Steiner
At Fossanova, Latitude 40N50', Longitude 14E15'	At Kraljavec/Yugoslavia, Latitude 46N22', Longitude 16E39'
Date: Wednesday, 7/MAR/1274, Julian	Date: Monday, 25/FEB/1861, Gregorian
Time: 3: 0, Local Time	Time: 23:25, Local Time
Sidereal Time 14:27:25, Vernal Point 15 ♓ 22'33"	Sidereal Time 9:47:41, Vernal Point 7 ♓ 11'52"

House System: Placidus, Zodiac: Sidereal SVP
Aspect set: Conjunction/Square/Opposition

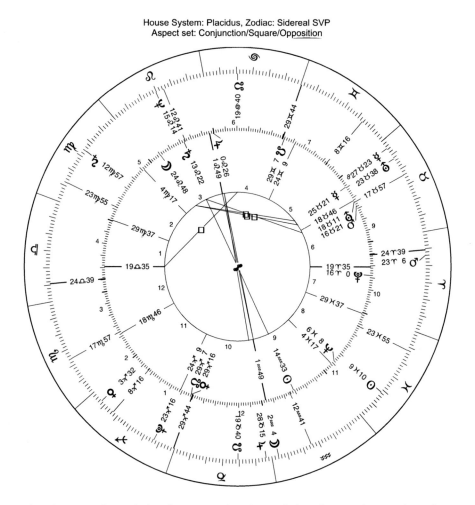

ing incarnation. A further examination of the charts shows that the second "law" is also fulfilled. In the hermetic (Tychonic) chart at St. Thomas Aquinas's death, Mercury and Uranus were in conjunction in the sidereal sign of Taurus, and in the hermetic chart at Rudolf Steiner's birth Mercury and Uranus were again close together in Taurus, the alignment of Mercury being almost exact (see hermetic comparison chart above: death St. Thomas Aquinas: h-Mercury = 27° Taurus / birth Rudolf Steiner: h-Mercury = 25° Taurus).

Looking at page 42, the probable conception chart of Rudolf Steiner (computed according to the hermetic rule for June 1, 1860), shows a geocentric conjunction between Mercury and Uranus in Taurus. This conjunction reflects the conjunction of Mercury and Uranus in Taurus in the hermetic chart at the death of St. Thomas Aquinas. Most striking at St. Thomas Aquinas's death was the conjunction (seen geocentrically) of the Moon with Venus and Jupiter. This geocentric conjunction of Venus and Jupiter recurred again in the conception chart of Rudolf Steiner computed for June 1, 1860—and then reappeared (metamorphosed) as a geocentric opposition between the two planets at Rudolf Steiner's birth. Moreover, the geocentric conjunction between the Moon and Venus at St. Thomas Aquinas's death reappeared as a conjunction in the hermetic chart at Steiner's conception.

From these astrological considerations, and with the addition of the argument of probability, June 1, 1860, is confirmed with a high degree of certainty as the date of Steiner's conception, or "epoch" (meaning etheric conception as computed by the hermetic rule). These indications show that, in the case of the individuality who incarnated in the thirteenth century as St. Thomas Aquinas and then reincarnated in the nineteenth to twentieth centuries as Rudolf Steiner, it is not only the birth chart but also the conception chart that bears a strong relationship to the death chart in the previous incarnation. (Unfortunately, the date of birth of St. Thomas Aquinas is not known, so it is impossible to undertake a comparison between Steiner's conception chart and the birth chart in the previous incarnation.) The conception chart computed by the hermetic rule can therefore be of value in reincarnation research and may be used in addition to the birth chart for comparisons of the birth/death charts of previous incarnations.

IMPLICATIONS OF THE ASTROLOGICAL RULES OF REINCARNATION

The examination of Rudolf Steiner's previous incarnation as Thomas Aquinas demonstrates that both rules of astrological reincarnation are fulfilled. This is a *scientific fact* that has an important implication—specifically, that in all probability there was no incarnation between those of Thomas Aquinas and Rudolf Steiner. This is confirmed by Steiner himself in a letter he wrote in 1904 to Doris and Franz Paulus at Stuttgart:

There was a person in my former life, centuries ago; she played the part of someone who tore me away from family connections and paved the way that led me to my calling that, at that time, was as a Catholic priest.[8]

Chapter 11 of the *Life of St. Thomas Aquinas* by William of Tocco describes the role of Thomas's mother, who in 1245 helped the twenty-one-year-old escape the situation in which he was held by his family, after which he returned to the Dominicans at Naples.[9] This indication of Rudolf Steiner concerning his previous incarnation as Thomas Aquinas may certainly be understood in the sense that he did not incarnate again between the thirteenth and nineteenth centuries.

While not completely beyond the bounds of possibility, in terms of probability it would be extremely unlikely that *both* astrological reincarnation rules would apply *again* in exactly the same way in the event of an incarnation between those of Thomas Aquinas and Rudolf Steiner. The fulfillment of these two rules from Thomas Aquinas's death to Rudolf Steiner's birth, together with Rudolf Steiner's statement, virtually excludes the possibility of an intervening incarnation.

The reader may begin to see the enormous potential of these two astrological reincarnation rules. Before we proceed to consider an application of these two rules to other reincarnation examples, however, we need to recall the consequence for the science of astrology. If the second astrological reincarnation rule holds true, it signifies that the sidereal zodiac is the authentic astrological zodiac. In order to embark upon a serious discussion of this issue, for the sake of comparison let us look at the same charts (Thomas Aquinas/Rudolf Steiner) in terms of the tropical zodiac (see tropical comparison chart on page 48).

A glance at the geocentric chart comparison between Thomas Aquinas and Rudolf Steiner shows a lineup of the Venus–Jupiter opposition at Rudolf Steiner's birth with the Venus–Jupiter conjunction at Thomas Aquinas's death (see page 99). At the same time, however, the sidereal line up of the Saturn–Sun opposition at Rudolf Steiner's birth with Neptune's sidereal position at Thomas Aquinas's death, disappears. And the fairly exact alignment (2° off) of h-Mercury in the sidereal zodiac at Rudolf Steiner's birth with its sidereal position at

---

8 Steiner, *From the History and Contents of the First Section of the Esoteric School 1904–1914*, p. 60.

9 Eckert, *Das Leben des heiligen Thomas von Aquino*.

Comparison Chart

Outer - Tychonic	Inner - Tychonic
Death of (St.) Thomas Aquinas (V. +)	Birth of Rudolf Steiner
At Fossanova, Latitude 40N50', Longitude 14E15'	At Kraljavec/Yugoslavia, Latitude 46N22', Longitude 16E39'
Date: Wednesday, 7/MAR/1274, Julian	Date: Monday, 25/FEB/1861, Gregorian
Time: 3: 0, Local Time	Time: 23:25, Local Time
Sidereal Time 14:27:25	Sidereal Time 9:47:41

House System: Placidus, Zodiac: Tropical
Aspect set: Conjunction/Square/Opposition

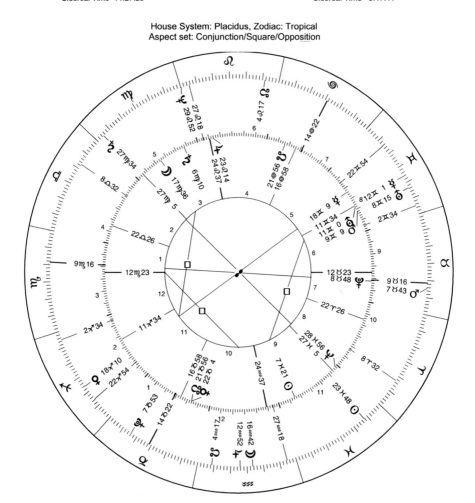

Thomas Aquinas's death becomes widened in the tropical zodiac to an orb of 6°. There are two possibilities here: that the sidereal zodiac and the tropical zodiac are both valid, but on different levels; or that one zodiac alone is authentic, in which case alignments in the other zodiac are pure coincidence. Let us consider these two possibilities.

The first point to note is that the method developed here for comparing reincarnation examples is something objective and scientific.

However, it depends on the truth of the reincarnation examples; the accuracy of the birth and death data of these examples; the accuracy of the astronomical calculations made on the basis of the birth and death data; and the correct interpretation of the chart comparisons.

With respect to the truth of the examples presented in this book, it is a matter of trusting Steiner's reincarnation research. This is the point of departure for the research presented here. The extraordinary thing is that, through this research, the first two rules of astrological reincarnation have been discovered. They in turn offer confirmation of the accuracy of Steiner's reincarnation research. Concerning the accuracy of the birth and death data of the examples, everything possible has been done to check this data for the reincarnation examples to exclude error. In the case of the astronomical calculations made on the basis of this data, the most up-to-date astronomical algorithms for computing the planetary positions have been used. With regard to the correct interpretation of the chart comparisons it is essentially a matter of clarifying a method and deciding which of the two possibilities mentioned above holds true.

FULFILLMENT OF THE RULES OF ASTROLOGICAL REINCARNATION

The method used to compare horoscopes from one incarnation to the next has already been illustrated with the example of Thomas Aquinas/Rudolf Steiner. Initially we looked in terms of sidereal horoscopes. Not knowing Thomas Aquinas's birth date we have only his death horoscope to go on, which we looked at geocentrically and heliocentrically (hermetically). These two sidereal horoscopes for Thomas Aquinas's date of death were compared with Rudolf Steiner's conception and birth sidereal horoscopes geocentrically and heliocentrically (hermetically), thus giving rise to four chart comparisons. In terms of the two rules of astrological reincarnation, we looked for something quite specific in making these comparisons. In the case of the first rule, we looked at the angular relationship between the Sun and Saturn from death (Thomas Aquinas) to birth (Rudolf Steiner), and we saw that in this example that it makes hardly any difference whether we read the Sun–Saturn angle geocentrically or heliocentrically (hermetically). In general, it should be noted that the difference between the geocentric and the heliocentric (hermetic) Sun–Saturn angle does not amount to more than about 6°. As this divergence is small, it usually makes little difference whether we look at the geocentric Sun–Saturn angle from death to the subsequent birth or whether we look at the heliocentric (hermetic) Sun–Saturn angle. In *Hermetic Astrology,* volume I, appendix III, the geocentric Sun–Saturn angle is used in twelve comparison examples. More research needs to be done, however, to clarify whether it is the geocentric or the hermetic Sun–Saturn angle that is most relevant when making such comparisons. About the significance of the Sun–Saturn angle, Steiner stated, "In the human being, this relationship of Saturn to the Sun comes to expression when the 'I' achieves an appropriate relationship to the astral body, and, above all, in the proper incorporation of the astral body into the whole human organization."[10] Note that, with this first astrological reincarnation rule, it does not matter whether the horoscopes are tropical or sidereal.

This is not the case, however, with the second rule of astrological reincarnation, which applies in terms of the sidereal zodiac. This is part of the *proof* of the sidereal zodiac as the authentic astrological zodiac.[11] With the second rule, it is not a matter of looking at angular relationships between planets, which are independent of zodiacal background. Rather, the important thing is the position of the planets—h-Mercury and/or h-Venus (h = heliocentric /hermetic)—in the sidereal zodiac.

As is seen from the example of Thomas Aquinas/Rudolf Steiner, the difference between h-Mercury at the birth of Rudolf Steiner is only 2° in the sidereal zodiac, whereas it amounts to 6° in the tropical zodiac. How does this discrepancy arise?

In the application of the second astrological reincarnation rule, we are usually looking for *zodiacal alignments* of h-Mercury and/or h-Venus at death in one incarnation to birth in the next incarnation, whereby an alignment can take place on the same side of the zodiac (conjunction) or on the opposite side (opposition). If we are looking in terms of the sidereal zodiac, the planet's location is in relation to the fixed stars. Thus, with the death of Thomas Aquinas and the birth of Rudolf Steiner, h-Mercury was approaching the stars marking the horns of the Bull (Taurus). This accords exactly with Rudolf Steiner's description, as follows.

---

10 Steiner, *Materialism and the Task of Anthroposophy*, p. 246.

11 See *Hermetic Astrology*, vol. I, appendix 4.

THE GROUND OF TRUE ASTROLOGY:
THE PLANETS IN THE CONSTELLATIONS

What is experienced both after death and in initiation is that one emerges from the body, and one's whole soul being expands....Human beings grow, in a spiritual sense, to gigantic dimensions. They grow out into the spheres....First it must be emphasized that, as we expand into other spheres, all our imperfections are inscribed there. We expand from the Moon sphere into the Mercury sphere. I am speaking entirely from the perspective of esotericism, not from that of ordinary astronomy. Something is inscribed by us in all the spheres—in the Mercury sphere, the Venus sphere, the Sun sphere, the Mars sphere, the Jupiter sphere, the Saturn sphere, and even beyond....

Let us say that a human being has inscribed a personal imperfection into the Moon sphere. While passing through the Mars sphere, that one inscribes a quality of individual character through the fact of having acquired in that sphere a certain element of aggressiveness previously absent. Now, on the return journey, one passes through the Mars sphere again and returns to the Earth. That individual lives on Earth and has received as karma what was inscribed in the Mars sphere, but at the same time, it stands recorded above one. Above is Mars in a certain relationship to the Moon. (The outer planets indicate the relative positions of the spheres.) Because Mars stands in a certain relationship to the Moon, the inscription of one's aggressive element and imperfections are, as it were, in the same constellation. Consequently, when one planet stands behind the other, they work in conjunction....In astrology, when we ascertain the positions of the planets and their positions relative to those of the *fixed stars,* it offers some indication of what we ourselves have inscribed....When the Moon stands in a certain relationship to Mars *and to some fixed star,* this constellation works as a whole. That is, the Mars quality, the Moon, *and the fixed star* work together on the an individual and bring about what this combined influence is capable of achieving.[12]

---

12 Steiner, *Life between Death and Rebirth,* pp. 247, 254–255 (translation revised; italics added by RP).

By emphasizing the fixed stars, Steiner clearly refers to planetary positions in the sidereal zodiac. In the following quote, again he speaks clearly about the sidereal zodiac, referring to the *sidereal sign* of Leo, since he talks about the Sun *covering* Leo:

> We were able to divide up the whole human form and connect its parts and members with *certain fixed stars, certain signs of the zodiac.*... Humanity's outer destiny can be connected with the *constellations of the stars,* just as we had to connect with the *constellations of the stars* what humanity has already become. If it was auspicious for the human organization that its Sun forces cooperated with those members of the human form to which we ascribed the *sign of Leo,* then it will also be auspicious today for certain human qualities and characteristics if some important moment of life, notably the moment of birth, occurs when the Sun is in the *sign of Leo*—that is, when the *Sun covers Leo,* so that these two forces mutually strengthen or in some way influence each other. Just as what humankind is today is written in the heavenly spaces in the *constellations of the stars,* so, too, what is yet to happen with humanity is also written there. This is the ground of true astrology.[13]

In the next quote, Steiner indicates how destiny is written in the stars and in the relationships between the planets:

> When we look up to the Sun, to the planetary system—*and the same applies to the rest of the starry heavens,* for they are connected in a very real way with the human being—we can witness how human karma takes shape in the cosmos. The Moon, the planets Venus, Jupiter—truly, these heavenly bodies are not as physical astronomy describes them. In their constellations, in their mutual relationships, in their radiance, in their whole existence, they are the builders and shapers of human destinies; they are the cosmic timepiece according to which we live out our karma.[14]

Rudolf Steiner's description of human life in the planetary spheres and in the world of the fixed stars after death is a key to understanding

---

13 Steiner, *Man in the Light of Occultism, Theosophy, and Philosophy*, pp. 169–170 (translation revised; italics added by RP).

14 Steiner, *Karmic Relationships*, vol. 7, pp. 32–33.

astrology as a science of destiny. He makes the analogy of the human being's perception of mountains, streams, woods, and fields during earthly life to beholding the spiritual aspects of the Sun, Moon, and planets as they move in relation to the fixed stars after his death and upon his return to earthly incarnation. "From that other world, while we are descending, we see the Sun from the other side; the Sun appears, the fixed stars appear, and behind them the planetary movements."[15]

At the moment of death, all of one's destiny lived through during that earthly life becomes imprinted into the starry heavens. The reincarnating soul seeks to be born at a moment when stars and planets are again aligned with their positions at the moment of death, so that the destiny is literally carried over from one incarnation to the next, via the stars. This then is the meaning of the second rule of astrological reincarnation.

APPLICATION OF THE SECOND RULE OF ASTROLOGICAL REINCARNATION

We return now to the question of how there could be only a 2° difference between h-Mercury at death Thomas Aquinas/birth Rudolf Steiner in the sidereal zodiac, while it amounted to a 6° difference in the tropical zodiac. h-Mercury was approaching the horns of the Bull at the death of Thomas Aquinas and at the birth of Rudolf Steiner. Rudolf Steiner's soul, spiritually beholding h-Mercury approaching the Bull's horns, chose to be born on February 25, 1861, when h-Mercury aligned with its position in the sidereal zodiac at the death of Thomas Aquinas. This alignment was fairly exact, the difference in position in the sidereal zodiac being only 2° (see comparison chart on page 45).

Now, looking at the *tropical* hermetic death horoscope of Thomas Aquinas, we see that h-Mercury was at 12° Gemini (see comparison chart on page 48). The signs of the tropical zodiac are actually spatial projections from the tropical calendar, where 30° arcs in space are measured from the vernal point.[16] 12° Gemini signifies that at the death of Thomas Aquinas h-Mercury was 72° East of the vernal point. At that time, the vernal point was located at about 15 ½° Pisces, and

---

15 Steiner, "Hidden Sides of Man's Existence and the Christ Impulse" (lecture of November 5, 1922), *Anthroposophical Quarterly*, vol. 17 (1972), p. 46.

16 Powell, *History of the Zodiac*, chapter 3.

at Rudolf Steiner's birth the vernal point was located at about 7½°
Pisces. In other words, between Thomas Aquinas's death (1274) and
Rudolf Steiner's birth (1861), 587 years had elapsed. Since the vernal
point moved back through Pisces at a rate of approximately 1° every
72 years, in 587 years it had moved back 587/72 = 8° 10′ in Pisces,
which is the difference in longitude of the vernal point between 1274
and 1861. This difference of more than 8° shows up in the comparison
of h-Mercury in the tropical and the sidereal zodiacs. In the sidereal
zodiac the difference is 2°, but in the tropical zodiac it amounts to
6°. If there had been an *exact* alignment of h-Mercury in the sidereal
zodiac from Thomas Aquinas's death to Rudolf Steiner's birth, the
discrepancy in the corresponding positions of h-Mercury in the tropical zodiac would have been just over 8°.

This example shows that chart comparisons of death in one incarnation with birth in the next incarnation (for both the tropical and
sidereal zodiacs) provide an objective means of assessing whether the
reincarnating soul chooses to be born when the planets align in the
sidereal rather than in the tropical zodiac. There are a number of conclusions that may be drawn from this objective finding, and they are
of extraordinary consequence for astrology. In summary, we can say

1. that the sidereal zodiac is the authentic astrological zodiac;
2. that in addition to the traditional geocentric sidereal birth horoscope, the heliocentric (hermetic) sidereal horoscope of birth
   also needs to be taken into consideration;
3. that the geocentric sidereal horoscope of conception is significant;
4. and that the heliocentric (hermetic) sidereal horoscope of conception is also important.

While the first and second conditions are proved by the second rule of
astrological reincarnation, the significance of the horoscope of conception remains, for the time being, of a more hypothetical nature.[17]

---

17 Powell, in *Elijah Come Again*, demonstrates the significance of the conception
horoscope in light of reincarnation examples from one life to the next. See also
the chapter on "Astrological Biography" in Powell, *Chronicle of the Living
Christ*, which shows the significance of the conception horoscope and briefly
describes the entire period of embryonic development between conception and
birth. Further, Powell, *Hermetic Astrology, Volume II*, treats in detail the karmic
significance of the conception horoscope.

FROM IMPERIAL ADVERSARIES TO ARTISTIC ALLIES:
A KARMIC PAIRING ACROSS TIME

When Rudolf Steiner began his *Karmic Relationships* lecture series, he never referred to individuals in the first six lectures, outlining general principles and processes instead. In the seventh lecture, when he did mention specific historical personalities, he seemed also to choose his first examples to illustrate general principles of reincarnation, always stressing the incredibly variegated and convoluted nature of each individual's path of destiny. As his second example, he spoke of the composer Franz Schubert, a European cultural icon whose music and biography would have been known to nearly every member of his audience in 1924. Schubert's exquisite music (Antonio Salieri once said about Schubert, "This one learned it from God") masked a personal life of tremendous turmoil, hardship, and even squalor. With his artistic friends, he was a frequenter of taverns and lived by the generosity of others much of his life. Taking issue with a biography of Schubert that cast aspersions on his physiognomy, Steiner said that Schubert had "a pleasing, attractive face," which could hardly have been caused by Schubert's poverty. Aside from his poverty, the aspect of Schubert's biography that most interested Steiner was his "inner, volcanic fire" that would occasionally burst out. Steiner—who had lived in Schubert's home city of Vienna for nearly twenty years—gave as example a story of how Schubert, having gone to hear Gluck's *Iphigenia,* was delighted with the opera and after the performance spoke enthusiastically of it in a Vienna club. As the story goes, a university professor at a neighboring table, listening to Schubert's enthusiastic account, jumped up, red-faced, and began loudly to proclaim his criticism of the performance and the lead singers. Schubert, unable to restrain himself, erupted like a volcano and had to be restrained as the dispute threatened to become physical.

Steiner's source for this story was a memoir written by Baron Joseph von Spaun, an art enthusiast and minor aristocrat who for many years was Schubert's most steadfast friend and patron. To demonstrate how intimate they were, Steiner recounted von Spaun's description of how Schubert would often spend the night at his home, and then witness in the morning how Schubert, upon rising, would go straight to the piano to compose "his beautiful motifs, as though they came straight out of sleep." In Steiner's research, Baron von Spaun quickly went from being a source of biographical information to an avenue of karmic research himself. Steiner was particularly struck by the contrast between von Spaun's passion for art, and his official position as Director of Lotteries for Austria, which trained him to deal with "the passions, the hopes, the blighted expectations, the disappointments, the dreams and superstitions of countless human beings." Schubert's poverty restricted the extent of his social circle and thus limited how often others were subjected to his "volcanic" outbursts. Von Spaun's aristocratic position and his particular experience as lottery director simultaneously acquainted him with and distanced him from the volatilities of human nature regarding matters of money. Seeing this combination of perspectives as uniquely karmic, Steiner posed a counterfactual scenario:

> If...the conditions had been different—if Schubert had not had the opportunity of expressing the musical talent within him, if he had not found a devoted friend in von Spaun—might he not have become a mere brawler in some lower station in life? What expressed itself as a volcano that evening in the club room— was it not a fundamental trait in Schubert's character? Human life defies explanation until we can answer the question: How does the metamorphosis come about whereby, in a certain life, a man does not, so to say, live out his pugnacity but becomes an exquisite musician, the pugnacity being transformed into subtle and delicate musical fantasy?[18]

When Steiner set out to do karmic research on Schubert, he discovered that "the tracks disappear; it is not easy to find him." This, however, was not the case with von Spaun, whom he traced to "an eighth- or ninth-century...prince of Castile who had a name for being extraordinarily wise." Steiner said that this prince had been an avid astrologer and astronomer, drawing up astronomical tables, and then noted that, at the end of his life, the prince was forced to flee his home and find refuge with a former enemy, a "tender-hearted Moor" who "cared for him with every kindness for many years, to the great joy of both."

Having sketched the outlines of this amazing relationship, Steiner neither identified by name the Castilian prince who reincarnated as

---

18 Steiner, *Karmic Relationships*, volume 1, p. 136 (translation revised).

Joseph von Spaun, nor named the "Moorish personality" who later reincarnated as Franz Schubert. The Castilian prince, who had once sought the Pope's recognition of him as emperor of the world, was wholly unknown to Steiner's listeners, more unknown certainly than Schubert's patron von Spaun, whose previous incarnation Steiner clearly implied had been this learned Castilian prince of the Middle Ages. The brief biographical details given by Steiner, however, unmistakably identify this individual as Alfonso X of Castile-Léon (1221–1284), known as *El Sabio* ("the Learned") for his profound cultivation and dissemination of knowledge in art, literature, music, law, astronomy, and other subjects. In addition to wise, Alfonso's contemporaries characterized him as generous, just, handsome, graceful, and elegant. One commentator astutely noted that Alfonso's generosity was "clothed by a sort of prodigality."

Alfonso's personality and life was marked by prodigality. Florentine poet Brunetto Latini declared:

> Under the moon no person has yet been found
> Who for noble lineage
> or high baronage
> was more worth of it
> than this King Alfonso.

Alfonso was a poet, or troubadour, himself, composing many of the celebrated *Cantigas de Santa Maria* ("Songs to the Virgin Mary"), one of the largest collections of monophonic songs to survive from Medieval times. Consisting of 420 poems written in Galician-Portuguese with musical notation, the *Cantigas* rhapsodize about miracles attributed to the Virgin Mary, including Alfonso's own healing in Puerto de Santa María. As "El Astrólogo" ("the astronomer" was another of Alfonso's nicknames during his lifetime), his most notable contribution was the *Tablas Alfonsies* (Alfonsine Tables), astronomical tables of planetary movements. The *Tablas* was the first European work to note the Andromeda Nebula, which was evidently unknown to Ptolemy, or at least he did not mention it.

In 1254 in Seville, Alfonso established a university intended to honor Latin and Arabic cultures equally. Alfonso's court was itself a university, and a host of scholarly works sprang from it that—along with promulgating new knowledge in the form of legal treatises, histories, translations of Arabic texts—established the Castilian language as a new lingua franca in Europe. Alfonso was even the author/compiler of *Libro de Juegos* ("Book of Games"), whose preface links God and gamesmanship: "Because God wanted that man have every manner of happiness, in himself naturally, so that he could suffer the cares and troubles when they came to them, therefore men sought out many ways that they could have this happiness completely."[19] That El Sabio could take as much note of javelins and spears, darts, chess, dice, and other diversions as studiously as he did stars, sacred song, and jurisprudence, underscores his exuberant "prodigality."

For all of his scholarly accomplishments, Alfonso was a king before he was a philosopher, and his reign was characterized by its own unique imperial prodigality. Shortly after his marriage at age twenty-three, Alfonso led his father's army to conquer the Mediterranean Islamic kingdom of Murcia. After inheriting the throne at thirty, Alfonso instigated armed adventures against Portugal on the west, Navarre and English Aquitaine in the north, and Morocco in the south. All during his reign, Alfonso faced assaults from neighboring Moorish kingdoms, as well as the threat of internal rebellion by the Mudéjars, the large Muslim population living under Castilian rule.

Alfonso's most formidable opponent was Abu Yusuf Ya'qub, emir of the Marinid sultanate from 1258 to 1286. The Marinids were a nomadic dynasty, originally from Zab in Algeria, who had in the thirteenth century invaded northeastern Morocco. While Abu Yusuf was ending Almohad rule in Morocco, Alfonso was preparing for the invasion of North Africa, a dream of his father, King Fernando III. In late 1259 or early 1260, Abu Yusuf asked Alfonso to send cavalry to help him take control of the port town of Salé. Alfonso seized the invitation as an opportunity to begin his North African crusade. On Friday, September 10, 1260, as the fast of Ramadan was ending, Alfonso's fleet of thirty-seven ships, rather than lending support to Abu Yusuf, delivered cavalry and archers who charged the town, surprising Abu Yusuf and the unarmed inhabitants. As Abu Yusuf watched helplessly from his citadel, women and children were herded into the town's principal mosque; Alfonso's troops sacked the town, taking gold, silver, other booty, and some 3,000 captives (including the chief judge), before Abu Yusuf's uncle arrived from nearby Rabat to repossess

19 Sonja Musser Golladay's English translation of *Libro de los Juegos* ("Book of Games") by Alfonso X (at www.u.arizona.edu/~smusser/ljtranslation.html).

Salé. In the wake of this attack, Abu Yusuf was chronicled as having exclaimed: "The tyrant [Alfonso]—may God annihilate him!"[20]

The hostile relationship between Alfonso and Abu Yusuf intensified when Marinid forces crossed the Straits of Gibraltar in 1275. The invading Marinids spread destruction far and wide. However, Alfonso X managed to arrange a two-year truce with Abu Yusuf, who withdrew back to Morocco in January 1276, after six months in Spain. He soon resumed hostilities, however, invading the Spanish peninsula again in the summer of 1277. Alfonso concluded another truce with Abu Yusuf in February 1278. This time it was Alfonso who broke the peace treaty by sending a fleet to blockade Algeciras in August 1278. The siege of Algeciras turned into a disaster a year later, when a Marinid fleet put the Castilian troops to flight. Abu Yusuf was at first unwilling to conclude another truce with Alfonso, but he finally agreed because of the continuing threat of opposition in Morocco.[21]

Meanwhile, Alfonso suffered a severe illness, and his son Sancho was concerned about his father's ability to govern Castile and Léon. The illness, apparently a malignant brain tumor, afflicted Alfonso to the extent that it forced his eye out of its socket. As his condition deteriorated, his wife and sons abandoned him, as did the monarchs— Dinis of Portugal, Pedro III of Aragón, and Edward I of England— whom he petitioned for support. He finally turned to his old nemesis, Abu Yusuf, sending his envoys to Marrakech in April 1282. According to the Moroccan historian Ibn Abi Zar, the envoys pleaded to Abu Yusuf, "O victorious king, the Christians have violated their oath of fidelity and have rebelled against me, together with my son. They say, 'He is an old man who has lost his judgment and whose reason is disturbed.' Aid me against them and I will go with you to meet them."

Crossing the strait to Algeciras in late summer, Abu Yusuf then received Alfonso near Seville, lending him 100,000 gold dinars and taking in return the Castilian crown in pledge. Staying four months with Abu Yusuf, Alfonso recovered his health to the point where he could walk and ride. On October 24, the two monarchs formed an alliance against all enemies, immediately besieging Cordoba together against Alfonso's renegade son Sancho. *Crónica de Alfonso* describes how Abu Yusuf and 4,000 Moorish knights were poised on a hill

---

20 O'Callaghan, *The Learned King*, p. 173.

21 Ibid., pp. 175–249.

above the city as Alfonso's troops assembled on the plain below. Alfonso sent in seven knights bearing his banner to demand entry to the city, but they were rebuffed, "and when the message reached King Aben Yuzaf, he ordered the war drums beaten and ordered all of his cavalry to go to war."[22]

By the time of his death two years later, Alfonso had a change of heart concerning Sancho. The *Crónica* concludes:

> And when he was stricken by his illness, he said before them all that he forgave Prince Don Sancho, his son and heir, because he acted due to his youthfulness. King Alfonso also said that he forgave all of the subjects of the kingdoms who had worked against him; and he quickly ordered documents written concerning this, sealed with his golden seals so that all the people of this kingdom would know that he had given up complaints against them and that he forgave them so that they would be safe from any vituperation whatsoever. After King Alfonso had finished and stated all this, he received very devoutly the Corpus Christi, and after part of an hour he gave his soul to God.[23]

ASTROLOGICAL REINCARNATION HOROSCOPE COMPARISONS

Alfonso "gave his soul to God" on April 4, 1284. Less than two years later, on Mocharrem 22, 1286, at Algeciras, Abu Yusuf gave his soul to *his* God. Rudolf Steiner, speaking of his karmic research on Franz Schubert, said that he had to take a "roundabout way" to discover Schubert's previous incarnation. But it was hardly a roundabout way in which the Christian and Moorish kings, in the thirteenth century, had established a deep karmic bridge across the Straits of Gibraltar. The relationship between Abu Yusuf and Alfonso X closely fits Rudolf Steiner's description of the karmic relationship between Franz Schubert and Joseph von Spaun in their previous incarnations.[24] Let

---

22 Shelby and Escobar, trans., *Chronicle of Alfonso X*, p. 248

23 Ibid., p. 258

24 Brian Hinderlider, an American curative eurythmist (movement therapist) living in Stuttgart, Germany, was the first to make the identification of Alfonso X as the previous incarnation of Joseph von Spaun. One detail does not fit Rudolf Steiner's description, namely that Alfonso X lived in the thirteenth century and not in the eighth/ninth centuries. Brian Hinderlider is preparing a

us now see if the laws of astrological reincarnation are borne out by an examination of the birth and death horoscopes of these two individualities (see following pages).

Alfonso X died at Seville April 4, 1284; Joseph von Spaun was born in Linz, Austria, November 11, 1788. In both cases, not knowing the times of death and birth, noon has been chosen as an "average time" on each day for casting the horoscopes. Looking at the geocentric comparison first (page 62), the angle between the Sun (7 ½° Aries) and Saturn (11 ½° Capricorn) at Alfonso's death amounts to 86°. At the birth of Joseph von Spaun, the angular relationship between the Sun (28° Libra) and Saturn (12 ½° Aquarius) was 104 ½° (see the geocentric comparison chart). The first rule of astrological reincarnation is fulfilled, although not exactly (orb: 10 ½°), since the sum of the two angles (86 + 104 ½) is 190 ½°, amounting to a difference of 10 ½° from 180°. (In order to have an exact fulfillment of this rule, the angles should be identical or their sum should be exactly 180°.)

Comparing the heliocentric/hermetic horoscopes in the sidereal zodiac (page 63), we see that h-Mercury at Joseph von Spaun's birth (11 ½° Pisces) aligned with h-Mercury at Alfonso X's death (10° Pisces), thus fulfilling the second rule of astrological reincarnation. Note that the range of h-Mercury on April 4, 1284, was between 7 ½° and 12 ½° Pisces. Similarly, the range of h-Mercury on November 11, 1788, was between 9° and 14° Pisces. Thus, according to the actual times of death and birth, the alignment could have been exact (0°) or it could have amounted to 6 ½° as the maximum possible separation. Note further that the consideration of time (on the day concerned) is significant in the case of the second rule, since h-Mercury can travel up to almost 6 ½° in the zodiac in one day. However, in relation to the first rule of astrological reincarnation, the time of day is not so significant as an influence upon the Sun/Saturn angle since the Sun travels merely about 1° in a day and Saturn's movement in the zodiac is hardly noticeable at all in one day.

The date of Abu Yusuf's death was Mocharrem 22, 1286.[25] As with the Hebrew and other lunar calendars, in the Muslim calendar the day

---

detailed study of his research findings in which he discusses this discrepancy, which may have been a transcription error on the part of the stenographer who recorded this lecture by Rudolf Steiner.

25 Wüstenfeld, *Vergleichungstabellen zur muslimischen und iranischen Zeitrechnung*, p. 15.

Comparison Chart

Outer - Geocentric	Inner - Geocentric
Death of (King) Alfonso X	Birth of Joseph von Spaun
At Seville, Latitude 37N23', Longitude 6W0'	At Linz, Latitude 48N19', Longitude 14E18'
Date: Tuesday, 4/APR/1284, Julian	Date: Tuesday, 11/NOV/1788, Gregorian
Time: 12: 0, Local Time	Time: 12: 0, Local Time
Sidereal Time 1:21:47, Vernal Point 15 ✕ 14' 8"	Sidereal Time 15:24:58, Vernal Point 8 ✕ 12'22"

House System: Placidus, Zodiac: Sidereal SVP
Aspect set: Conjunction/Square/Opposition

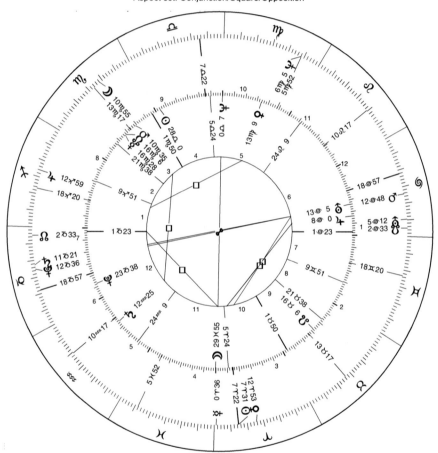

begins at dusk and continues until sunset the next day. Thus, Mochar-rem 22, 1286, began around 6 p.m. on March 20 and continued until about 6 p.m. on March 21. For computational purposes, let us take the midpoint of this "lunar day," i.e. 6 a.m. on March 21, as an average. Therefore the horoscope at the death of Abu Yusuf Ya'qub is cast for 6 a.m. on Thursday, March 21, 1286, at Algeciras, Spain. How does this compare with Franz Schubert's birth horoscope?

Comparison Chart

Outer - Tychonic
Death of (King) Alfonso X
At Seville, Latitude 37N23', Longitude 6W0'
Date: Tuesday, 4/APR/1284, Julian
Time: 12: 0, Local Time
Sidereal Time   1:21:47, Vernal Point 15 ♓ 14' 8"

Inner - Tychonic
Birth of Joseph von Spaun
At Linz, Latitude 48N19', Longitude 14E18'
Date: Tuesday, 11/NOV/1788, Gregorian
Time: 12: 0, Local Time
Sidereal Time 15:24:58, Vernal Point 8 ♓ 12'22"

House System: Placidus, Zodiac: Sidereal SVP
Aspect set: Conjunction/Square/Opposition

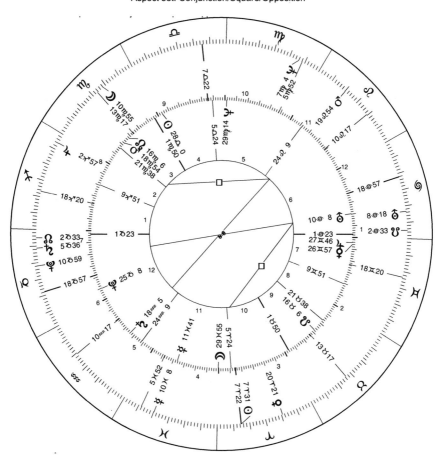

According to the family bible, Franz Schubert was born at 1:30 p.m. on January 31, 1797, in Vienna.[26] Applying the hermetic rule to his birth horoscope, the birth time has to be corrected to 1:27 p.m. (see the geocentric comparison horoscope, next page: Schubert's birth horoscope in the inner circle and Abu Yusuf's death horoscope in the outer circle). Looking first at the comparison of the geocentric

26 Taeger, *Internationales Horoskope-Lexikon*, vol. 3, p. 1361.

Comparison Chart

Outer - Geocentric	Inner - Geocentric

Outer - Geocentric
Death of (Emir) Abu Yusuf Ya'kub
At Algeciras, Latitude 36N08', Longitude 5W30'
Date: Thursday, 21/MAR/1286, Julian
Time: 6: 0, Local Time
Sidereal Time 18:23:42, Vernal Point 15 ♓ 12'30"

Inner - Geocentric
Birth of Franz Schubert
At Vienna, Austria, Latitude 48N13', Longitude 16E22'
Date: Tuesday, 31/JAN/1797, Gregorian
Time: 13:27, Local Time
Sidereal Time 22:12: 5, Vernal Point 8 ♓ 5'29"

House System: Placidus, Zodiac: Sidereal SVP
Aspect set: Conjunction/Square/Opposition

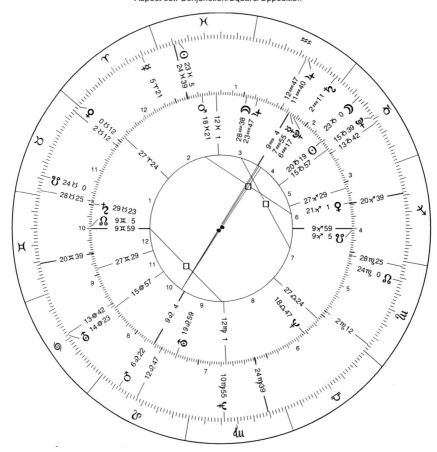

horoscopes, we see that the angle between the Sun (23° Pisces) and Saturn (2° Aquarius) at Abu Yusuf's death amounts to 51°. At Franz Schubert's birth the angle between the Sun (20° Capricorn) and Saturn (29° Taurus) amounts to 129°. This fulfills the first rule of astrological reincarnation, since the sum of the two angles (51 + 129) amounts to 180°.

Looking now at the comparison of the heliocentric/hermetic horoscopes in the sidereal zodiac (next page), we see that h-Mercury at the

Comparison Chart

Outer - Tychonic
Death of (Emir) Abu Yusuf Ya'kub
At Algeciras, Latitude 36N08', Longitude 5W30'
Date: Thursday, 21/MAR/1286, Julian
Time: 6: 0, Local Time
Sidereal Time 18:23:42, Vernal Point 15 ♓ 12'30"

Inner - Tychonic
Birth of Franz Schubert
At Lichtental, Latitude 48N13', Longitude 16E22'
Date: Tuesday, 31/JAN/1797, Gregorian
Time: 13:27, Local Time
Sidereal Time 22:12: 5, Vernal Point 8 ♓ 5'29"

House System: Placidus, Zodiac: Sidereal SVP
Aspect set: Conjunction/Square/Opposition

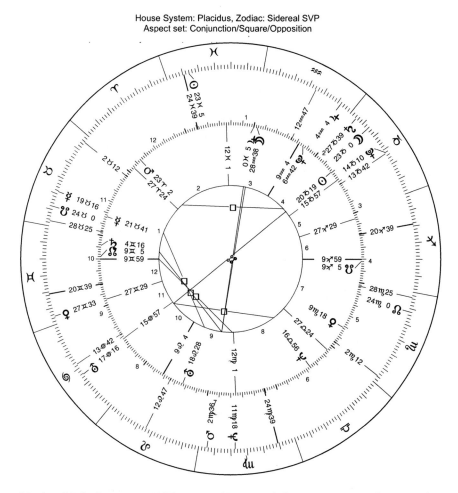

birth of Schubert (21 ½° Taurus) aligns with h-Mercury at Abu Yusuf's death (19° Taurus) to within 2 ½°, thus fulfilling the second rule of astrological reincarnation. However, we have to bear in mind that, whereas the position of h-Mercury at Schubert's birth is exact since the birth time is known, the position of h-Mercury at Abu Yusuf's death is an average one since only the day and not the time of death is known. If Abu Yusuf died at the start of the lunar day Mocharrem 22, the position of h-Mercury would have been 16° Taurus, i.e. 5 ½°

less than the position at Schubert's birth. And if Abu Yusuf died at the close of Mocharrem 22, the position of h-Mercury would have been 22 ½° Taurus, i.e. 1° advanced from the position at Schubert's birth. In any case, it is possible to speak of an alignment in the sidereal zodiac of h-Mercury at Schubert's birth with its position at the death of Abu Yusuf, with the alignment being more exact if Abu Yusuf died during the second half of Mocharrem 22.

When considering the angular relationships expressed in the birth and death horoscopes of any human individuality, one must guard against a kind of "bookkeeping" attitude. It is all too easy to become enamored of the neatly fitting numerical relationships and, in the process, lose track of the sublime and still wholly mysterious cosmic activity behind those "numbers." In a sense, we are presented with two distinct "streams" of activity. One stream is the intricate, truly baroque karmic history of any human being (this chapter's examples—Thomas Aquinas, Alfonso X, and Abu Yusuf—are admittedly spectacularly prominent historical characters, but clearly any human life is a "tangled bank" of karmic details). The other stream is the movement of planets against the stars and the consequent activity of the ranks of spiritual beings guiding and guarding the processes of repeated earthly lives for *every* human being.

One of the most significant truths about history brought to light by Rudolf Steiner is that the human being's journey—expressed so beautifully in the New Testament fable of the prodigal son—has both an outward and inward pulsing arc, an evolution outward from spirit into matter, and then back to spirit from matter. Indeed, the "loss" of the brick pillar of ancient star wisdom is one necessary historical development on this journey, for coincident with this loss was a substantial gain in human freedom, a standing up into selfhood apart from the wisdom imparted by the holy living creatures, the spiritual beings (Seraphim, Cherubim, Thrones) working through the twelve zodiacal constellations. Rudolf Steiner also established through his teachings about karma that all prodigal sons and daughters on their journey experience a rhythmic point/counterpoint "logic" from incarnation to incarnation, so that they are afforded the opportunity to balance in one lifetime the deeds of the previous lifetime. In the great individualities of human history, this contrapuntal dance takes on virtuoso form, leaping forth so spectacularly as to leave a wake that entire civilizations and cultures take centuries and millennia to fulfill.

There is perhaps no more stunning example of this than Steiner himself, who, from the midst of the war-torn, materialistic, and deeply somnambulant decades of early-twentieth-century Europe, gave to the world a scientific path from the physical world into the spiritual world by spiritualizing his own intellect, while showing how others might follow this path. Six centuries earlier, in the person of Thomas Aquinas, this same individuality had, by Christianizing Aristotelian philosophy, shepherded human intelligence through lofty realms of knowledge. However, he then shrank back from the realm of revelation, convinced that human beings had to wait until after death to experience the highest realms of knowledge. For all of his great learning, Aquinas was not an initiate, nor was he clairvoyant. Although he fulfilled a monumental spiritual task during his lifetime, after his death he carried into the spiritual world a longing to penetrate the spiritual world while still incarnated. He fulfilled this task in his incarnation as Rudolf Steiner, forging a path that stands as an archetype for all humanity.

If Thomas Aquinas was one of the premier contemplatives of thirteenth century Europe, his contemporaries Alfonso X and Abu Yusuf were two of the premier "actors"—their imperial exploits setting in motion great political, social, and historical forces. In their next incarnation, the two kings chose genteel Vienna as their meeting ground, and music became the vehicle for the author and patron of the Cantigas de Santa Maria to provide support for a new troubadour named Franz Schubert. Music has been an avenue into the spiritual world during every century and in every corner of the planet. This, of course, includes Alfonso's cantigas; the nûbas and other Andalusian music that would have been heard throughout Abu Yusuf's Islamic kingdom; as well as Schubert's songs and piano sonatas. Whether harmonizing within one individuality's karmic journey from life to life (Thomas Aquinas–Rudolf Steiner) or harmonizing between individualities (Alfonso X–Joseph von Spaun and Abu Yusuf–Franz Schubert), human destiny is deeply "musical" in its composition. As a life unfolds, discrete pitches and tempos ray out and in, melodies come into being and fade away, and harmonies both expected and unexpected burst into song, and then are gone. At this moment of time, the long lost strains of star wisdom in its relation to human destiny are just becoming audible once more, but there is a grand cosmic symphony that is undoubtedly yet to be heard.

CHAPTER THREE

STAYING THE COURSE:
AVOIDING ILLUSION IN KARMIC RESEARCH

In his book *Return of the Revolutionaries,* Dr. Walter Semkiw claims that he is the reincarnation of John Adams, the second president of the United States. He claims, too, that fellow American Revolutionaries have reincarnated, as well, in the present time as George W. Bush, Bill Clinton, Al Gore, Ross Perot, and Ralph Nader. In their previous incarnations, Shirley MacLaine, Oprah Winfrey, and Gary Zukav were all signers of the Declaration of Independence. Retired General Tommy Franks, who led US forces in the 2003 invasion of Iraq, was George Washington.[1]

Based on communications from "Ahtun Re," the channeled ancient Egyptian "spirit guide" of medium Kevin Ryerson (who was Shirley MacLaine's trance channeler for twenty years), Semkiw identifies radio host George Noory as William Whipple, a shipmaster and merchant captain who became New Hampshire's delegate to the Continental Congress. Ahtun Re also made past-life matches in Revolutionary era America for Carl Sagan, Steve Jobs, Steve Wozniak, and New Age writer Neale Donald Walsch. Nor does Semkiw stop there; he goes beyond the Revolutionary generation to identify mystery writer Michael Crichton as Rabelais; Ariel Sharon as Napoleon III; Uri Geller as medium Daniel Dunglas Home. Semkiw confirms Ahtun Re's identifications by comparing facial appearance, personal interests, and writing styles. Along with finding "nearly identical facial architecture" for Al Gore and General Horatio Gates, for example, Semkiw reasons that Gates was a "master of military organization," and Gore was a "master of the intricacies of government." [2]

This sort of simplistic causal calculus of reincarnation was already afoot in the early twentieth-century revival of Western interest in reincarnation. Thus, it is unsurprising that Rudolf Steiner began his *Karmic*

---

1 Semkiw, *Return of the Revolutionaries,* xiii–xiv.

2 Ibid., pp. 234–235.

Relationships series with a devastating critique of the cause-and-effect logic of modern science. Having clearly shown the limitations of biology to explain plants or animals (much less human beings) based on principles and forces restricted to mineral nature, Steiner prepared his audiences for the kind of unorthodox causal observations he would make throughout the karmic lectures. "What was head-organization in the previous life becomes foot- or limb-organization," in the subsequent life, and vice versa (Steiner discovered this while doing karmic research on his geometry teacher, who had a club foot). Founders and devotees of important historical movements become separated from the movement (for example, Ignatius of Loyola, founder of the Jesuit Order, who reincarnated as Emmanuel Swedenborg). Moreover, through the action of Mercury beings, illnesses from one incarnation are transformed into moral and spiritual qualities.

The human mind, when predisposed to a certain belief, has a tendency (for example, in making biographical or horoscopic comparisons) to seize upon any correlation as a substantiation of that belief. The reincarnation statements made in *Return of the Revolutionaries* are glaring examples of this sort of mistaken correlational activity. Similarly, one can fall into a subjective tendency when working with horoscopes. It is quite possible for two horoscopes to display a number of correlations purely by chance. It would be dangerous and misleading to take such agreements between two horoscopes as proof in itself of a particular example of reincarnation.

KAMALOCA CONFUSION

The guiding role played in *Return of the Revolutionaries* by the channeled entity Ahtun Re points to a much more serious danger than mere sloppy causal thinking—one that has plagued modern thinking about reincarnation. Ever since the Fox sisters let the Spiritualist genie out of the bottle in 1846, a cacophony of so-called spirits have been playing havoc with beliefs about the life between death and rebirth. Although Spiritualists in the nineteenth-century largely denounced reincarnation, preferring fantasies of various highly materialistic "Summerlands" on the other side, by the early twentieth century, Anglo-American Spiritualists were becoming the most active evangelists for reincarnation. In almost every decade of the twentieth century, there has been some media frenzy about a spectacular case of supposed reincarnation. In the teens and twenties, Pearl Lenore Curran, a St. Louis housewife, became the vehicle for "Patience Worth," a seventeenth-century English schoolgirl, using "automatic writing" to produce six novels and hundreds of pages of poetry, proverbs, prayers, and conversation. Beginning in 1923, the "Sleeping Prophet" Edgar Cayce delivered thousands of "Life Readings," in which he gave details about individual past incarnations in Atlantis, ancient Egypt, colonial America, and other times and places. In 1952, after being hypnotized, Colorado housewife Virginia Tighe claimed to be the reincarnation of Bridey Murphy, a girl from Cork, Ireland. In the 1970s, "Seth" through Jane Roberts, "Ramtha" through J. Z. Knight, and dozens of other channeled, discarnate, wise entities held forth on the intricate mechanics of reincarnation. By the time Shirley MacLaine, with the help of trance medium Kevin Ryerson, "discovered" her past lives and wrote about them in *Out On a Limb* (1983), "past life regression" was a full-blown American fad, and today there are probably more than a million people who claim to have some knowledge of their previous incarnations.[3]

Even a cursory examination of the history of the mediumistic conjuring of "spirits" during the nineteenth and twentieth centuries—from Mormon "Prophet" Joseph Smith's "Moroni" and "Poughkeepsie Seer" Andrew Jackson Davis's "Swedenborg" and "Galen" to Barbara Marciniak's "Pleiadeans" and Esther Hicks's "Abraham" (this last one played a role in the recent New Age craze "The Secret")—gives one the image of Walt Disney's Sorcerer's Apprentice episode in *Fantasia,* in which hapless wizard Mickey Mouse is surrounded by out-of-control astral critters. The "magic" that released such a menagerie of past-life characters has been consistently the grey magic of somnambulists, hypnotists, and mediums. While Pearl Curran and Jane Roberts used Ouija boards, the vast majority of "reincarnation" tales have come from hypnotized individuals, whose individual self,

---

3 As an example of how widespread "past-life regression" has become, consider Richard Sutphen, who in 1972 developed a technique to simultaneously regress large groups of people to alleged former lifetimes. After his book *You Were Born Again to Be Together* became a bestseller in 1978, Sutphen began holding past-life seminars in major cities throughout the United States, with an annual Super Seminar in Arizona. By the 1990s, more than 100,000 people had attended a Sutphen seminar, and hundreds of thousands more experienced past life regression through his eighteen books and more than 350 audio and video titles, which include the first prerecorded hypnosis tapes.

the "I," is placed at the mercy of a host of invisible beings who delight in deceiving human beings by feeding them bogus information about both themselves and spiritual realms.

And what deceptions! Unfortunately, the *Complete Idiot's Guide to Past Life Regression* is just what the title declares. The book accepts the premise that one can gain knowledge of previous incarnations merely by entering a hypnotic state. Invariably, the resulting identities are notable. Shirley MacLaine published *Out on a Limb,* in which she claims to have been the lover of Charlemagne in a past life, as well as that of his current reincarnation, Swedish Prime Minister Olaf Palme. In a reading devoted to Woodrow Wilson, Edgar Cayce proclaimed Wilson a vehicle of Christ.[4] The tragedy of such an epidemic of illusion about reincarnation is threefold. First, seeking glorious and wholly imaginary past incarnations prevents people from fulfilling their present unique destinies. Second, the "past life therapy" movement believes it is ushering in a "new age" of heightened spirituality, whereas it actually shepherds humanity into an even more materialistic future. Finally, the victims of reincarnation illusions have not only populated the astral realm with polluted thought forms that can continue to deceive future unprepared vagabonds, but they in fact also supply material for what ancient Israel called "the pit" and modern esotericism names the "eighth sphere,"[5] a subterranean prison planet.

In the entire witches brew of past-life regression and channeling, one finds that Christ is either ignored or caricatured, because the source for the channeled messages are primarily regressive beings that lack proper knowledge and experience of the Christ. Such regressive beings have fallen away from the divine plan of evolution. St. Paul referred to them as "spiritual hosts of wickedness in the heavenly places" and recommends that we gird ourselves with truth and the "breastplate of righteousness" (Ephesians 6:12–14) in order to deal with those deceptive forces. In addition to the traditional view of contending with fallen

---

4 Cayce, *Life Reading 3976–12.* Steiner, on the other hand, in a lecture in Zurich, October 16, 1918, pointed emphatically to the fact that his spiritual-scientific research showed that President Wilson was "possessed in his subconscious."

5 There are seven spheres of evolution—these being the seven pillars in the temple referred to in *Proverbs* 9:1. The eighth sphere is a "disposal pit" for all that falls away from the course of evolution mapped out as the seven spheres, or pillars, according to the divine plan.

beings during earthly life through prayer, truthfulness, and a moral way of life, it is also helpful to consider how human beings in the life after death may encounter those beings' influence in the Moon sphere during *kamaloca,* the period of purification that human souls enter after leaving the Earth. During kamaloca, one casts off the negative shadow of oneself (known esoterically as "the double") to enter gradually the heavenly aspect of existence. In this process of purification, known to Roman Catholics as "purgatory," we essentially divest ourselves of all the negative karma accumulated during life on Earth before journeying through the planetary spheres beyond the Moon and up to the higher heavenly realm represented outwardly by the fixed stars.

At some point on this journey of the soul into higher realms, the decision is made to return to incarnation on the Earth. On the inward return to the next incarnation, the soul passes back down through the planetary spheres, and the Moon sphere is the last planetary realm through which one passes during the time leading up to conception (prior to birth), where it meets and "gathers up" the negative karma from the past. It is possible for certain souls, just before reincarnating, to "pick up" memories from newly discarnate human beings in kamaloca and to carry those memories into the next life *as if they were their own.* This seems to be the explanation for cases such as that of Barbro Karlén, who has received much attention for her claim to be the reincarnation of Anne Frank.[6]

There is a much darker dimension to the deceptions played out in the sphere of the Moon and encouraged (from there) right here on Earth. As Rudolf Steiner so courageously pointed out in his lectures *The Occult Movement in the Nineteenth Century,* the Spiritualist movement—which encouraged millions of Americans and other Westerners to adopt a mediumistic approach to the spiritual world—was manipulated by "brothers of the left," occult lodges keen to keep the true concepts of karma and reincarnation—and Christ—away from humanity. With the modern epidemic of trance channeling and hypnotic regression "therapies," these brotherhoods continue to thwart the recognition of Christ, and thus derail humanity from its proper destiny. The esoteric Tower of Babel that they have helped to unleash

---

6 See Karlén, *And the Wolves Howled: Fragments of Two Lifetimes.* This may also be the explanation for another recent notorious case of alleged reincarnation of individuals from the Nazi era, Yonassan Gershom's *Beyond the Ashes: Cases of Reincarnation from the Holocaust.*

also simultaneously provides cover for their own illicit activity. Ultimately, the many competing and conflicting voices from the world of the Moon sphere obscure the one true voice, that of the Logos. The pervasiveness in Western popular culture of this kamalocan garbage tossed up by mediumistic activity only deepens the problem. Rather than being merely flaky illusions that prevent proper consideration of authentic research into karma and reincarnation, channeling has become an incredibly persistent avenue for influences that lead at best to delusion, and at worst to demonic possession, and unfortunately it is almost wholly unrecognized as being such an avenue.[7]

THE SHUFFLING EFFECT OF THE LUCIFERIC SPHERE

As Rudolf Steiner describes,

> Through the temptation of Lucifer, what we may call the "expulsion from Paradise" has come about.... Expulsion from Paradise means that the human being was originally in the spiritual world, that is, in Paradise, and consisted of *Imagination, Inspiration,* and *Intuition* in an entirely supra-earthly existence.... Under the luciferic influence, the human being received an inrush...of matter. Thus, we are filled with matter, but it does not belong to us. We bear this matter within us, and because we bear it in us we must die a physical death."[8]

Not only did a great change come about in human beings, but also, at the time of this ancient event known as the Fall, a great change took place in the relationship between the Earth and the cosmos. Lucifer (the being responsible for the Fall and depicted in the Bible in the image

---

7 It is possible to understand much of Rudolf Steiner's mission as one of correcting the untruths about the life after death that had been introduced by the secret lodges not only via Spiritualism, but also via H. P. Blavatsky who, though outspoken about the grave errors of Spiritualists in attributing paranormal phenomena to "spirits of the dead" (rather than to the activities of fallen elementals and astral shells), was herself a victim of occult manipulation, particularly regarding her conceptions of reincarnation. The Eastern lodges were keen that humanity would not learn the truth about the human being's life after death in the planetary spheres and also that humankind should be kept ignorant about the importance of Christ as the Lord of Karma.

8 Steiner, *World of the Senses and World of the Spirit*, lectures of December 28 and 29, 1911 (translation revised).

of a serpent) inserted himself between the Earth and the cosmos. This created a sphere around the Earth, which some call the luciferic sphere.[9] When we search for knowledge regarding karma we need to understand that the luciferic sphere has to be traversed to reach pure truth.

The luciferic sphere has a "shuffling" effect that is especially dangerous to those conducting karmic research. Rudolf Steiner gives as an example in *Karmic Relationships* the Roman emperor Julian the Apostate, who was a nephew of the emperor Constantine the Great. Julian was born in A.D. 331 or 332 and died 363. He was emperor from 360 to 363 and tried to reinstate the pagan mystery religion in place of Christianity. Schooled in Neoplatonism, he was familiar with the teaching of reincarnation. Through the shuffling effect of the luciferic sphere, he came to believe that he was the reincarnation of Alexander the Great. According to Socrates Scholasticus, also known as Socrates of Constantinople (fourth to fifth centuries A.D.), Julian believed himself to be Alexander the Great in another body via soul transmigration as taught by Plato and Pythagoras.[10]

In fact, Julian the Apostate actually did have a spiritual connection with Alexander the Great, and the "inspiration" (actually the force of illusion) working from the luciferic sphere acted through the spiritual connection between Julian the Apostate and Alexander the Great to shuffle, or distort, matters. This caused a shift in Julian's consciousness to believing he was Alexander the Great. Generally, the luciferic sphere uses a real connection, then shuffles things around to cause a very powerful illusion that is a distortion of the truth.

According to Rudolf Steiner, Julian the Apostate reincarnated in the ninth century as Herzeloyde, the mother of Parzival.[11] In notes published in 1976 by Margarete and Erich Kirchner-Bockholt, Steiner indicates that Alexander the Great reincarnated as Sigune, a cousin of Parzival; she was therefore a niece of Herzeloyde.[12] In Wolfram von Eschenbach's account, Sigune, upon the death of her mother Schoy-

---

9 Tomberg, *Christ and Sophia* (pp. 43–46), describes the this sphere: "The luciferic sphere is not merely a ring moving round the Earth; it is also the sum of the forces that influence earthly events."

10 Socrates and Sozomenus, *Ecclesiastical Histories,* trans. Philip Schaff, book 3, chapter 21.

11 Steiner, *Karmic Relationships,* vol. 4, p. 82.

12 Kirchner-Bockholt, *Rudolf Steiner's Mission and Ita Wegman,* pp. 72–79.

siane, was given into Herzeloyde's care.[13] Hence there was a very close relationship between Herzeloyde and Sigune, reflecting the close spiritual relationship between Julian the Apostate and Alexander the Great. Herzeloyde and Sigune are closely connected but not identical. Julian the Apostate sensed the close connection with Alexander the Great on a spiritual level, yet through the influence of the luciferic sphere fell into the illusion that he was identical with Alexander the Great.

This example warns of the danger of falling into illusions about oneself. It is a sort of spiritual illness by which one human "I" comes to identify with another false "I." It is very difficult to heal someone of this spiritual illness, and indeed a person may even become aggressive when the truth is pointed out, because they prefer to cling to the illusion. Moreover, once the door has been opened to connect oneself with the luciferic sphere by way of illusion, a veritable flood of false inspirations may stream from that sphere into the person's consciousness. The results may border on mental illness.

Increasingly, people are becoming subject to illusory thoughts concerning one or more of their previous incarnations, and often the illusion is not restricted to themselves but includes the previous incarnations of others around them. Such spiritual illness is assuming epidemic proportions. One purpose of this book is to help awaken people to this serious danger and to indicate a path that enables one to circumnavigate the pitfalls of this domain.

GROUP ILLUSION

Sometimes an entire group of people can come under the influence of a luciferic inspiration concerning a certain individual—usually a spiritual teacher. In 1910, C. W. Leadbeater, a leading Theosophist, began a series of articles in *The Theosophist* that claimed to describe previous lives of Jiddhu Krishnamurti, an individual he called "Alcyone" (from the brightest star in the Pleiades cluster in the constellation Taurus). Leadbeater went on to give star names to all of the characters in his tale of Krishnamurti's past incarnations. At the time, Alcyone was a thirteen-year-old boy whom Leadbeater met in Adyar, India, when the boy came to the beach after school with friends. In Leadbeater's account, Alcyone's biography begins in the Gobi Desert

13 Von Eschenbach, *Parzival*, p. 477.

around 70,000 B.C. and goes through forty-eight incarnations before appearing in Kannauj, India, in 624 B.C. In his thirteenth incarnation, in 27,527 B.C. in Ireland, Alcyone was the grandson of a priest named Surya, who with the help of the Tuatha-de-Danaan (the nature spirits) founded a series of sacred sites through which magnetic power would be radiated. Alcyone would carry on this tradition. In the nineteenth incarnation, Alcyone was a female priest possessed of great psychic powers and living in an area west of the Rocky Mountains. In life number forty-six, in the mid-second millennium B.C., Alcyone (then called Maidhyairnaongha) was an admiring cousin of Zarathustra.[14]

In his penultimate life, according to Leadbeater, Alcyone met Lord Buddha, became a devotee, traveled the Ganges Valley with him, and was then told he would become the Maitreya Bodhisattva, who is yet to come. Indeed, Leadbeater and the Theosophical Society president Annie Besant devoted the next fifteen years to promoting Krishnamurti as the reincarnated Jesus, or Jeshu, in whom the Maitreya Bodhisattva (for Leadbeater, identical with Christ) would incarnate. Krishnamurti was thus heralded as the vessel for the new World Teacher, and the Order of the Star of the East was founded in his honor to support his world mission. Thousands of people were taken in by this illusory "inspiration" from the luciferic sphere, until on August 3, 1929, the thirty-four-year-old Krishnamurti disbanded the order and declared that his sole purpose was to set human beings free, absolutely and unconditionally. By that time he had been the figurehead of the order for eighteen years.

In the Krishnamurti affair, the force of this illusion worked powerfully because of the heightened mood of expectation among Theosophists for the coming of the Maitreya Boddhisattva at the beginning of the twentieth century. Guided by Leadbeater, Krishnamurti became the unwitting object, and victim, of that subconscious projection of expectation. Luciferic inspiration can work wherever there is a mood of expectation to create a "substitute" avatar, which diverts

---

14 Along with the spurious karmic history of Krishnamurti, Leadbeater's *Lives of Alcyone* makes many false statements about other individuals, a number of who were among Leadbeater's Theosophical circle. The character "Venus" in *Lives of Alcyone* is said to have had these incarnations: A.D. 1214 in England as Roger Bacon; A.D. 1375 in Germany, as Christian Rosenkreutz; A.D. 1425 in Hungary as John Hunyadi; A.D. 1500 in Germany as Monk Roberts; A.D. 1561 in England as Francis Bacon; and last, as the eighteenth century adept Count St. Germain. (Besant and Leadbeater, *Lives of Alcyone*, vol. 1, p. 305.)

attention away from the true expected one. In a remark to Friedrich Rittelmeyer in August 1921, Rudolf Steiner referred to an earlier incarnation of the Maitreya Bodhisattva as Jeshu ben Pandira, the teacher of the Essenes: "Jeshu ben Pandira was born at the beginning of this [the twentieth] century, and if we live another fifteen years, we shall notice his activity."[15] This points to a birth around 1900; Krishnamurti was born on May 12, 1895. Acting under luciferic inspiration, C. W. Leadbeater presented Krishnamurti as a "substitute" for the real reincarnated Jeshu ben Pandira, thus diverting the attention of many people from the truth.

DISTINGUISHING BETWEEN REINCARNATION AND THE PASSING OF THE ASTRAL OR ETHERIC BODY

There is yet another subtle point that calls for our attention. We need to understand that it is the "I" that reincarnates from life to life. The "I" is the true self, the kernel or core, of the human being, which indwells all the bodies—astral, etheric, and physical. The "I" is much more than the ordinary ego. In keeping with Jungian psychology, the ego relates to the self as the part to the whole. Therefore, to make a reincarnation statement such as "Elijah = John the Baptist" means strictly that the "I" of Elijah reappeared as the "I" of John the Baptist, as indicated by Christ himself:

> For all the prophets and the law prophesied until John. And if ye will receive it, this is Elijah, which was for to come. He that hath ears to hear, let him hear. (Matthew 11:13–15)

In addition to reincarnation of the "I," or self, however, it is possible for a person's astral or etheric body to be passed on to someone else. A classic example is Zarathustra, founder of the Persian religion, who passed his astral body on to Hermes, the teacher of the Egyptian mysteries, and his etheric body to Moses, the teacher of the people of Israel.[16] Another example that Rudolf Steiner gives is the German cardinal, philosopher, jurist, mathematician, and astronomer Nicolaus Cusanus (1402–1464), whose astral body was passed on to Nico-

---

15 Powell, *Hermetic Astrology*, vol. 1, p. 78.

16 See Steiner, *According to Matthew*, lecture 2.

laus Copernicus (1473–1543).[17] Almost two years later, in his lecture series *Occult History,* Rudolf Steiner made a statement concerning the polymath Nicolaus Cusanus: "He was born again—it was a case of a very quick reincarnation—as Nicolaus Copernicus."[18]

What are we to make of such a statement? If the reincarnation statement "Nicolaus Cusanus = Nicolaus Copernicus" is true, then there is an identity on the level of the "I." However, Steiner's statement from 1909 implies that it is not a matter of an identity on the level of the "I," but that Nicolaus Copernicus received the astral body of Nicolaus Cusanus.

In the comparison of Copernicus's birth horoscope with Cusanus's death horoscope, the first "law" of astrological reincarnation is not fulfilled (see the geocentric comparison chart on page 80). The second "law" is fulfilled, however, since h-Mercury (10° Cancer) at the birth of Copernicus is opposite h-Mercury (10° Capricorn) at the death of Cusanus (see the hermetic comparison chart, page 81). Does this alignment provide confirmation that Copernicus was the reincarnation of Cusanus, or does it simply say that Copernicus received the astral body of Cusanus?

Another striking feature in this chart comparison is that the geocentric conjunction of the Moon and Jupiter at Copernicus's birth aligned closely with the position of the Moon in Scorpio at the death of Cusanus. Moreover, the Sun in Aquarius at Copernicus's birth aligned closely with geocentric Jupiter's position at Cusanus's death. In Copernicus's birth horoscope the Sun and Pluto are in opposition, whereas the Sun and Pluto are in conjunction at Cusanus's death.

The chart comparison alone, however—striking though it may be—does not help solve the question implied by Rudolf Steiner's two different statements (from 1909 and 1910). We are faced with a real dilemma. This example illustrates the fact that it is impossible to know, based only on a chart comparison, whether there is an actual reincarnation or the passing on of an etheric or astral body, in this case a matter of passing on the astral body.

Now let's approach the validity of the reincarnation statement "Nicolaus Cusanus = Nicolaus Copernicus" from a different angle. Cusanus was born in 1401 and was therefore sixty-two or sixty-three

---

17 Steiner, *The Principle of Spiritual Economy,* January 21, 1909.

18 Steiner, *Occult History,* p. 94.

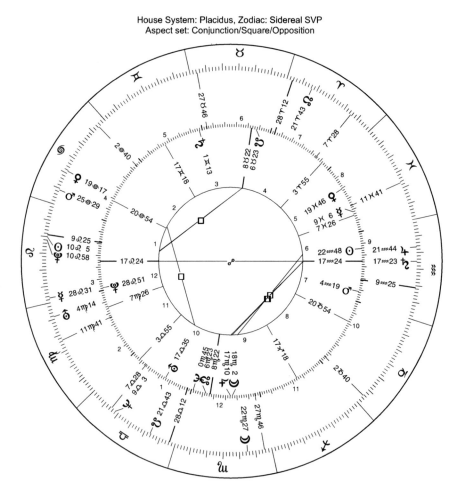

Comparison Chart

Outer - Geocentric
Death of (Cardinal) Nicolaus Cusanus
At Todi, Latitude 42N47', Longitude 12E24'
Date: Saturday, 11/AUG/1464, Julian
Time: 12: 0, Local Time
Sidereal Time 9:55:42, Vernal Point 12 ♓ 43'29"

Inner - Geocentric
Birth of Nicolaus Copernicus
At Thorn, Poland, Latitude 53N01', Longitude 18E35'
Date: Friday, 19/FEB/1473, Julian
Time: 17: 0, Local Time
Sidereal Time 3:33:40, Vernal Point 12 ♓ 36'22"

House System: Placidus, Zodiac: Sidereal SVP
Aspect set: Conjunction/Square/Opposition

years old at his death on August 11, 1464. After death, human beings
undergo the kamaloca period, which, according to Steiner, lasts
approximately one-third the length of one's life. For Cusanus, kamaloca should have lasted for about twenty years. However, Nicolaus
Copernicus was born 8 ½ years after Cusanus's death. If Cusanus reincarnated as Copernicus, this would have signified a breach of karmic
laws, according to which the human being lives through kamaloca
before reincarnating.

Comparison Chart

Outer - Tychonic	Inner - Tychonic
Death of (Cardinal) Nicolaus Cusanus	Birth of Nicolaus Copernicus
At Todi, Latitude 42N47', Longitude 12E24'	At Thorn, Poland, Latitude 53N01', Longitude 18E35'
Date: Saturday, 11/AUG/1464, Julian	Date: Friday, 19/FEB/1473, Julian
Time: 12: 0, Local Time	Time: 17: 0, Local Time
Sidereal Time 9:55:42, Vernal Point 12 ♓ 43'29"	Sidereal Time 3:33:40, Vernal Point 12 ♓ 36'22"

House System: Placidus, Zodiac: Sidereal SVP
Aspect set: Conjunction/Square/Opposition

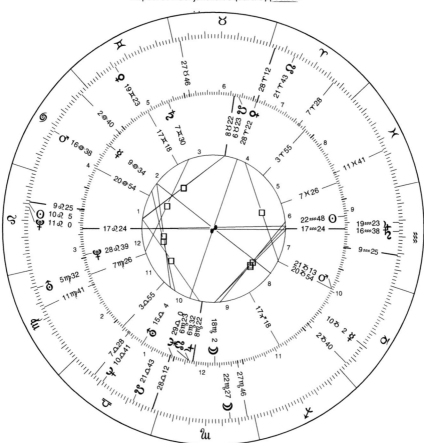

In the twentieth and twenty-first centuries, the laws of karma are being modified, with human beings reincarnating rapidly, without living through kamaloca. So what happens in such cases?

Let's suppose that someone lives through life "A" during the first half of the twentieth century and then reincarnates during the second half of the century (life "B") without having completed the normal period of kamaloca. One must make up for this somehow. When life "B" follows shortly after life "A," breaking the normal laws of karma, kamaloca for life "B" and life "A" must then be lived through, as though "A" and "B" were two halves of a single long life. Ultimately, the laws of karma cannot be circumvented. Thus, the kamaloca period that should have followed the end of life "A" is simply postponed until the end of life "B." The question is: Was this the case with Cusanus–Copernicus?

This question makes sense only if Copernicus was the reincarnation of Cusanus, as Rudolf Steiner seems to say in *Occult History*. Steiner was not the first esotericist to speak of a connection between Cusanus and Copernicus. H. P. Blavatsky, too, spoke of Copernicus as the reincarnated Cusanus in her lectures. She wrote about Cusanus as an adept who, in the face Church tyranny, sought intellectual recuperation and respite in the body of Copernicus.[19]

Rudolf Steiner made it a principle not to simply take over the findings of others, but always to pursue his own independent investigations. While it may appear that he took over Blavatsky's statement, he was very clear that this was not the case. In a lecture of January 21, 1909, he says:

> The soul body [astral body] of Cusanus did actually become passed on to Copernicus, although the "I" of Copernicus was quite another one than that of Cusanus.[20]

So we see clearly here that Steiner saw this as a matter of two separate "I" beings. Therefore we cannot say, "Nicolaus Cusanus = Nicolaus Copernicus." What we can say is that several years after his death, Cusanus's astral body was passed on to Copernicus, and that, from spiritual realms, the "I" of Cusanus closely followed the unfolding of Copernicus's life on Earth. Thus, it was not a matter of a rapid reincarnation and the breaking of the normal laws of reincarnation and kamaloca.

Clearly, the comparison of horoscopes is insufficient to distinguish the reincarnation of the "I" from the passing on of the astral or etheric bodies. The ability to make this distinction requires well-developed faculties of subtle perception—an intuitive "sixth sense." Without this, astrological reincarnation research can be highly misleading. Here lies another subtle danger in addition to the illusion of luciferic inspiration.

---

19 Blavatsky, *Secret Doctrine*, vol. 3, 377–378

20 Steiner, *The Principle of Spiritual Economy*, January 21, 1909.

THE TROPICAL ZODIAC: A LUCIFERIC INSPIRATION?

Earlier we considered the process of how the tropical zodiac was introduced. Left unanswered is the question of why. One possibility has to do with humanity's spiritual evolution and the attainment of spiritual freedom. This perspective can be grasped by way of analogy with the Fall. From one perspective, the Fall was a tragedy. Lucifer's intervention (symbolized by the temptation of the snake in Genesis 3:1–7) means that humankind fell from its harmonious union with higher spiritual reality. A separation occurred, and human beings felt cut off from the Divine. Yet this is precisely what allowed freedom and the attainment of self-consciousness. Without Lucifer's intervention, we would have remained in a condition of unconscious union with higher spiritual reality, rather like the relationship between a baby and the mother.

Analogously, it is possible to see a higher purpose here—that the tropical zodiac was introduced to cut us off from the world of stars in order for us to attain freedom from this higher world and reach a new level of self-awareness as earthly human beings. Ptolemy was unwittingly instrumental in the fulfillment of this divine purpose. The projection of the tropical calendar into space created a veil between humanity and the world of stars.[21] Now, however, it is time to penetrate this veil and return to a connection with divine spiritual reality. How is this possible? It is possible through Christ,[22] through Christ's will in us, as indicated by this meditative verse by Steiner:

> Isis–Sophia
> Wisdom of God:
> Lucifer hath slain her
> And on the wings of Worldwide Forces
> Carried her forth into cosmic Space.
> Christ Will,

---

21 Powell, *History of the Zodiac*, chapter 3 describes that originally the tropical zodiac was not a zodiac but a calendar dividing the cycle of the year into twelve solar months named after the zodiacal constellations according to the method of correspondences ("as above, so below"). The tropical calendar, a division of time, was subsequently projected into space, thus creating the tropical zodiac familiar to modern astrology. See also appendix 1 of this volume.

22 References to Christ in this book are to be understood in the sense of the Cosmic Christ, who is the Spirit of the Universe, and whose Being is Divine Love.

> Working in human beings,
> Shall wrest from Lucifer
> And on the sails of Spirit knowledge
> Call to new life in human souls
> Isis–Sophia,
> Wisdom of God.[23]

Steiner conveys the appeal to us to penetrate the veil and reach the Divine Sophia, or "Wisdom of God." What has happened from the time of ancient Egypt to render us generally unaware of Sophia? She is still there in cosmic space, but Lucifer has "slain" her—not literally, but in terms of Sophia's relationship to humanity. A veil has been placed between human consciousness and Divine Sophia, and the tropical zodiac is an expression of this veil. It is an intellectual construct that has taken hold in human consciousness, blocking perception of the spiritual reality of the cosmos. In writing these words, one knows that it may be difficult for some readers to accept them. Nonetheless, it is solely the truth that counts, not any attachment based on "sympathy for the known" or "antipathy for the unknown." The truth may be hard to accept, but most people would agree it is better to know the truth rather than to live in illusion.[24] Moreover, on the spiritual path, it is a normal practice to use one's intelligence and conscience to discover the illusions one holds, proceeding from illusion to truth, the realm of the Holy Spirit. The advance from illusion to truth requires discernment of the illusory, followed by cognition of the illusion as a reflection of the truth.

> To reach the sphere of the Holy Spirit, consciousness must first pass through the luciferic sphere that covers it. To arrive at truth, it must first conquer the surrounding lies. The conquest requires that the power of conscience recognizes the fact that the luciferic sphere is a mere reflection and thus advances to the truth reflected by it.[25]

---

23 Steiner, *Verses and Meditations*, p. 123. Divine Sophia was known as Isis to the ancient Egyptians.

24 Powell, *History of the Zodiac* gives extensive background concerning the origin of the sidereal zodiac and of the tropical zodiac.

25 Tomberg, *Christ and Sophia*, p. 45.

As pointed out, both the tropical zodiac and the astronomical zodiac are intellectual constructs (products initially from the minds of Hipparchus and, later, Ptolemy) that work to veil our perception of spiritual reality. Examples of this are the Virgin seen as reclining (instead of standing); the fact that "the Balance Holder" (Archangel Michael in Christian iconography) holding the Scales has been banished from the zodiac; and that some zodiacal constellations are seen as "large" and others as "small," whereas in reality they are each 30° long in terms of their spiritual influence.

To grasp the effects of intellectual constructs such as the astronomical and the tropical zodiacs, which then become vehicles for Lucifer's inspiration, it is helpful to consider this descending sequence from the Divine down to the level of human consciousness (see diagram). Lucifer has inserted himself between Sophia and human consciousness, so that inspiration proceeding from Sophia becomes "deflected" by Lucifer before it reaches human consciousness. Through deflection a caricature is created, a caricature that mirrors divine spiritual reality but is not the Divine Spiritual itself; rather, it is a "construction." The tropical zodiac is an example of such a construction of an intellectual nature.

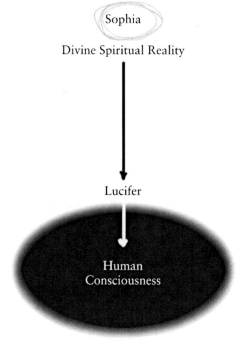

Sophia

Divine Spiritual Reality

Lucifer

Human
Consciousness

By contrast, the sidereal zodiac was not constructed intellectually. As pointed out earlier, it is an expression of the spiritual reality of the "holy living creatures" (*Seraphim, Cherubim, Thrones*) mentioned in the book of Ezekiel and in the fourth chapter of the book of Revelation as the *Zoa* around the throne of God.

> The living ones.... By this name they are called in the visions of St. John and of Ezekiel. The Greek word *Zoa* applied to them by St. John exactly corresponds to the Hebrew word *Chayoth,* by which Ezekiel calls them. Both mean living creatures.[26]

As mentioned, it was Zaratas, known to the Greeks as Zoroaster, who indicated the original definition of the sidereal zodiac in terms of the fixed stars Aldebaran and Antares. This great initiate, Zoroaster, clairvoyantly penetrated to the level of divine spiritual reality of the Zoa ("the holy living creatures") and communicated what he found to the Babylonian priesthood. This is the origin of the sidereal zodiac, as the "circle of the Zoa" with the twelve signs to indicate the spheres of influence of the twelve groupings of the Zoa.

The tropical zodiac originated during Ptolemy's lifetime as a projection of the tropical calendar, when this projection coincided more or less with the sidereal zodiac. With this coincidence an opportunity arose to substitute a caricature (the tropical zodiac) for the true expression of Divine Spiritual reality (the sidereal zodiac). This opportunity arose with the Arabs, who, not knowing of the original zodiac, adopted the tropical zodiac in their practice of astrology. Thus, a caricature (the tropical zodiac) was substituted for the authentic, sidereal zodiac. Most of the attributes associated with the original, sidereal zodiac became "deflected" onto the tropical zodiac. For example, the Babylonians saw the "exaltation" of the Moon at 3° in the sidereal sign of Taurus, close to the Pleiades at 5° Taurus, and a cuneiform tablet depicts the Moon at exaltation alongside the Pleiades.[27] By way of deflection, the exaltation of the Moon in tropical astrology is considered to be at 3° of the tropical sign of Taurus, which now equates with 8° of sidereal Aries, near the star Mesartim in the horns of the Ram, about 27° distant from the Pleiades.

---

26 Smith, *The Zodia*, p. 2.

27 Weidner, *Gestirn-Darstellungen auf babylonischen Tontafeln*, p.5.

REDISCOVERING ASTRO-SOPHIA

The tropical zodiac, as an intellectual construct of the Greek mind,[28] has become firmly established in the minds of today's Western astrologers. Practicing astrologers have a vested interest in maintaining the status quo. An astrologer who has been paid for advice to clients will not find it easy to say to a client, "All of these years I have been saying to you that you are an Aquarius, but the Sun was actually in Capricorn when you were born." To make such a statement requires courage. How much easier it is to ignore the "zodiac question" and continue practicing tropical astrology. A frequently used line of justification is, "They cannot all be wrong, all those millions of people who believe in tropical astrology, and all the books written on tropical astrology." As pointed out, the spiritual reality underlying the belief of these millions is actually the *tropical calendar*. The tropical calendar is real; as a spatial projection of the tropical calendar, the tropical zodiac is solely an intellectual construct. But because there is a reality underlying this intellectual construct, and because of the spiritual reality of the sidereal zodiac, deflected onto the tropical zodiac, the latter appears real. It is a "floating reality," however, uprooted and disconnected from divine spiritual reality.

In comparing tropical and sidereal astrology, it should be borne in mind that the only difference between a tropical and a sidereal horoscope is the *zodiacal location* of the planets and other elements in the horoscope. Otherwise, in terms of planetary aspects, houses, and so on, they are identical. Therefore, tropical astrologers are still able to make many true statements, even if their art rests on an erroneous foundation. Many tropical astrologers are gifted with intuition and are able to make true pronouncements despite the tropical system. How much more their natural gift could blossom if they were to make the transition from tropical to sidereal astrology.

In a conversation several years ago, the French sidereal astrologer Jacques Dorsan—who had practiced tropical astrology for about ten years before beginning his career as a "siderealist"—was asked how,

---

28 It seems that the tropical zodiac originated with the Greek astronomer Hipparchus (second century B.C.). He used it purely as a coordinate system. It was much later, through Ptolemy (second century A.D.), that the tropical zodiac was introduced into astrology. See Powell, *History of the Zodiac*, pp. 7–15.

in looking back, he viewed his time as a "tropicalist."[29] He replied that the transition from tropical to sidereal astrology for him was comparable to initially believing that the Earth is flat and then discovering it is round.

To return to the historical reason for the introduction of the tropical zodiac into astrology, it has had the consequence of helping to cut humanity off from the spiritual reality of the starry heavens, where Divine Sophia is to be found. Lucifer has created a veil between humanity and Divine Sophia, thus rendering Sophia impotent, by using intellectual constructs such as the tropical zodiac as a foothold in human consciousness. However, as indicated in Rudolf Steiner's verse quoted earlier, the relationship between humankind and Sophia will be restored through the "Christ will working in human beings." With the help of Christ's will, we can break through the veil of illusions in human consciousness to find a new relationship with the divine spiritual reality of the world of stars, to find Sophia. Having been cut off from Sophia and the star world, we acquired freedom and consciousness of ourselves as earthly beings, and we are able to take the step of rediscovering Sophia in a conscious way, to give rise to *Astro-Sophia*, or star wisdom.

SIGNS AND CONSTELLATIONS

Earlier researchers inspired by the work of Rudolf Steiner—such as Elisabeth Vreede, Günther Wachsmuth, and Willi Sucher—without knowing about the sidereal zodiac, were limited to casting horoscopes in terms of the conventional tropical zodiac and then adding in the zodiacal constellations around the outside. Each of them realized the importance of the sidereal frame of reference; however, not knowing of the equal-division constellations/signs of the sidereal zodiac, they were obliged to work with the unequal-division constellations of the astronomical zodiac. The only way of drawing a horoscope showing the location of the planets in the constellations was first to draw the horoscope showing the planets in the signs of the tropical zodiac and then to draw the unequal constellations around the outside. In this way there arose the convention of speaking about the "constellations"

---

29 See Dorsan, *The Clockwise House System*, as well as articles about him and his work in *Journal for Star Wisdom 2011*.

(unequal, astronomical) and the "signs" (equal, tropical). If, however, the sidereal zodiac is employed, all talk about "signs" and "constellations" as separate entities is superfluous, as the zodiacal constellations in terms of the sidereal zodiac are equal-division sidereal signs. Moreover, because of the way in which the sidereal signs are defined, each 30° long, they can be used to specify the locations of the planets in degrees and minutes within the signs. Just as with the tropical zodiac, therefore, the sidereal zodiac is a completely adequate horoscopic frame of reference, as we have seen already in relation to the various horoscopes we have looked at so far.

Moreover, we have also seen that the sidereal zodiac enables comparisons to be made between horoscopes belonging to different historical times. Exact comparisons can be made between planets, since in the sidereal zodiac each planet's location against the background of the zodiacal constellations is recorded to degree and minute. By contrast, the system of "signs and constellations" used by Elisabeth Vreede, Günther Wachsmuth, and Willi Sucher permitted only an inexact comparison between planetary positions in the zodiacal constellations. Without reference to degrees and minutes, as in the signs of the sidereal zodiac, it is only possible to say that a planet is near the beginning, in the middle, or near the end of a zodiacal constellation, or some such approximate statement—that is, a rather vague reference to its location in the astronomical zodiac.

RUDOLF STEINER, PENTECOST, AND THE GALACTIC CENTER

To illustrate the power of the sidereal zodiac to make such comparisons, let us consider Rudolf Steiner's birth horoscope once again, this time in relation to the planetary configuration at Pentecost, when the descent of the Holy Spirit upon the disciples took place. This event was on May 24, A.D. 33, forty-nine days after Easter Sunday, April 5, A.D. 33.[30] From the chart comparison (next page), we see that there was an exact alignment in the sidereal zodiac of the Moon at Steiner's birth (25° Leo) with the Moon at Pentecost (25° Leo). What is the significance of this?

One possible interpretation is that there was a resonance between the descent of the Holy Spirit at Pentecost and the birth of Rudolf

---

30 Powell, *Chronicle of the Living Christ*, p. 178.

Comparison Chart

Outer - Geocentric	Inner - Geocentric
Pentecost of Descent of Holy Spirit	Birth of Rudolf Steiner
At Mt. Zion, Latitude 31N46', Longitude 35E14'	At Kraljavec/Yugoslavia, Latitude 46N22', Longitude 16E39'
Date: Sunday, 24/MAY/33, Julian	Date: Monday, 25/FEB/1861, Gregorian
Time: 5: 0, Local Time	Time: 23:25, Local Time
Sidereal Time 20:58:19, Vernal Point 2♈35'39"	Sidereal Time 9:47:41, Vernal Point 7♓11'52"

House System: Placidus, Zodiac: Sidereal SVP
Aspect set: Conjunction/Square/Opposition

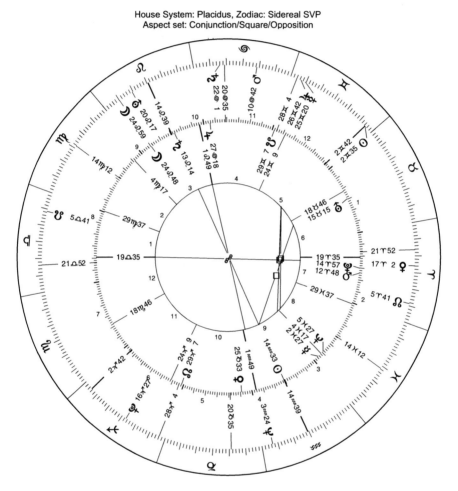

Steiner. According to esoteric teaching, everything that takes place is recorded in the cosmic memory, known as the akashic chronicle. The starry heavens, according to esoteric tradition, are an outer manifestation of the akashic chronicle. When an event takes place, the sidereal horoscope of that event is a kind of cosmic "diary entry" into the akashic chronicle of that event. And certain events are outstanding, radiant memories in the akashic chronicle. Pentecost was such an event. Therefore, when the one or the other planet returns to the same part of the zodiac where it was at a great event, it activates, by way of resonance, the memory of that event. Such was the case with the return of the Moon at Steiner's birth to its precise location at the event of Pentecost. In this sense it is possible to speak of a resonance between Rudolf Steiner's birth and the occurrence of Pentecost. Perhaps this helps to explain the extraordinary spirit power at work in Rudolf Steiner's life? Perhaps he acted as a kind of "ambassador" for the Holy Spirit?

In working with the sidereal zodiac, extraordinary connections such as the one just mentioned come to the light of day. For example, seeing that the Sun was at 2 ½° Gemini at Pentecost,[31] this means that the Earth (always diametrically opposite the Sun in the zodiac) was at 2 ½° Sagittarius. And 2° Sagittarius is the location in the sidereal zodiac of the galactic center around which our galaxy revolves![32] In fact, the galactic center is just below the Sun's path (ecliptic); it is located just in front (southwest) of the tip of the Archer's arrow. So the Archer's arrow is aimed at the galactic center (see figure on the next page). Transposed to the ecliptic from the tip of the arrow, the longitude of the galactic center is 2° in the sidereal sign of Sagittarius, which was almost exactly the location of the Earth at Pentecost, and signifying that the Earth was right "on target" at this event. Such a statement, with this degree of precision, could not be made in terms of the unequal-division astronomical zodiac. For this reason we can be grateful that the Babylonians devised such an accurate sidereal measuring system. This has opened up the possibility of doing historical chart comparisons, and thus made astrological reincarnation research possible.

PLANETARY ALIGNMENTS IN THE SIDEREAL ZODIAC

Readers may well understand that the second astrological rule validates the sidereal zodiac, yet they may also think that it does not disprove the tropical zodiac. Convinced that the tropical zodiac must hold true on some level, the following hypothesis (or something similar to it) is sometimes presented. *Although the sidereal zodiac clearly applies on the level of the individuality reincarnating from life to*

---

31 Ibid.

32 Michelsen, *The American Sidereal Ephemeris, 1976–2000*, p. 5.

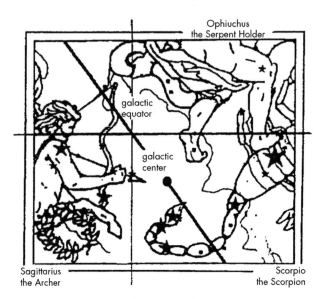

Ophiuchus
the Serpent Holder

galactic
equator

galactic
center

Sagittarius
the Archer

Scorpio
the Scorpion

The Archer Aims His Arrow
(*With grateful acknowledgment to Raymond Mardyks for this graphic.*)

life, the tropical zodiac surely holds on the level of the personality.
This hypothesis, or other similar hypotheses, are often put forward in
favor of retaining the tropical zodiac. We will see how the following
considerations show that this hypothesis leads to absurdity, if certain
conclusions of astrological reincarnation research are accepted.

One of the conclusions presented in *Hermetic Astrology*, volume
II is that there is not only a relationship between the death horoscope
in one incarnation and the birth horoscope in the next incarnation,
but also that there is a relationship between the birth horoscope in
one incarnation and the conception horoscope in the next incarnation.
This I have called the "fundamental principle of astrological biography" (see following figure).

THE FUNDAMENTAL PRINCIPLE OF ASTROLOGICAL BIOGRAPHY

The basic principle is that of comparing the horoscope of death in one
incarnation (†A) with the horoscope of birth in the following incarnation (*B). This rule is extended to include the comparison of the
birth horoscope (*A) with the conception horoscope of the following
incarnation (ØB):

Ø = conception/epoch; * = birth; † = death

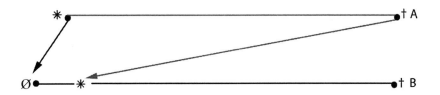

One way that these relationships (from birth to conception, and from death to birth) show up is in terms of planetary alignments in the sidereal zodiac such as comes to expression in the second rule of astrological reincarnation. It was the discovery of consistent planetary alignments in the sidereal zodiac from one incarnation to the next, which provided the empirical proof that the sidereal zodiac is the authentic astrological zodiac.[33] Given the importance of this discovery, it would be appropriate to discuss it in detail.

Like almost everyone else who becomes interested in astrology, at least in the West, my initial introduction was in terms of tropical astrology.[34] However, I could not simply accept the tropical zodiac as the fundamental framework for horoscopes without investigating to find out where it originated. It was then that I embarked on the research that led to my Ph.D. thesis on the history of the zodiac and discovered that the sidereal zodiac, long antecedent to the tropical zodiac, was the zodiac used in the astrology of the Babylonians, Egyptians, Greeks, Romans, and Hindus. Thus I came to know the original astrology based on the ancient sidereal zodiac. When I first encountered sidereal astrology, I continued to cast horoscopes tropically, as well as sidereally, convinced that there was truth in both, on different levels. However, I discovered planetary alignments in the sidereal zodiac from one incarnation to the next, and then I discovered the fundamental principle of astrological biography. These two discover-

---

33 Powell, *Elijah Come Again: A Scientific Study of Reincarnation* shows many examples of the heliocentric planetary alignments of Mercury and Venus between successive incarnations of the same individuality—incarnations often widely separated in time, also in the horoscope comparisons taking account of conception horoscopes as well as horoscopes of birth and death—showing the fulfillment of the second rule of astrological reincarnation.

34 This section of the book is written by Robert Powell.

ies, taken together, showed me the absurdity of my hypothesis that the sidereal and tropical horoscopes relate to different levels: to the individuality and the personality, as I had believed. The conclusion of the following discussion will show why this hypothesis is untenable.

As a clear illustration of planetary alignment, let us consider a reincarnation example spoken of by Rudolf Steiner: Caliph Mu'awiya, who reincarnated as President Woodrow Wilson.[35] Mu'awiya died on or around April 4, 680. As we shall focus on the slow-moving planets Uranus and Neptune, it does not matter that the date of death is not known exactly to the day, since the motion of Uranus and Neptune cannot exceed more than ½° in the space of a week. Comparing the outer circle, the geocentric death configuration of Mu'awiya, with the inner circle, the geocentric birth configuration of President Wilson, we see that the Moon at Woodrow Wilson's birth aligned exactly in the sidereal zodiac with Neptune at Mu'awiya's death (see geocentric comparison chart opposite).

Note that Uranus at President Wilson's birth aligned with the sidereal position of Uranus at Mu'awiya's death. Leaving other alignments out of consideration, we shall now focus on this Uranus alignment in the sidereal zodiac. (Note that the corresponding geocentric positions of Uranus in the tropical zodiac are 5 ½° Taurus at Mu'awiya's death and 21 ½° Taurus at President Wilson's birth, some 16° apart and therefore nowhere near an alignment—see page 96.) Since Uranus takes almost 84 years to complete one orbit of the sidereal zodiac, this means that between the death of Mu'awiya and the birth of Woodrow Wilson, Uranus completed fourteen orbits of the zodiac (1,856 − 680 = 1,176 ÷ 84 = 14). The soul of Mu'awiya remained in spiritual realms during the time interval that Uranus orbited fourteen times around the sidereal zodiac (unless there was some unknown intervening incarnation).

The fundamental principle of astrological biography states that such alignments take place in the sidereal zodiac. What this expresses is that the reincarnating soul endeavors to connect at conception onto the previous birth configuration and at birth onto the previous death configuration. Let us bear in mind, also, that such alignments can be geocentric or heliocentric (hermetic), giving rise to four possibilities:

---

35 Steiner, *Karmic Relationships*, vol. 1, pp. 169–171.

Comparison Chart

Outer - Geocentric	Inner - Geocentric
Death of (Caliph) Mu'awiya	Birth of (President) Woodrow Wilson
At Nr. Damascus, Latitude 33N30', Longitude 36E19'	At Staunton, VA, USA, Latitude 38N10', Longitude 79W05'
Date: Wednesday, 4/APR/680, Julian	Date: Sunday, 28/DEC/1856, Gregorian
Time: 12: 0, Local Time	Time: 23:40, Local Time
Sidereal Time 25: 2:55, Vernal Point 23 ♓ 37'46"	Sidereal Time 6:11:43, Vernal Point 7 ♓ 15'21"

House System: Placidus, Zodiac: Sidereal SVP
Aspect set: Conjunction/Square/Opposition

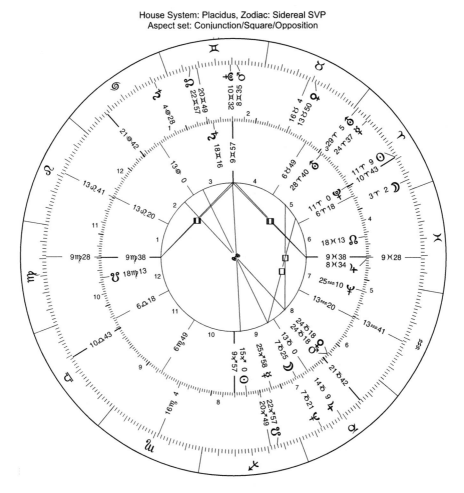

1. birth to next conception, geocentric
2. death to next birth, geocentric
3. birth to next conception, heliocentric (hermetic)
4. death to next birth, heliocentric (hermetic)

The Uranus alignment from Mu'awiya's death to President Wilson's birth is an example of the fulfillment of case 2. Let us recall Rudolf Steiner's statement concerning the reincarnating soul, "From that

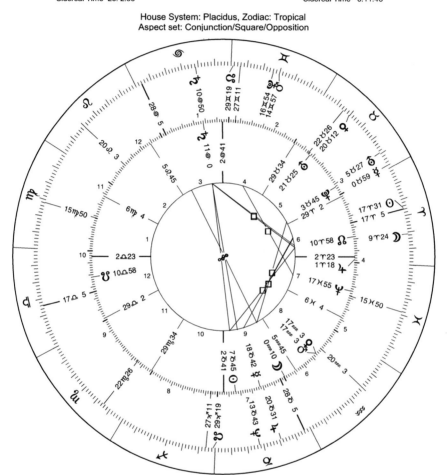

Comparison Chart

Outer - Geocentric
Death of (Caliph) Mu'awiya
At Nr. Damascus, Latitude 33N30', Longitude 36E19'
Date: Wednesday, 4/APR/680, Julian
Time: 12: 0, Local Time
Sidereal Time 25: 2:55

Inner - Geocentric
Birth of (President) Woodrow Wilson
At Staunton, VA, USA, Latitude 38N10', Longitude 79W05'
Date: Sunday, 28/DEC/1856, Gregorian
Time: 23:40, Local Time
Sidereal Time 6:11:43

House System: Placidus, Zodiac: Tropical
Aspect set: Conjunction/Square/Opposition

other world, while we are descending, we see the Sun from the other side; the Sun appears, the fixed stars appear, and behind them the planetary movements."[36] In light of this statement the reincarnating soul has a perception of the movements of the planets in relation to the fixed stars of the sidereal zodiac. We can conclude that the reincarnating soul of President Wilson chose to incarnate so as to be born when

---

36 Steiner, "Hidden Sides of Man's Existence and the Christ Impulse" (lecture of November 5, 1922), *Anthroposophical Quarterly*, vol. 17 (1972), p. 46.

Uranus would return to exactly the same position in the sidereal zodiac as at the time of death in the incarnation as Mu'awiya. (As Mu'awiya's date of birth is not known, it is not possible to undertake a comparison between Mu'awiya's birth configuration and Woodrow Wilson's conception configuration corresponding to cases 1 and 3.)

Similarly, in the case of Rudolf Steiner he chose to be born when heliocentric Mercury aligned in the sidereal zodiac with its position at death in the preceding incarnation—this being an example of fulfillment of case 4 above. (Note also that at Rudolf Steiner's birth Uranus returned close to its position at death in the preceding incarnation.) Again, not knowing Thomas Aquinas's date of birth, it is not possible to do a comparison with Steiner's conception configuration.

Given that cases 1 through 4 hold true for alignments in the sidereal zodiac, this means that the reincarnating soul has these various possibilities in view. Since conception and birth are linked, being always approximately nine months apart, it is evident that the reincarnating soul focuses upon the entire period of incarnation between conception and birth, aligning it with the course of life between birth and death in the foregoing incarnation. However, there are two levels to this focus: Sun centered (heliocentric–hermetic) and Earth centered (geocentric). In *Hermetic Astrology,* volume 1, these two levels are related on the one hand to the higher self that is more connected with the Sun, and on the other hand to the earthly personality that comes to expression on Earth during earthly incarnation. Taking this as a hypothesis, this would explain why both levels: heliocentric (hermetic) and geocentric, are significant. We can think of this as analogous to two "eyes"—the higher "I" and the lower "I"—one above the other, each focusing upon planetary alignments in the sidereal zodiac on its own level, heliocentric and geocentric. This, then, is the spiritual background underlying the occurrence of cases 1, 2, 3, and 4.

Suppose, now, that someone were to believe that both the tropical and the sidereal zodiacs hold true. If it were so that planetary alignments were to be sought out by the reincarnating soul not only in the sidereal zodiac but also in the tropical zodiac, then we would have to conceive of cases 5 to 8 of planetary alignments in the tropical zodiac in addition to cases 1 to 4 in the sidereal zodiac. Yet this would be absurd! It would mean that the reincarnating soul would be searching for alignments not only in terms of two levels (heliocentric = higher self, and geocentric = earthly personality) but also simultaneously in two different coordinate systems (sidereal = measured in relation to the fixed stars, and tropical = measured from the vernal point). And it is precisely the second astrological rule of reincarnation, which demonstrates that this is not the case; i.e. that planetary alignment is sought in the sidereal zodiac, *not in the tropical zodiac*. This conclusion shows the far-reaching significance of the second rule: not only does it establish the sidereal zodiac as the authentic astrological zodiac, but it also proves the validity of the heliocentric (hermetic) perspective in addition to the geocentric one.

SUMMARY

Those readers who have carefully studied the reincarnation comparison charts already presented in this book will have noticed that there are also alignments between the tropical charts. Thus there is an exact alignment of Saturn (11° Cancer) in the tropical zodiac from Mu'awiya's death to Woodrow Wilson's birth (see tropical comparison chart, page 96). Moreover, there is a close opposition alignment in the tropical zodiac of Jupiter (19° Aquarius) from Thomas Aquinas's death to Jupiter (20° Leo) at Rudolf Steiner's birth (opposite).

Having researched reincarnation comparison charts for more than thirty years, the conclusion is that these alignments in the tropical zodiac are purely chance. The second rule of astrological reincarnation has shown itself consistent in terms of heliocentric planetary alignments in the sidereal zodiac (see *Elijah Come Again* and *Hermetic Astrology*, vol. 1, appendix 4). If it were true that planetary alignments take place *consistently* also in the tropical zodiac, it would be a different story. However, there is nothing to show that such alignments take place consistently in the tropical zodiac. Moreover, as long as no such evidence in favor of the tropical zodiac exists, it would be untenable to maintain that four additional kinds of alignments (cases 5, 6, 7, and 8) exist in addition to the four cases 1, 2, 3, and 4 already mentioned.

One general criticism that may be leveled at the research presented in this book is that it relies too much on Rudolf Steiner, the source of the reincarnation examples presented here,[37] and that the number

---

37 Steiner spoke of the previous incarnations of Franz Schubert and Joseph von Spaun, but did not name them. Thanks to astrological reincarnation research, we

Comparison Chart

Outer - Geocentric
Death of (St.) Thomas Aquinas
At Fossanova, Latitude 40N50', Longitude 14E15'
Date: Wednesday, 7/MAR/1274, Julian
Time: 6:15, Local Time
Sidereal Time 17:42:57

Inner - Geocentric
Birth of Rudolf Steiner
At Kraljavec/Yugoslavia, Latitude 46N22', Longitude 16E39'
Date: Monday, 25/FEB/1861, Gregorian
Time: 23:25, Local Time
Sidereal Time 9:47:41

House System: Placidus, Zodiac: Tropical
Aspect set: Conjunction/Square/Opposition

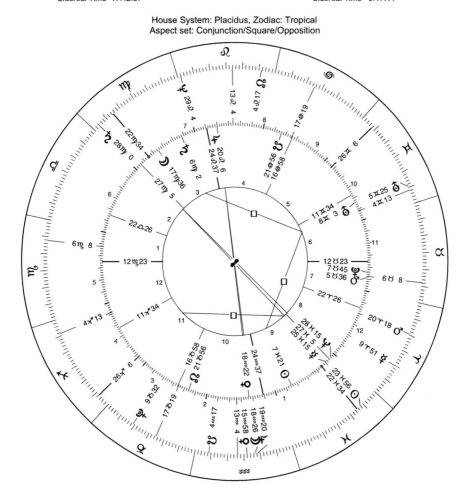

of examples is too small to have any real significance. Admittedly the
sample is small. Nevertheless, it is of very "high quality" in the sense
that Steiner was truly capable of reincarnation research in a fully conscious way. Therefore, what he presents is reliable, as may be ascer-
tained through a thorough study of his life's work. When one studies

---

can be certain that the previous incarnation of von Spaun was as Alfonso, the
king of Castile and Léon from 1252 to 1284, and that the former incarnation of
Franz Schubert was as Abu Yusuf, the sultan of Morocco from 1258 to 1286.

Steiner's statements through more than thirty-five years, one gains confidence in their truth and trusts the accuracy of his reincarnation examples. Moreover, it is preferable to work with a small sample of trustworthy examples in contrast to a larger sample of questionable reliability. The conclusions from research into this small sample are thoroughly reliable, despite the small sample size, and undoubtedly they will eventually be confirmed by independent research.

Once one reaches generally valid conclusions (such as the first and second rules of astrological reincarnation), it becomes possible to apply those rules. A few examples of this were presented in *Hermetic Astrology,* volume 1: Francis Bacon, Friedrich Nietzsche, and Vladimir Soloviev. As with Franz Schubert and Joseph von Spaun, Rudolf Steiner referred to the previous incarnations of Nietzsche and Soloviev in a non-explicit manner, characterizing them but without naming them and, although Rudolf Steiner referred to Francis Bacon's preceding incarnation as Haroun al-Rashid, he did not speak of Francis Bacon's reincarnation (as British mathematician and philosopher Bertrand Russell) in the twentieth century, because Rudolf Steiner chose not to speak publicly about the karmic background and preceding incarnations of his contemporaries. In the case of President Woodrow Wilson, who was a contemporary of Rudolf Steiner, he did not speak of Woodrow Wilson's preceding incarnation as Mu'awiya until after the president's death in February 1924.

Both Friedrich Nietzsche and Vladimir Soloviev were contemporaries of Rudolf Steiner, but both died already in 1900, when Steiner began his lecturing activity. In each case Rudolf Steiner spoke in 1924 of their preceding incarnations but without specifying the names of these historical personalities. In *Hermetic Astrology,* volume I, through the application of the new science of the stars (hermetic astrology) as a new science of reincarnation and karma, these historical personalities are identified with a high degree of certainty. These examples show the potential for hermetic astrology as a new science of reincarnation and karma. *Hermetic Astrology,* volume II expanded upon these examples, investigating—among others—the preceding incarnation and the destiny of the great nineteenth-century composer Richard Wagner and also of two individuals in Wagner's karmic circle: Friedrich Nietzsche and King Ludwig II of Bavaria. These two volumes on hermetic astrology—followed by *Elijah Come Again: A Scientific*

Study of Reincarnation together with the present volume containing further examples—thus represent the founding (laying the foundation) of a new science of the stars and the systematic, step-by-step application of this as a new science of reincarnation and karma.

CHAPTER FOUR

THE NEW GOSPEL IN THE STARS

Look as they rise, up rise
Over the line where sky meets the Earth;
Seven Stars!
Lo! They are ascending, come to guide us,
Leading us safely, keeping us one.
Oh, Seven Stars,
Teach us to be, like you, united.
—PAWNEE CEREMONIAL SONG

For the modern materialistic mind, which dismisses both the constellations and their associated myths and legends as human fabrications, there should be something deeply unsettling about the repeated convergence across time and space both of name and of narratives describing the starry heavens. The Pawnee song, chanted for generations "where sky meets Earth" upon the grassy great plains of Turtle Island, immediately strikes even untutored ears as an echo of the Greek conception of the Pleiades as the "Seven Sisters"—Alcyone, Asterope, Celaeno, Elektra, Maia, Merope, and Taygeta. Daughters of Atlas and Pleione, they were also the half-sisters of the Hyades and the Hesperides. Though Greek, Pawnee, Hindu, and other myths call the Pleiades the "seven stars" (the number seen with the naked eye; a telescope reveals a great many more stars in this region), their Greek name signifies "multitude," or "abundance," as does the Arabic *Al Thuraiya*. Whatever the number, the Pleiades form the most storied constellation in the night sky. References to the Pleiades appear in Mesopotamian and Chinese writings dated to the third millennium B.C., as well as in aboriginal myth and early Hindu and Egyptian texts, the Talmud, Qur'an, the Bible, and Homer's *Iliad* and *Odyssey*. In the New World, a variety of ancient structures line up with the Pleiades, including a

Nazca desert feature (ca. 500—700 A.D.) and the streets and build-
ings of Teotihuacan (150—750 A.D.). The Maya sacred calendar, the
Tzol'kin, is based on the cycles of the Pleiades. Mexican emperor
Moctezuma regarded the Pleiades as an omen of great significance.
One finds the Pleiades illustrated in the Night Sky figures of Navajo
sand paintings, on the masks of Pueblo *kachinas,* and on the painted
interior "sky" of Blackfeet lodges. As expressed in the ceremonial
song above, the Pawnee attended faithfully to the Pleiades, even laying out some of their villages in a pattern reflecting the arrangement
of the seven sisters.

For agricultural peoples of northeastern America, the star cluster guided their planting activity, as the Pleiades' disappearance and
reappearance coincided with the limits of the frost-free season. One
Algonquian name, *asishquattouog* ("the boundary mark"), suggests
their prominent position. That prominence is more emphatically
affirmed in the Arabic *Al Wasat* ("the central one"), a name given by
the fifteenth-century astronomer Ulugh Beigh.[1] But it is God's astral
challenge to Job—"Canst thou bind the sweet influences of the Plefa-
des, or loose the bands of Orion?"—that most beautifully illustrates
the ancient knowledge of the Pleiades. The Arabic *kam* (translated
here as "sweet influences") refers to a thing or person pivoting about
a fixed point, calling most elementally to mind the stake tethering a
camel to a "sweet" area of grazing. [2]

This pervasive sense of the Pleiades as the starry stake about
which worlds and systems of worlds moved led the English astronomer Thomas Wright to propose in *An Original Theory or New
Hypothesis of the Universe* (1850) that the Pleiades are at the center
of the universe. In 1848, German astronomer Johann Heinrich von
Mädler narrowed this further, suggesting that the entire universe
revolves around Alcyone. By the early twentieth century, the notion
was well-established both in scientific circles and by popular opinion.

---

1 A Latin name for the Pleiades, *Vergiliae* ("center of the revolving"), conveys
the same sense that has been attributed to the largest star of the cluster, Alcyone,
and moreover the Arabic *Al Cyone* means "center star" (Frances Rolleston,
Mazzaroth, part 2, p. 10.) This gives some insight into C. W. Leadbeater's choice
of the name for the supposed avatar, Krishnamurti.

2 John G. Lansing, "Pleiades, Orion and Mazzaroth," *Hebraica,* 1(4) (April
1885), pp. 236–241.

MODERN ASTRONOMY AND THE SIDEREAL ZODIAC

Do these ideas about the Pleaides as cosmic axis find affirmation from modern astronomy? To answer this question let us consider the structure of the Milky Way Galaxy, to which our solar system belongs. The Milky Way is a spiral galaxy with several arms (see figure opposite). The arm that lies between the galactic center and the Earth is called the Sagittarius arm. The Perseus arm wraps itself behind us. Our Sun is located on the inside edge of the Orion arm.

The Milky Way Galaxy lies more or less on a plane that, if we could see it from afar, would look like a flat disk with a bulge in the center where the galactic center is located. The central plane of the Milky Way is called the galactic equator, and it rotates like a giant wheel with the galactic center at its hub. This wheel is about one hundred thousand light years across.

Looking up at the night sky beholding the girdle of the Milky Way, we can imagine the galactic equator running through the center of the galaxy. In the evening sky during spring we can see the Milky Way intersecting the zodiac between the horns of the Bull (Taurus) and the feet of the Twins (Gemini). The galactic equator intersects the sidereal zodiac at 5° Gemini. In the old Zoroastrian astrology, the Milky Way was called the "brilliance of the dragon."[3] The dragon was pictured as enveloping the orb of the celestial sphere, intersecting the zodiac at 3° Gemini (the dragon's head) and at 3° Sagittarius (the dragon's tail). And the exaltation of the Moon's North Node, where the Moon's ascending orbit intersects the ecliptic running through the middle of the zodiac, was said to be at 3° Gemini—likewise the Moon's South Node, where the Moon's descending orbit crosses the central path (ecliptic) of the zodiac, was located at 3° Sagittarius. By way of assimilation into tropical astrology, the Moon's North and South Nodes are said to be exalted at 3° Gemini and 3° Sagittarius in the tropical zodiac, placing the North Node's exaltation now close to the Pleiades in Taurus, far-removed from the galactic equator running through the center of the Milky Way. For the ancient clairvoyant consciousness, it was highly significant wherever the Moon's nodal axis closely aligned with the Milky Way. Yet this relationship of the sidereal zodiac to the galaxy became completely obscured by the introduction of the tropical zodiac into astrology.

---

3 D. N. MacKenzie, "Zoroastrian Astrology in the Bundahisn," *Bulletin of the School of Oriental and African Studies* 27 (1964), p. 522.

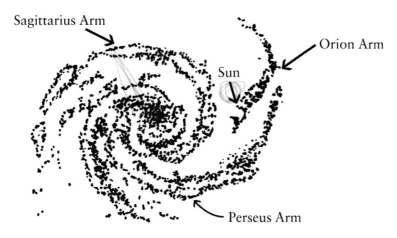

Sagittarius Arm

Orion Arm

Sun

Perseus Arm

The Milky Way Galaxy, with spiral arms

As stated earlier, the galactic center lies at 2° Sagittarius, which is strikingly close to the ancient point of exaltation (3° Sagittarius) of the Moon's South Node. To grasp the relationship between the zodiacal location of the galactic center (2° Sagittarius) and the place where the galactic equator intersects the zodiac (5° Sagittarius) it is helpful to think of the ecliptic as a line running through the center of the zodiac. Positions of stars can be described in terms of longitude in the sidereal zodiac together with latitude, which measures the distance North or South of the ecliptic. The galactic equator intersects the ecliptic at 5° Sagittarius (0° latitude) and the galactic center is at 2° Sagittarius (5 ½° latitude South). The angle of intersection between the ecliptic and the galactic equator is about 60°. The figure on page 92 also shows the remarkable fact of the tip of the Archer's arrow pointing to the galactic center. On December 18/19 each year the Sun is at 2° Sagittarius in conjunction with the galactic center.

Our solar system races at about 140 miles (220 kilometers) per second around the galactic center, taking about 225 million years for a complete circuit of the galaxy. The direction in which the solar system moves lies 90° along the galactic equator from the galactic center, in the direction of the constellation of the Swan (see figure, page 106). The exact focus of this movement in the direction of the Swan, called the vertex, is near the star Deneb forming the tail of the Swan.

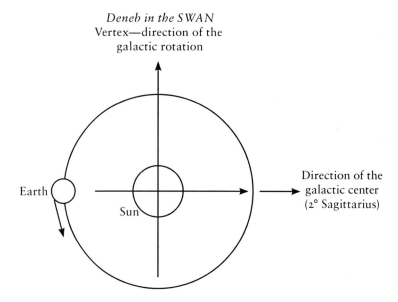

*The position of the Earth in relation to the Sun on December 18/19
each year and the direction of the Sun's movement toward the Vertex*

The Sun, Earth, and other planets move together with neighboring stars around the galactic center in the direction of the vertex near Deneb. On closer observation, however, it is evident that the Sun has its own movement within the cluster of neighboring stars moving toward the star Vega in the constellation of the Lyre (see opposite). This movement of our solar system relative to the neighboring stars amounts to about twelve and a half miles (twenty kilometers) per second. By coincidence, the direction of this "local movement" of the Sun toward the solar apex is close to the vertex of the galactic rotation, since the solar apex is not far from the star Vega in the constellation of the Lyre, directly adjacent to the constellation of the Swan. The actual location of the solar apex is close to the star Omicron Herculis in the left hand of Hercules, which appears to reach out toward Vega in the Lyre, the neighboring constellation (page 107). On the opposite side of the heavens, in the constellation of Columba, the Dove, below the brightest star in the night sky, Sirius, is the solar antapex, the point from which the Sun is receding.

Thus, there are two independent movements of our solar system to be considered. Imagine driving in a car and various other cars are all

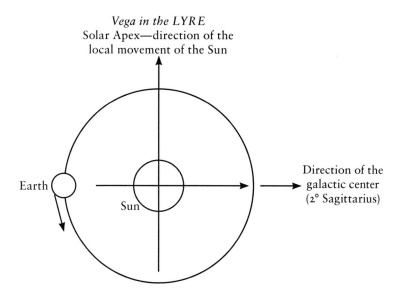

The position of the Earth in relation to the Sun on December 18/19 each year and the direction of the Sun's local movement toward the Solar Apex

traveling in the same direction at approximately the same speed. This would correspond to the first movement of our Sun and neighboring stars in the direction of the vertex near to Deneb at a speed of about 140 miles (220 kilometers) per second. Then imagine that our car (our solar system) is moving slightly faster than the average speed of the other cars—twelve and a half miles (twenty kilometers) per second faster—and that our car is moving in a direction that deviates slightly from that of the other cars (corresponding to the local movement of our Sun in relation to neighboring stars—this local movement being in the direction of Vega in the Lyre). With the help of this analogy it is possible to grasp that our solar system is drifting along at a speed of about 150 miles (240 kilometers) per second toward the stars Deneb and Vega, the largest component of this speed being the movement toward Deneb. The direction of this movement is marked by the "summer triangle," of which Deneb and Vega are the most striking, with Altair in the constellation of the Eagle as the third star making up the summer triangle. This region lies far from the Pleiades in Taurus, and thus would seem to contradict the unanimous assertion by ancient peoples of the seven sisters as our solar system's focal point.

It would also seem to contradict a statement made by Rudolf Steiner: "The next solar system will take place in the Pleiades. The entire solar system is moving toward the Pleiades."[4] Even if we take into account a third movement, that of our Milky Way Galaxy together with our whole local group of galaxies, moving toward the constellation of Leo at about 400 miles (640 kilometers) per second, this does not astronomically explain either the ancient myths or Rudolf Steiner's statement. We must search further for the meaning of his statement by considering Rudolf Steiner's description of the origin of our solar system through the four stages of cosmic evolution, which he termed "Ancient Saturn," "Ancient Sun," "Ancient Moon," and "Present Earth."[5] In other words, the Pleiades are not a spatial, but a temporal pivot point.

THE STAGES OF COSMIC EVOLUTION

What one calls old Saturn in its beginning stage was about as large as our solar system. But we should not simply imagine it as a material globe. You will remember that, on ancient Saturn, nothing existed yet of what we have today as the three physical states—solid, fluid, and gaseous. There was only warmth, or fire. Let us represent this primeval globe of warmth by a circle....At the point where the primeval globe of Saturn develops into the Sun globe, those beings who form the zodiac appear, surrounding the Sun globe. I indicated, however, that the zodiac already surrounded ancient Saturn, though not as compactly as during the evolutionary stage of the old Sun. Around ancient Saturn, therefore, we must picture the activity of Thrones, Cherubim, and Seraphim, who spiritually represent the zodiac. The outer circle in the diagram represents the zodiac spiritually. You might ask, "How does this agree with the modern view of the zodiac?" It agrees completely.[6]

---

4 Steiner, oral communication transmitted by Imma von Eckhardtstein, *Beiträge zur Rudolf Steiner Gesamtausgabe*, vol. 37/38 (1972), p. 81

5 For readers unfamiliar with Steiner's cosmology of evolution unfolding through seven stages—Saturn, Sun, Moon, Earth, Jupiter, Venus, Vulcan—his book *An Outline of Esoteric Science* gives a basic overview.

6 Steiner, *The Spiritual Hierarchies and the Physical World*, p. 97.

This important statement shows that there is complete continuity regarding the zodiac from the time of Ancient Saturn until modern times. It is the same zodiac now, spiritually representing the Seraphim, Cherubim, and Thrones, as at the time of Ancient Saturn. And this is the sidereal zodiac, as Rudolf Steiner makes clear:

> In order to locate particular Thrones, Cherubim and Seraphim, one denotes them by a particular constellation. It is like a signpost. In that direction over there we see the Thrones, Cherubim and Seraphim known as the Twins, over there, the Lion, and so on. The constellations of the zodiac are more than mere signposts but, as a first stage, it is important to realize that, when we refer to the zodiac, we are speaking of spiritual beings.[7]

After pointing out that when we look up to the constellations of the zodiac we are actually beholding the outer aspect or manifestations of the Seraphim, Cherubim and Thrones, Steiner goes on to describe how these beings were active in the formation of the various globes named Saturn, Sun, Moon, and Earth:

> While this globe, corresponding to the primal condition of Saturn, is revolving, a kind of girdle is being formed; it does not surround the whole of the egg; it is like a broad band. Everything that is being formed around about is gathered within the girdle. This girdle formation represents a general cosmic law. You can see this law relating to accumulation in the form of an equator or girdle exemplified in the cosmos as far as the eye can see, for the Milky Way owes its existence to it. The Milky Way is like an outermost girdle surrounding cosmic space with stars sparsely distributed in between, and is the result of the law that causes things to be gathered together in a belt as soon as a rotary motion sets in. Because of this, our cosmic system is lentil-shaped. It is not spherical as is usually accepted, and the girdle is gathered together at the equator.[8]

Here Rudolf Steiner accurately described the lentil shape of our Milky Way Galaxy, as a rotating belt or girdle through the center

---

7 Ibid., p. 99.

8 Ibid., pp. 111–112.

of which runs the galactic equator, and how this corresponds to the primal globe of Saturn with its revolving girdle. This description exemplifies Steiner's extraordinary gift of penetrating beyond the science of his time to reach higher spiritual reality. According to Steiner it was during the revolution of this globe of Saturn through the signs of the sidereal zodiac that the foundations of the human physical body were laid:

> During Ancient Saturn the human physical body was gradually prepared for its later task; each part was formed in a rudimentary way as Ancient Saturn revolved from one sign of the zodiac to the next. During the period that Saturn stood in the sign of the Lion, the outline of the heart was formed; the beginnings of the rib cage came about as Saturn passed through the sign of the Crab. The predisposition to symmetry in the human physical form took place when Saturn stood in the sign of the Twins. We could thus trace every part of the human body. Looking up to the Ram, we find the sign of the zodiac that gave birth, when ancient Saturn stood in it, to the upper part of the head. The foundations of our speech organs were laid down when Ancient Saturn stood in the sign of the Bull. If you now imagine the human being distributed in this way, you will find in the zodiac the creative forces that gave rise to each of these parts.[9]

The first thing to become aware of in the above description is that Rudolf Steiner clearly refers to "signs of the zodiac" in the whole context, however, of the zodiacal constellations. So this description applies to the sidereal signs. Then in his description of the rotation of the globe of Ancient Saturn he indicates that the rotation started and also stopped when Ancient Saturn was in the sign of Leo.[10] If we subsequently view Ancient Saturn in connection with our Milky Way Galaxy, it is most extraordinary that in 1977 the American cosmologist and Nobel laureate George Smoot and his colleagues discovered the movement of the Milky Way Galaxy moving toward the constellation of Leo at about 400 miles (640 kilometers) per second! They explained that the movement toward Leo is the result of gravitational

---

9 Ibid., p. 113.

10 Ibid., pp. 101–104.

pull toward what they called the Great Attractor, estimated to be about 150 million light years across, and equally far away. This is more than one thousand times larger than the diameter of the Milky Way Galaxy!

Here we see an agreement between Rudolf Steiner's description of the formation of the solar system and the findings of modern astronomy. This agreement applies to the globe of ancient Saturn—and therewith the Milky Way Galaxy—being related to Leo. Having arrived at this point, we shall omit the next two stages of cosmic evolution—Ancient Sun, related to Scorpio, and Ancient Moon, related to Aquarius—in order to come to the present stage of cosmic evolution (Earth), related to Taurus, the Bull.[11] The sidereal sign of Taurus, containing the star cluster of the Pleiades at 5° Taurus, plays a similar role in relation to the present Earth globe as Leo did for the Ancient Saturn globe. It is here that we find the deeper significance of the words, "The entire solar system is moving toward the Pleiades," as well as the confirmation of the ancients' mythology and nomenclature for the Pleiades. The primary impulse of Earth evolution proceeded from Taurus—in particular from the Pleiades star cluster located at 5° Taurus—and will finish with the same. It is conceivable that the motion of our Sun—now toward Deneb (through the rotation of our Milky Way Galaxy) and toward Vega (movement of our Sun in relation to neighboring stars)— will one day be in the direction of the Pleiades, in millions of years time, through the further rotation of our Milky Way Galaxy, having perhaps once been aligned with the Pleiades in the far distant past, at the beginning of Earth evolution. Be that as it may, on a spiritual level the entire Earth evolution stands under the sign of Taurus where the Pleiades are an important star cluster. In this sense the Pleiades are both the hub and the goal of the spiritual evolution of the Earth and humanity. God's challenge to Job—"Canst thou bind the sweet influences of the Pleiades?"—is not about the Atlas-like task of holding in place the physical starry heavens, but an invocation of the steadfastness of the plan of cosmic evolution, and thus, of human destiny, which is eternally guided and witnessed by the stars.

Undoubtedly, it is for this reason that the Pleiades are the stellar determinants of Krittika, the first nakshatra in Vedic star lore.[12] The

11 Ibid., pp. 106–108.

12 *Surya-Siddhanta*, translated by E. Burgess, p. 324.

twenty-eight lunar mansions or nakshatras, the Indian equivalent to the thirty-six solar decans of the ancient Egyptians, are alluded to in the Vedas, each nakshatra having a presiding deity.[13] The Hindu sages, out of a profound spiritual intuition concerning the central role of the Pleiades in Earth evolution, started their lunar zodiac of 28 nakshatras with the lunar mansion Krittika, containing the Pleiades. Perhaps it was out of a similar profound intuition that the Egyptian priests started their solar equivalent of the zodiac, the thirty-six decans, with Sothis as the first decan, containing Sirius, the brightest star in the heavens. Especially interesting is the discovery of modern astronomy that the direction of the local movement of our solar system toward the solar apex near Vega proceeds from the solar antapex in the constellation of Columba, the Dove, located beneath Sirius.

Readers who are accustomed to the tropical zodiac may wonder what the relevance of this information drawn from modern astronomy is to astrology. It makes little sense in terms of the tropical zodiac. But in relation to the sidereal zodiac it is highly significant. For the Babylonians there was not any fundamental difference between astrology and astronomy, and if one works with the sidereal zodiac as a basic astronomical reference, the whole world of astronomy suddenly opens up in an approachable way. The rediscovery of the original Babylonian sidereal zodiac helps heal the split that emerged between astronomy and astrology through Ptolemy's introduction of the tropical zodiac into astrology. Hopefully the interweaving of these ancient sister sciences may resume now with renewed intensity and continue into the future for the mutual benefit and fructification of both, giving rise to true *Astrosophy,* or "star wisdom."

STAR MYTHS IN TERMS OF THE SIDEREAL ZODIAC

When Rudolf Steiner made the assertion that the solar system is moving toward the Pleiades, he drew the following figure, which clearly applies to the signs of the sidereal zodiac (see following figure).

In this diagram, therefore, Steiner emphasizes the importance of the Pleiades. As mentioned earlier, he said in connection with this diagram, "The next solar system will take place in the Pleiades. The entire solar system is moving toward the Pleiades." On another

---

13 Powell, *History of the Zodiac,* pp. 114–124.

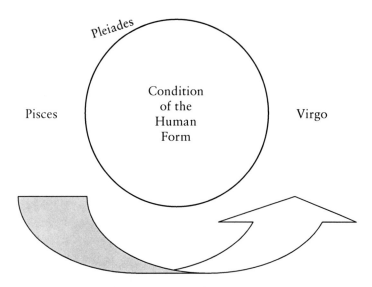

*Figure similar to one drawn by Rudolf Steiner. The arrow from Pisces
to Virgo goes through the development of the human form.
Pisces is the repetition of the Saturn period*

occasion he said: "The Pleiades…is moreover the region where the
whole solar system entered into the universe to which we belong."[14]
These two statements taken together are a clear affirmation of what
has been presented in the foregoing: that the primary impulse of Earth
evolution proceeded from Taurus and the Pleiades and will finish in
that same region of the heavens, which enables us to understand the
extraordinary significance of this star cluster throughout antiquity
and down to the present day.

Also the Babylonian priest-astronomers were very much focused
upon the Pleiades. They determined the "exaltation" of the Moon to
be at 3° Taurus alongside the Pleiades. In the sidereal zodiac the Pleiades are located at 5° Taurus. Supposing that the Babylonian priest-
astronomers knew that our solar system originated from and will
eventually return back to the region of the Pleiades, they would have
felt it to be special when the Moon passed by the Pleiades, aligning
with the past and also with the future in a cosmic evolutionary sense.
The experience of the Moon in (or near) the Pleiades would thus have
been a time of "exaltation" for them.

---

14 Steiner, *Background to the Gospel of St. Mark*, p. 207.

Elisabeth Vreede draws our attention to another interesting star myth mentioning the Pleiades as referred to by Rudolf Steiner:

> It is related that the death of Osiris took place as the Sun stood in the seventeenth degree of Scorpio and the Full Moon rose on the opposite side. We have here an assertion [it is to be found in Plutarch, among others, "Concerning Isis and Osiris"] that is made quite in the sense of the later astrological method of thought....Let us take the picture of the setting Sun in the Sign of Scorpio, which was the Sign of the Underworld and of Death. The Sun stands not far from the red-colored Antares. Osiris disappears in the Underworld, but soon afterward he rises again as Full Moon in the eastern sky....The constellation depicted here: the Sun in 17° Scorpio, the Full Moon in Taurus by the Pleiades, is again no unique one.[15]

This description makes sense only in terms of the sidereal zodiac, in which Antares, marking the Scorpion's heart, is located at 15° Scorpio, and Rudolf Steiner's statement was:

> Those whose thoughts centered on the Osiris myth looked back to a very definite star constellation. They said that Osiris was slain, by which they meant: the old life in the Imaginations vanished when the setting Sun in autumn stood at 17° of Scorpio and, in the opposite point of the heavens, the Full Moon rose in Taurus, or in the Pleiades.[16]

In the sidereal zodiac Antares, "the heart of the Scorpion," is located at 15° Scorpio. The Sun at 17° Scorpio would be "close to the red Antares," as described by Elisabeth Vreede. "The setting Sun in autumn" would signify that the Sun must have been close to the autumnal point, which offers a key to the historical period under consideration. In fact, the autumnal point was at 17° Scorpio in the course of the century from 3200 to 3100 B.C.

The other clue that is given is that "the old life of Imagination vanished." In Hindu chronology, the loss of the ancient clairvoyance (Imagination) signified the start of Kali Yuga, the Dark Age, dated to midnight February 17/18, 3102 B.C. (= -3101 astronomically):

---

15 Vreede, *Astronomy and Spiritual Science*, p. 127.

16 Steiner, *Ancient Myths and the New Isis Mystery*, p. 38.

...midnight between Thursday and Friday, the 17th and 18th of February -3101; this is the beginning of Kaliyuga according to the arddharatrika system of Aryabhata and the original Old Suryasiddhanta.... Sripati's Siddhantasekhara provides us with their [the planets'] mean positions at the beginning of the present Kaliyuga according to the system of the Paitamahasiddhanta = Brahmasphutasiddhanta = Sindhind:

Saturn	Pisces 28; 46, 33, 36
Jupiter	Pisces 29; 27, 36
Mars	Pisces 29; 3, 50, 24
Venus (conj.)	Pisces 28; 42, 14, 24
Mercury (conj.)	Pisces 27; 24, 28, 48

The mean Sun and the mean Moon are both at Aries 0°.[17]

As we can see from the sidereal horoscope for midnight from Thursday/Friday, February 17/18, 3102 B.C. (= -3101 astronomically), there was indeed a conjunction of the planets in the last half of Pisces and beginning of Aries, with the exception of Saturn (22 ½° Aquarius) and Mercury (5 ½° Pisces); see horoscope on page 117.

Returning to the Egyptian myth of the death of Osiris, one may ask: Was there such a configuration around the time that Kali Yuga began? At sunset on October 16, 3104 B.C. (that is, less than 1 ½ years prior to the Hindu date for the beginning of Kali Yuga), the Sun set at 16° Scorpio, exactly conjunct the autumnal point. Simultaneously, the (nearly) Full Moon rose in the East at 3 ½° Taurus alongside the Pleiades (see horoscope, next page). Even more striking, the next evening (October 17) the Sun set at 17° Scorpio and the Full Moon rose in the East at 15° Taurus in conjunction with Aldebaran (the eye of the Bull), accompanied by an eclipse of the Moon. As Elisabeth Vreede pointed out, the configuration of the Full Moon in Taurus, with the Sun at 17° Scorpio, is not unique, and so it is difficult to pinpoint it exactly. Nevertheless, the foregoing configuration of the lunar eclipse on the evening of October 17, 3104 B.C. fits the

---

17 Pingree, *The Thousands of Abu Ma'shar*, p. 35—planetary sidereal longitudes in *Siddhantasekhara* 2, 52–53.

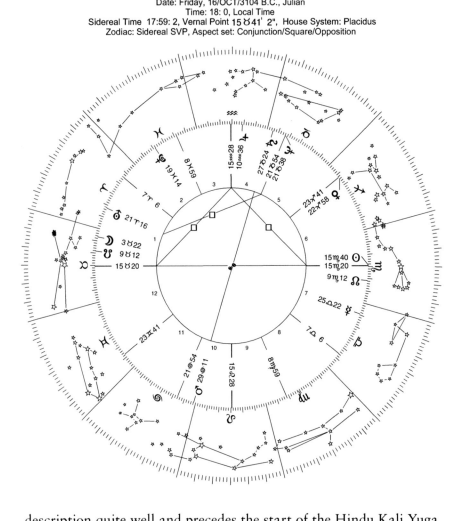

Death of Osiris - Geocentric
At Heliopolis, Latitude 30N06', Longitude 31E19'
Date: Friday, 16/OCT/3104 B.C., Julian
Time: 18: 0, Local Time
Sidereal Time 17:59: 2, Vernal Point 15 ♉41' 2", House System: Placidus
Zodiac: Sidereal SVP, Aspect set: Conjunction/Square/Opposition

description quite well and precedes the start of the Hindu Kali Yuga
by less than 1 ½ years.

Whether Pawnee, Hindu, or Egyptian myth, or the voice of God
speaking to Job, only by returning to the ancient sidereal zodiac can
one hope to decode the language of the stars.

Start of Kali Yuga - Geocentric
At Benares, India, Latitude 25N17', Longitude 83E8'
Date: Friday, 18/FEB/3102 B.C., Julian
Time: 0: 0, Local Time
Sidereal Time 8: 7:22, Vernal Point 15 ♉ 39'56", House System: Placidus
Zodiac: Sidereal SVP, Aspect set: Conjunction/Square/Opposition

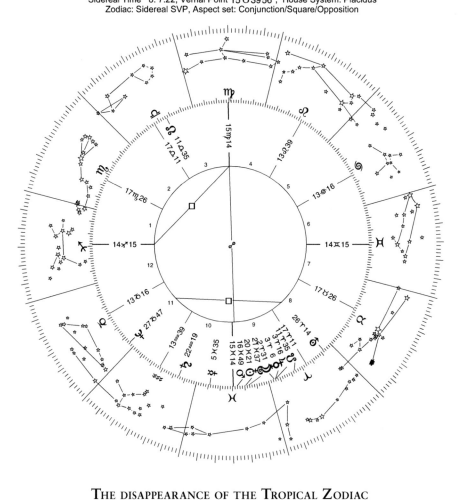

THE DISAPPEARANCE OF THE TROPICAL ZODIAC
AND THE TROPICAL CALENDAR IN THE FUTURE

Certain discoveries in the realm of modern astronomy, such as the galactic movement referred to above, are of extraordinary significance for the renewal of astrology as a true science. A recent finding of modern astronomy points to a time when the tropical calendar—and with it the tropical zodiac—may disappear altogether, leaving only the sidereal zodiac. According to Rudolf Steiner's words quoted earlier, the zodiacal constellations forming the sidereal zodiac have always been and will always be there. But how is it possible that the tropical calendar could disappear at some time in the future?

To grasp this concept, we need to recall that the tropical calendar arises through the Sun's movement in declination.[18] In the Northern Hemisphere, when the Sun reaches maximum northerly declination at the summer solstice (June 21/22), it is about 23 ½° North of the equator—that is, 23 ½° northerly declination. This occurs because the Earth's axis of rotation points toward the Pole star Polaris, which is inclined at an angle of 23 ½° to the Sun–Earth plane of the ecliptic. Correspondingly, the Earth's equator is inclined at 23 ½° to the plane of the ecliptic, denoting the apparent orbit of the Sun around the Earth (top figure, opposite). It is interesting to note that modern astronomy defines the ecliptic in relation to the Earth's orbit around the Sun.

Recent research shows that climatic changes in prehistoric times were influenced by changes in the inclination of the Earth's axis. It has now been estimated that the inclination of the Earth's axis around 750 to 550 million years ago amounted to 54° (lower figure).

This meant that on average the poles received more sun during the course of the year than the equatorial regions, which correspondingly were colder than polar regions. Therefore the polar regions had a more tropical climate while there was large-scale icing over our present tropical regions during the time paleontologists refer to as the Neoproterozoical period. Geologically speaking, this was the time of transition from the Pre-Cambrian to the Cambrian period. This recent research pointing to a pole shift at that time confirms Rudolf Steiner's indications, albeit Steiner's dating of this event is different:

> The Earth's axis shifted gradually. In earlier times there was a tropical climate at the North Pole; later, through a pole shift, the tropical climate came to the middle. This transition proceeded relatively quickly, but it lasted perhaps four million years. The Lemurian Age was twenty-two million years ago. The Lunar Pitris took four million years to shift the axis.[19]

Here Steiner indicates that the change to the Earth's axis took place during the Lemurian Age some 22 million years ago, whereas modern research places it more than 500 million years ago. However,

18 Powell, *History of the Zodiac*, pp. 64–74.
19 Steiner, *Foundations of Esotericism*, October 25, 1905.

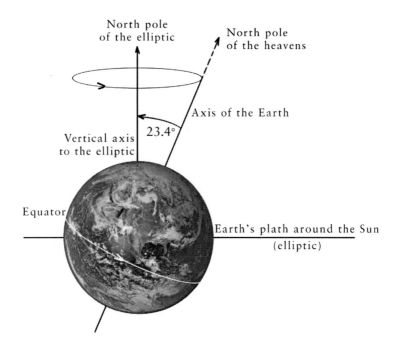

Present inclination of the Earth's axis

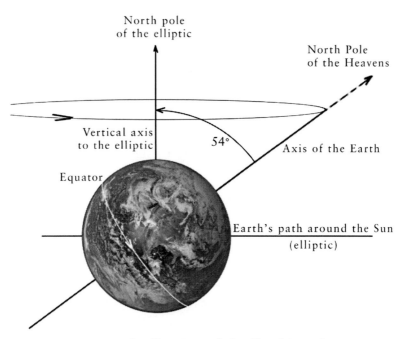

Inclination of the Earth's axis
approximately 500,000,000 years ago

as he mentioned on various occasions, the planetary periods, rate of precession, and so on, were different in those times, and the scientific method of counting years can be inaccurate when not considering these differences. Apart from the difference in the dating of the pole shift, there is also an astonishing agreement, as Rudolf Steiner also spoke of a tropical climate in the polar regions prior to the pole shift.[20]

For our considerations, the important point is the scientific estimate that the pole was previously inclined at 54° whereas now its inclination is 23 ½°, and that it is predicted that the inclination will be less in the future. It could even shift to 0°. If such a pole shift were to take place so that the inclination of the Earth's axis were less than a few degrees (or even 0°), there would be no seasons to speak of. The fact that the Earth's equator would coincide with the plane of its ecliptic and the Sun's declination would be very minimal or at 0° all year round, would effectively eliminate seasons. Without movement of the Sun in declination, there would be no tropical calendar and correspondingly no tropical zodiac (which is simply a projection into space of the Northern Hemisphere's tropical calendar). This would then end the tropical/sidereal controversy by default, since only the sidereal zodiac would remain.

PREJUDICE AND PRECONCEPTIONS:
HINDRANCES TO KNOWLEDGE OF THE TRUTH

Despite the above-mentioned perspectives, it is understandable for astrologers using the tropical zodiac to respond that when one has observed many people over a long period of time in relation to their horoscopes, including one's own horoscope, it is an undeniable fact that the tropical horoscopes reveal truth about character with predictions that are accurate. From the point of their own empirical experience they feel that tropical astrology works, whatever new evidence comes into play. However, if one inquires about the nature of the empirical experience in favor of tropical astrology, one often hears the type of response such as that of a famous German astrologer who had practiced tropical astrology for over fifty years. She said that she knows that tropical astrology is true because her two grandchildren, who are both born under Leo, roar like lions. This kind of response is an

---

20 Ibid.

example of an underlying prejudice. The preference may be to think of oneself as a tropical Leo rather than a sidereal Cancer. Unfortunately the zodiacal images themselves evoke sympathy and antipathy: One may assume that the image of a lion is more magnificent than that of a crab. To overcome this subjective prejudice it may be helpful to recall that the circle of the twelve sidereal signs of the zodiac represents the holy living creatures—the Seraphim, Cherubim, and Thrones (according to Rudolf Steiner)—around the throne of God (Revelation 4:6–8). The animal images—bull, crab, lion, and so on—stem from clairvoyant perception of the spiritual beings belonging to this elevated level of the Divine, and we need to conceive of these holy living creatures as majestic, exalted, divine beings, each as magnificent as the next. When we think of the holy living creature manifesting through the sidereal sign of the Crab, therefore, it is as majestic as the holy living creature manifesting through the sidereal sign of the Lion. Each has the same 30° range of influence as the other, and there is not a diminutive little constellation of the Crab and a grand lengthy constellation of the Lion, as Ptolemy's astronomical zodiac implies.

Underlying this prejudice (sympathy and antipathy in relation to the signs of the zodiac) is the problem of fixed ideas (preconceptions) that one is rarely willing to renounce—especially if it means rethinking all that one has believed thus far. It is much easier just to ignore the rediscovery of the Babylonian sidereal zodiac, because it entails a great deal of difficult mental work to rethink horoscopes in this new context. So those who believe they are Aquarian because they were born in early February may still say that they *know* they are Aquarian when hearing that the Sun was actually in the sidereal sign of Capricorn at their birth. It is possible only to suggest that they lay all preconceptions aside and attempt to weigh up Capricorn and Aquarius objectively. If they are able to do this, they often say some time later, "You know, I really am a Capricorn!"

Apart from anything else, it may be that a *compensation* takes place when a horoscope is transposed from the tropical to the sidereal zodiac. For example, in the above instance it could be that the Sun is in sidereal Capricorn (transposed from tropical Aquarius) but that the Ascendant is now in sidereal Aquarius (transposed from tropical Pisces). In this case, then, the subjective feeling of "being Aquarian" would be accurate, but for a different reason than originally believed.

In the case of Goethe who was born on August 28, 1749, the tropical Sun in Virgo becomes sidereal Leo, with the Sun in the middle of sidereal Leo. At the same time, however, Venus in Goethe's sidereal horoscope is in Virgo, so it is still accurate—in relation to Venus—to speak of a Virgo quality in Goethe's nature.

The fundamental problem is the subjective nature of it all. Though it is not possible to prove that Goethe was a Leo rather than a Virgo personality, the fact is that our preconceptions influence the way we see things. If a tropical astrologer believes that Goethe is a Virgo, he or she will look in Goethe's biography for descriptions that will support that a priori belief. Generally the passages that do not fit with preconceived beliefs will be ignored. So the preconception "Goethe is a Virgo" is for the mind like a pair of sunglasses for the eyes—coloring the way one sees. If this tropical astrologer were then to take up sidereal astrology, a new pair of glasses would be worn to adopt the preconception "Goethe is a Leo." Suddenly everything read about Goethe will confirm this preconception of Leo, just as previously it confirmed the preconception of Virgo.

Perhaps the reader who has followed this so far will grasp how extraordinary it was to discover the rules (or "laws") of astrological reincarnation—in particular the second rule—showing objectively that the soul chooses to be born, to reincarnate, when *planets align in the sidereal zodiac*. Here, for the first time in the history of astrology, there is objective proof of the authentic astrological zodiac, rather than subjective feelings about the qualities of the zodiacal signs (tropical or sidereal). This is a decisive breakthrough to a new science of the stars referred to as hermetic astrology. And this new science of the stars is also a science of reincarnation and karma.

HISTORICAL SHIFT IN THE CHARACTERIZATION
OF THE ZODIACAL SIGNS

Despite any evidence to the contrary, tropical astrologers will assert their subjective feeling that the tropical zodiac is "obviously right." The situation is further complicated by the shift in characterization of the zodiacal signs that has taken place through tropical astrology. The Greek classical scholar Rupert Gleadow drew attention to this shift:

People fail to realize that sidereal Cancer cannot possibly have the same character as the old tropical Cancer. For a person's character is not going to change just because he is classified under a different sign. And the fact is that tropical Leo and sidereal Cancer are two different ways of referring to the same part of the sky, so obviously the character of the people born under that piece of sky must be the same, whether we label them Leo or Cancer. And so in fact it is. For while the characters of the constellations have remained unaltered, the characters of the tropical signs have gradually changed, at any rate in some cases. The Virgin, for instance, has been interpreted as a hard, domineering middle-aged spinster, by astrologers of the tropical zodiac who did not know that two thousand years ago she was a pretty maid, affable and willing to help. And tropical Cancer, supposedly soft, sentimental, maternal and fond of children, corresponds much better to the playful and childish sidereal Gemini than to sidereal Cancer, which is said to be very hard-shelled. There are certain things in the usual tropical characters that really do not fit the symbol: in particular Cancer has been called soft in spite of the crab's hardness, Virgo harsh instead of amiable and Scorpio profound instead of martial.[21]

Gleadow draws attention to the fact that, owing to the precession of the equinoxes, each tropical sign more or less now coincides with the preceding sidereal sign. He states that tropical astrologers have subconsciously compensated for this, altering the qualities of the zodiacal signs accordingly. Gleadow discovered this shift by comparing the Greek and Roman astrologers' descriptions of the zodiacal signs with those of modern tropical astrologers. In order to illustrate the shift that has occurred through tropical astrology let us consider a specific. Here is Alan Leo's description of Scorpio published at the beginning of the twentieth century:

The Sun in the sign Scorpio gives a very firm, determined and reserved individuality, with an inclination to be very dignified, secretive and full of desire. It gives pride to the individual, and tends toward much self-control with regard to each of the lunar indications; the individuality may be either very well disposed or

21 Gleadow, *Your Character in the Zodiac*, p. 30.

very selfish, according to progress. Scorpio is a sign of strength, independence and industry.

Now follows Gleadow's comment:

> This character is all very well in itself, but completely different from the ancient writers, and has nothing Martian about it! To call it 'ruled by Mars' comes dangerously close to hypocrisy. But the explanation is, of course, that Alan Leo's 'Scorpio natives' were only so in the tropical zodiac; really they were Librans, and not ruled by Mars at all but by Venus, hence their un-Martian behavior. So, having cleared away these centuries of misconception, perhaps we may discover by observation what Scorpio natives are really like....
>
> On the whole, then, the ancients were quite right to make Scorpio quick to act, adaptable, proud, courageous and generous, whereas the modern books make it deep and mysterious, obstinate, hard working but not very active. None of the ancients suggest that Scorpio is in any way mysterious or profound, and doubtless the notion was invented because so many alleged Scorpios failed to show the typical forthright and courageous Martian character. A sidereal astrologer would say that these Scorpios are not deep and mysterious at all—they are just simply Librans.[22]

In this description Rupert Gleadow refers to the ancient astrological conception—confirmed by Rudolf Steiner—that each sidereal zodiacal sign has a ruling planet: The Moon ruling sidereal Cancer, the Sun sidereal Leo, Mercury sidereal Virgo, Venus sidereal Libra, Mars sidereal Scorpio, and so forth. [23]

What has taken place is that the real qualities of the zodiacal signs have become obscured through this shift that the tropical zodiac introduced into astrology. The description of tropical Scorpio given in modern astrological textbooks is generally a mixture of sidereal Scorpio and sidereal Libra. The further the tropical sign of Scorpio slips back to coincide with the sidereal sign of Libra (at present tropical Scorpio is covering 25° of sidereal Libra) the more qualities of sidereal Libra enter in. The characterizations of the zodiacal signs are therefore no

---

22 Ibid, pp. 109–110, 112.

23 Steiner, *Ancient Myths*, pp. 48–62.

longer pure, but mixed. The task is to recover the pure characterizations. Rupert Gleadow indicates that the way to do this is to "discover
by observation." Although this is a major task, it is a necessary one if
a true astrology is ever to arise again in the West. This can happen if
sufficient numbers of people again adopt the sidereal zodiac, like our
ancestors in antiquity—including the magi. It would then be possible
to reopen the cosmic dimension of Christianity, which was also accessible to the magi, giving rise to Cosmic Christianity.[24]

The Incarnation of Christ from Space into Time

The story of the magi following the star to find and worship the new-
born savior is one that has held its power even in this most secular and
skeptical of times. For the nineteenth-century pioneer restorers of the
"gospel in the stars"—faithful scholars who courageously defended
ancient star wisdom from the rising tide of both scientific skepticism
as well as the fearful conservatism of fellow Christians—the star of
Bethlehem tale was a helpful aide to open their contemporaries to
contemplation of Biblical affirmation of astrology. Frances Rolleston's
Mazzaroth: or the Constellations (1862) found its original inspiration
in her simple observations of: (1) the concordance with the zodiac
of the abundant instances of "twelves" in the scriptures; (2) John's
and Ezekiel's Holy Living Creatures being positioned near where the
four equinox and solstice points were some 3,000 years before Christ;
(3) the three constellational heroes—Hercules, Ophiucus, and Leo—
crushing the heads of monsters—Draco, Scorpio, and Hydra—remi-
niscent of the promise given to Eve that her seed would bruise the
serpent's head even though the serpent would bruise her heel (Genesis
3:15); and (4) the diverse sources that attributed the origin of the constellations either to Seth or his descendant Enoch.

Rolleston conceived of the zodiacal constellations—beginning
with Virgo—as expressing a summary of the entire gospel tale, and
then filled in detail by drawing upon the ninth-century Arab astronomer Albumazar's designations for the decans.[25] In *The Gospel in the*

---

24 Powell, *Christian Hermetic Astrology.*

25 Powell, *History of the Zodiac* (pp. 87–95), describes the Egyptian decans.
Originally the decans were a set of thirty-six extra-zodiacal constellations.
Later, when the zodiac was introduced to Egypt from Babylon, the decans were

Stars (1862), the popular American Lutheran preacher Joseph Seiss added astronomical detail and narrative continuity to Rolleston's work. A decade later, E. W. Bullinger's *The Witness of the Stars* (1893) closely examined Psalm 19 ("The heavens declare the glory of God"), then drew upon both classical authors and Egyptian hieroglyphs to support his interpretation that the constellations did indeed tell the Christian story.

Reading these three works today, one is struck by how very "cosmic" they seem, as they are keen on deciphering the grand narrative written in the heavens, rather than obsessing (as does most twentieth century "Sun Sign" astrology) on the cult of individual human personality. But the truly cosmic dimension of Christianity reentered the modern world only with the teachings of Rudolf Steiner, who expressed over and again that the sacrifice of Christ on Golgotha changed the entire Earth forever. At Easter 1924 Steiner described Christ's coming as something that brought about a passage or transition of perception from space to time:

> In the old initiation centers, neophytes gazed up to the Sun and through initiation became aware of the Christ. To find him they looked out into space, so to speak. In order to show later developments...[after] the Mystery of Golgotha had already taken place: human beings, instead of seeking Christ in the Sun from a Mystery temple, now look back toward the turning point of time, to the beginning of the Christian era. They look back in time toward the Mystery of Golgotha and there find Christ performing an earthly deed. The significance of the Mystery of Golgotha was that it changed a previously spatial perception into perception through time.[26]

The momentous event of the Incarnation of Christ thus signified "the turning point of time," a coming down from cosmic space to enter into the stream of time. This had to be prepared for. Looked at in this light, the introduction of the tropical calendar by Euctemon in the fifth century B.C. was a preparation for the event of Christ entering the stream of time. The tropical calendar is a seasonal calendar that helps us to attune to the cosmic reality underlying the unfolding of

---

assimilated to the zodiac as 10° divisions, three to each zodiacal sign.

26 Steiner, *The Easter Festival in the Evolution of the Mysteries*, p. 10.

the year.[27] Yet what took place through Ptolemy—the introduction of the tropical zodiac into astrology—effectively obscured the tropical calendar. Let us now consider this more closely.

THE ASTRONOMICAL AND THE ASTROLOGICAL TROPICAL ZODIAC

Euctemon, a Greek astronomer living in Athens around 430 B.C., presented the tropical calendar. However, it seems that he was inspired to do this without knowing the deeper reason for this: to help carry over consciousness from space to the stream of time as a preparation for the coming of Christ. We may note that the tropical calendar and the sidereal zodiac, the latter relating to the spatially perceptible spiritual reality of the twelve zodiacal constellations, coexisted for several centuries until the coming of Christ. Indeed, there was no rivalry between them, since they clearly refer to different levels and different experiences of reality. The sidereal zodiac refers to the reality of the "holy living creatures"—Seraphim, Cherubim, and Thrones—manifesting outwardly in space through the visible constellations of the zodiac, through the twelve 30° signs of the sidereal zodiac as a spatial reality. The tropical calendar refers to a perception of the different qualities of Nature experienced during the cycle of the year, which is a temporal reality. In so far as these different qualities of Nature are designated each month by naming them after the signs of the sidereal zodiac, there is a clear correspondence between the months of the tropical calendar and the signs of the sidereal zodiac.

Astronomically, the point of intersection between the tropical calendar and the sidereal zodiac is the vernal point, the location of the Sun on the day of the vernal equinox and the first day in the tropical calendar. At the time of Euctemon the vernal point was located at 9° Aries. In the following centuries the vernal point traversed the early part of Aries drawing toward Pisces, which it reached around A.D. 215, beginning the Age of Pisces.

Earlier it was mentioned that the tropical zodiac originated during the second century B.C. with the Greek astronomer Hipparchus, and that Ptolemy (second century A.D.) introduced it into astrology. It is helpful to make a clear distinction here between

---

27 Powell, *History of the Zodiac*, pp. 64–74.

the astronomical tropical zodiac of Hipparchus and the astrological tropical zodiac of Ptolemy.

The astronomical use of the tropical zodiac as introduced into astronomy by Hipparchus is simply a way of measuring the longitude and latitude of planets and fixed stars. It is a coordinate system based on the ecliptic (the apparent path of the Sun against the background of the zodiacal constellations). In this system the customary starting position is the vernal point, designated as 0° Aries. From this point 30° arcs in space are measured along the ecliptic—the first 30° arc being called "the sign of Aries," the second 30° arc called "the sign of Taurus," and so on. This is purely an astronomical convention since Hipparchus used the expression "zodiacal signs" to mean any 30° arc on the celestial sphere. Although the introduction of this astronomical convention is attributed to Hipparchus, it is a fact that in his star catalog he did not use ecliptic longitudes but rather gave stellar coordinates primarily in right ascension and declination. This is an alternative astronomical coordinate system utilizing the celestial equator rather than the ecliptic.

It was only with Ptolemy, through his introduction of the tropical zodiac into astrology, that the signs of the tropical zodiac acquired a qualitative significance. Prior to Ptolemy, following Hipparchus, they had only an astronomical function; and this applies right up to the present time in modern astronomy. For an astronomer the zodiacal signs are nothing more than a coordinate system, just as they were for Ptolemy in his star catalog in the *Almagest,* which gives stellar coordinates in ecliptic longitude and latitude.

The tropical zodiacal signs acquired qualities only by virtue of Ptolemy's statement in the *Tetrabiblos* that the sign of Aries begins with the vernal point. However, Ptolemy had not intended to introduce a new zodiac into astrology. What happened—as is evident through later Arabic astrology—is that the description of the astrological qualities of the sidereal signs of the zodiac became transferred to the astronomical tropical zodiac coordinate system of Hipparchus, thus creating the astrological tropical zodiac.

Summary of Historical Steps

Let us summarize the steps that took place historically:

1. In the sixth to early fifth century B.C., the Babylonians began using the sidereal zodiac, a division of the zodiacal constellations into twelve 30° signs (equal-length constellations), which were the original zodiacal signs. Based on their clairvoyant perception of the spiritual influences proceeding from the twelve signs/constellations of the sidereal zodiac, spiritual qualities were attributed to the zodiacal signs, and this was foundational for the new science of astrology—entailing the casting of horoscopes—inaugurated by the Babylonians. Astrology spread from Babylon throughout the ancient world, as far as India, where it is still practiced using the sidereal zodiac to the present day. At the same time as its deployment astrologically, the sidereal zodiac was used by the Babylonians as their astronomical coordinate system, giving ecliptic longitudes and latitudes of planets and stars measured from 0° sidereal Aries—the advantage of this system being that the ecliptic longitudes and latitudes of the stars remain fixed and do not need to be periodically adjusted on account of precession. The importance of the sidereal zodiac is that it accurately describes, in terms of the sidereal signs, the differentiated qualities ("beingness") of the various regions of space that are endowed with these qualities by spiritual beings.

2. Around 430 B.C., the Greek astronomer Euctemon introduced the tropical calendar that accurately describes—in terms of the solar months—the qualities of time belonging to the cycle of the year. Evidently Euctemon was inspired to introduce the tropical calendar by way of preparation for the coming of Christ descending from cosmic space to enter into the stream of time over four hundred years later. The tropical calendar is of a purely temporal nature based on a specification of the four major turning points of the solar year: the vernal equinox, the summer solstice, the autumnal equinox, and the winter solstice, which denote Day 1 in the solar months of Aries, Cancer, Libra, and Capricorn, respectively—these being the pivotal days in the tropical calendar. With the approach of Christ into the stream of time, there arose a need for a way to relate to the spiritual qualities

active in Nature during the cycle of the year. Euctemon's solar calendar helped to prepare for this (which application has to be reversed for the Southern Hemisphere).

3. In the second century B.C., the Greek astronomer Hipparchus introduced an astronomical coordinate system different from the Babylonian sidereal zodiac. This new system of Hipparchus could be called the astronomical tropical zodiac. Along with the coordinate system of right ascension and declination, it is the standard astronomical coordinate system used to the present day. It begins with the vernal point and measures off 30° arcs in space along the ecliptic. Originally it had no astrological connotations and was not used at all by early astrologers. Among its first recorded astrological applications is that of the eighth century Byzantine astrologer Stephanus the Philosopher in casting the "horoscope of Islam" for the year A.D. 621.[28] He was most certainly led to apply this purely astronomical coordinate system in an astrological way from Ptolemy's reference in the astrological textbook *Tetrabiblos* to the "sign of Aries" beginning with the vernal point. Also in the eighth century there began the practice of Islamic astrology with Masha'allah, who inherited the legacy of Hellenistic astrology, primarily Ptolemy's *Tetrabiblos*.[29] Arab astrologers, and this holds true for all subsequent practitioners of tropical astrology, clearly did not realize that Ptolemy was referring to the sidereal sign of Aries in which the vernal point was located more or less exactly at 0°, when Ptolemy wrote the *Tetrabiblos* and placed the vernal point at 0° of Aries.[30]

4. Thus, Ptolemy unwittingly introduced the tropical zodiac into astrology in the second century A.D. through his "academic" astrological textbook the *Tetrabiblos*, whereby the spiritual qualities of the sidereal signs became transferred to the astronomical tropical coordinate system. This created a new astrological zodiac with the tragic effect of obscuring the tropical calendar, since in effect the tropical zodiac is simply a spatial projection of the

28 Neugebauer and van Hoesen, *Greek Horoscopes*, pp. 158–160, 190.

29 Kennedy and Pingree, *The Astrological History of Masha'allah*.

30 Powell, *History of the Zodiac*, p. 80: "At the time Ptolemy wrote the *Tetrabiblos* (ca. A.D. 150), the vernal point was located at 1° of the sign of Aries in the sidereal zodiac, making it quite accurate (to within 1°) to say that the sign of Aries began with the vernal equinox."

(Northern Hemisphere) tropical calendar. Despite being obscured in this way, various cathedrals later portrayed something of the mystery of Christ's entrance into the stream of time, giving a new experience of the cycle of the year. An example is the famous West portal of Chartres cathedral with its magnificent statues and depictions of spiritual truths sculpted in stone. Arched around the left side of the portal are "allegories" of the twelve months of the year showing activities characteristic of each month and above most of them corresponding zodiacal images, e.g. a crab (Cancer) above a man cutting wheat, relating to the period June 22—July 23 in the tropical calendar, and Christ himself as a gardener, beneath the image of a ram (Aries), relating to the period March 21—April 20 in the tropical calendar.

The Incarnation of Christ Did Not Change the Reincarnation of the Soul in Relation to the Sidereal Zodiac

Now we should consider the widespread belief that at the Mystery of Golgotha the being of Christ, coming down from cosmic space (the signs of the sidereal zodiac), became impressed into the signs of the tropical zodiac; and that thereby, since Christ's death and resurrection, the tropical signs are believed to be significant for the soul and spirit of each human being. This belief comes to expression in the following quote:

> In a lecture held on June 30, 1956 (in the working group of anthroposophical doctors in Witten), Rudolf Hauschka mentioned what had become clear to him in a conversation with Dr. Ita Wegman. "I had always struggled against the idea that astrology should still hold any truth, since it no longer has a cosmic reality underlying it. I was taught otherwise, that indeed a reality exists that is more significant than the constellations visible in the starry heavens—namely, the configuration at the time of the life of Christ. When his blood flowed on Golgotha, the macrocosm imprinted itself into the Earth's aura and is effective since then in the Earth or from the Earth's aura."

Somewhat later, in a letter, Hauschka formulated this as follows:

Then certainly a mysterious perspective will emerge, that one will be able to attribute spiritual significance to these two entities: the constellations and the signs, and one will scarcely abstain, when one sees the effect of the zodiacal *constellations* upon Nature, from commemorating here the heavenly and there the earthly offspring of the Elohim. At the turning point of time the representative of the Macrocosm united himself with the Earth and imprinted the stellar constellations into the Earth's aura for all time. Thus, it seems to me that the zodiacal *constellations* work upon the physical–etheric side of Nature, and the signs have to do with the soul–spiritual constitution.[31]

What is expressed here is the idea that, with the Incarnation of Christ, the reality of the sidereal world of the zodiacal constellations was brought down and impressed into the tropical signs. The conclusion is that both the tropical signs and the sidereal constellations are valid, but on different levels. According to this concept Christ brought something of eternal value down from the world of stars into earthly reality, thus imbuing the earthly reality connected with the tropical signs with eternal validity. So what does this idea really express?

There are actually two ideas interwoven here. The first is the conception that Christ brought down something of eternal significance into earthly reality from the world of stars. The second is the conclusion drawn from this, that thereby the tropical signs became imbued with higher reality. The first idea is central to Rudolf Steiner's teaching. He expressed over and again that the sacrifice of Christ on Golgotha changed the entire Earth forever. As referred to earlier, at Easter 1924 Steiner described Christ's coming as something that brought about a passage or transition of perception from space to time.

However, in light of the four points enumerated above, it is evident that the tropical zodiac only *seems* to be related to time (bearing in mind Christ's entrance into the stream of time). In fact the tropical zodiac is *another spatial division* interpolated between the Earth and the real zodiacal signs, the sidereal signs that express the spiritual qualities of cosmic space. So the tropical zodiac obscures both the tropical calendar and the sidereal zodiac. It is only by returning to the original divisions of time and space—the tropical calendar and the

---

31 Novalis—*Zeitschrift für spirituelles Denken*, p. 61.

sidereal zodiac—that we can truly begin to appreciate the spiritual qualities of time and space.[32]

Thus, upon closer inspection the thesis often put forward that Christ's descent to unite with the Earth at Golgotha has imbued the tropical zodiac with a spiritual reality is not substantiated. It is not the signs of the tropical zodiac but the solar months of the tropical calendar that became imbued with spiritual significance through Christ's entrance into the stream of time. Moreover, if the signs of the tropical zodiac were actually relevant astrologically, then this would show up in terms of reincarnation research. But it has not shown up. On the contrary, it is the signs of the sidereal zodiac that show up as significant when the birth horoscope is compared with the horoscope of death from the preceding incarnation. Christ's descent from cosmic space did not put a stop to the work of the lofty spiritual beings called Seraphim, Cherubim, and Thrones, which is to guide the reincarnating human being from life to life in relation to the movements of the planets against the background of the sidereal signs.

The second rule of astrological reincarnation described in chapter 1 is an expression of this sublime work of the Seraphim, Cherubim and Thrones. The incarnation of Christ did not stop the work of the spiritual hierarchies. However, it did imbue the fundamental experience of earthly reality—the cycle of the year—with new spiritual reality. At the same time, Christ has continued to work in conjunction with the hosts of the heavenly hierarchies. He has become the Lord of Karma and thus oversees the destiny of every reincarnating human being. In doing so, Christ unites with the spiritual hierarchies in the great work of regulating reincarnation and karma.

The fact that there are *rules* of astrological reincarnation is an expression of the work of Christ and the spiritual hierarchies. The second rule of astrological reincarnation is formulated in terms of the sidereal zodiac. This did not change at the time of the Mystery of Golgotha. The sidereal zodiac is and always was the authentic astrological zodiac. This is evident when we compare the birth and death horoscopes of individuals from pre-Christian to post-Christian times, one example being that of John the Baptist (born in 2 B.C.), who

32 A still earlier division of the cycle of the year (preceding Euctemon's tropical calendar) was the ancient lunar calendar of the Babylonians, adopted in the sixth century B.C. also by the people of Israel. The lunar calendar is discussed in *Hermetic Astrology*, vol.2, chapter 10.

Comparison Chart

Outer - Geocentric	Inner - Geocentric
Birth of John the Baptist	Birth of Raphael
At Jutta (Yattah), Latitude 31N32', Longitude 35E6'	At Urbino/Italy, Latitude 43N44', Longitude 12E38'
Date: Wednesday, 4/JUN/2 B.C., Julian	Date: Friday, 28/MAR/1483, Julian
Time: 0:37, Local Time	Time: 21:30, Local Time
Sidereal Time 17:15:23, Vernal Point 3♈ 3'52"	Sidereal Time 10:28:41, Vernal Point 12♓27'56"

House System: Placidus, Zodiac: Sidereal SVP
Aspect set: Conjunction/Square/Opposition

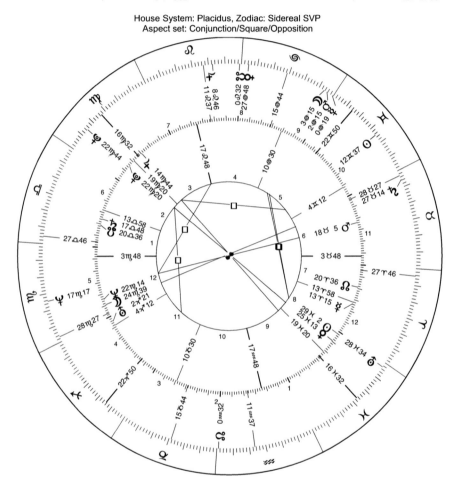

reincarnated as the Renaissance painter Raphael (born in 1483). That the planet Pluto lines up exactly between the two birth horoscopes in the sidereal zodiac (comparison horoscope above) shows that the occurrence of the Mystery of Golgotha between the birth of John the Baptist and the birth of Raphael did not change anything astrologically. Moreover, the second rule of astrological reincarnation shows the continuity in the path of reincarnation for human beings, and that there was no "switch" from the sidereal to the tropical zodiac following the

Mystery of Golgotha. The sidereal zodiac is as valid now as it was at the time of the Babylonians. The following words of Rudolf Steiner confirm the validity of the sidereal perspective:

> If one were to photograph a person's brain at the moment of birth and then photograph also the heavens lying exactly over the person's birthplace, this latter picture would be of exactly the same appearance as that of the human brain. As certain centers were arranged in the latter, so would the stars be in the photograph of the heavens. The human being has within himself a picture of the heavens, and every person has a different one, according to whether he was born in this place or that, and at this or that time. This is one indication that the human being is born from out of the whole cosmos.[33]

This indication by Rudolf Steiner is a confirmation that the sidereal horoscope is the valid horoscope of birth as it gives a photo-like picture of the starry heavens at the moment of one's birth. Thus, if the constellation of Leo were rising on the eastern horizon at the moment of birth, the Ascendant would comprise the stars of Leo rather than tropical Virgo. Rudolf Steiner's clairvoyant perception of the imprint of the sidereal heavens in the brain at birth gives direct confirmation of the validity of the Babylonian sidereal zodiac as providing a true basis for astrology. It is as if each human being, within the vault of his or her own skull, has preserved an important facet of Seth's stone pillar of star wisdom.

That Seth's pillar is of stone does not mean that it is static and lifeless! It is stone in the sense that it is permanent, eternal. In our time, another facet of Seth's stone pillar has come into view, which reflects the incarnation of Christ from space into time. The emerging Cosmic Christianity, the new "gospel in the stars," demonstrates decisively that the deeds of Christ two thousand years ago reverberate down through time, and are effective and alive today, having become renewed since Christ's return in the etheric—beginning in 1933.[34] This renewed presence of Christ—the *parousia*—is the process by which the etheric body of Christ (which incorporates all the events through

---

33 Steiner, *The Spiritual Guidance of the Individual and Humanity*, p. 63.

34 Powell, *The Christ Mystery*, discusses the dating of Christ's second coming to 1933. The rhythm of Christ's life confirms this date and thus supports Rudolf Steiner's prophecy that the second coming of Christ would commence in 1933.

which Christ lived) is membered into the Earth's etheric aura. Since the images of the events in Christ's etheric body are related wholly to the cosmic world, they are activated at each recurrence of the cosmic configurations from Christ's life. For example, the crucifixion took place at Full Moon; today, at every Full Moon, there is a "cosmic echo" of this event, and one may thus, at each Full Moon, live meditatively into the Crucifixion. The raising of Lazarus, having taken place at New Moon, is "remembered" in our own time at each New Moon.[35]

Two foundational concepts of conventional astrology are the significance of: (1) planetary transits; and (2) recurring aspects; these principles of course hold in a new and profound manner relative to the new gospel of the stars. Within the context of the new star wisdom, a transit occurs whenever a planet crosses over a particular position in the sidereal zodiac that it (or another planet) occupied at the time of an event in Christ's life. Such events—including Jesus' conception and birth, the baptism in the Jordan, Christ's healing miracles, the Mystery of Golgotha, and other events (for example, Ascension and Pentecost)—would also include the principle events in the lives of Mary and John the Baptist and other significant individuals in the life of Jesus Christ for whom accurate dates can be found.

As an example of a transit, let us consider the great event of the baptism of Jesus in the River Jordan, which signified the start of his 3½-year ministry. Accompanied by Lazarus, Jesus set out from Lazarus's home in Bethany on the night of September 22, A.D. 29, proceeding east toward the Jordan, arriving at the place of baptism around dawn the next morning. The baptism took place later that morning of September 23, around 10 a.m. At that time the Sun had just entered sidereal Libra (1°), and the waning crescent Moon was at 16° Leo. At the baptism the Cosmic Christ descended in the form of a dove of light to unite with Jesus; thus the "conception" of Christ Jesus occurred "on the cusp," i.e., just as the Sun entered sidereal Libra. This single event shows how finely attuned the rhythm of Christ's ministry is to the passage of the Sun through the sidereal zodiac. If we had transposed ourselves from the Earth to the Sun at the moment when the Sun was entering Libra, we would have seen the Earth just entering Aries, the zodiacal point that has always signified the start of a new cycle.

---

35 Powell, *Chronicle of the Living Christ,* gives an exact dating of the events in the life of Christ and presents the horoscopes of the corresponding planetary configurations on those dates.

Again and again one finds such correspondences in Christ's ministry to the passage of the Sun through the sidereal signs of the zodiac,
and one can through conscious attention to these archetypes, pro-
foundly experience the events in this ministry, in our own time. Since
the stellar archetype of the baptism occurred on the cusp of Virgo/
Libra in the sidereal zodiac, one need only identify the date—October
18/19—in our own epoch when this cusp recurs.[36]

The same principle applies to the recurring aspects between two
planets, particularly conjunctions and oppositions. The New Moon
(Sun/Moon conjunction) and Full Moon (Sun/Moon opposition) are
the most common recurring aspects, and, as mentioned above, they
commemorate, respectively, the raising of Lazarus and the crucifixion.
Moreover, on the day of Christ's raising Lazarus from the dead there
was a close conjunction of Venus and Uranus in Leo; and it is possible
in our day to consult an ephemeris to discover on which date such a
conjunction falls.

As another example: at Christ's healing of the blind youth of
Manahem, there was a superior conjunction of Mercury with the
Sun in Libra. In 2007, this configuration recurred on October 23.
One can consult an ephemeris each year to discover when the same
planetary configuration returns and prepare oneself to attune to
the cosmic recurrences commemorating events in the life of Christ.
Thus, for example, three momentous miracles in the life of Christ—
the baptism; the healing of the blind youth of Manahem; and the
raising of Lazarus—were thus "remembered" in 2007, in just a single week (October 18—October 25). Over an entire year, a majestic
pageant of Christ's life unfolds within the etheric tableau, and each
event is available to us as a path to attune to the cosmic dimension
of Christ's ministry. This is truly a new gospel of the stars, one made
possible to read only through recognition of the sidereal zodiac and
the importance of the heliocentric, as well as geocentric, perspectives for those events.[37]

---

36 The Sun is at this time in the first decan of Libra, associated with the
constellation of Boötes, the Ploughman. The deeper meaning of *Boötes* has to
do with the Hebrew *Bo*, which means "coming"; hence, *Boötes* is the "Coming
One"—a perfect sidereal picture for the event of Christ's baptism.

37 None of this knowledge would be possible without a precise and accurate
calendar of the events in Christ's life, which has been available since the
publication in 1996 of Robert Powell's *Chronicle of the Living Christ;*. see also

This new gospel of the stars calls out to each of us not only from the calendar, in conjunction with the horoscopes of the events in the life of Christ, but *from our own horoscope.* There lies before us the possibility to rediscover in what particular ways we ourselves are in cosmic communion with Christ, via the examination of our own sidereal horoscopes of birth and conception. The sidereal horoscopes of great individuals can provide initial signposts to this exploration. As discussed in chapter 3, Rudolf Steiner was born with the Moon at 25° Leo, the exact position of the Moon at the event of Pentecost, and it was suggested that this indicated a resonance between the descent of the Holy Spirit at Pentecost and the birth of Rudolf Steiner. Even a cursory examination of Rudolf Steiner's biography will reveal the many ways in which his life bore the stamp of the Holy Spirit.

Remarkably, almost *all* of the planets in Rudolf Steiner's sidereal natal chart stand at positions where there had been planets at seminal events in the life of Christ. The position of Mercury at Rudolf Steiner's birth is within 1° of the position of the Moon (3 ½° Pisces) at the miracle of the changing of water into wine at Cana. Venus, at 25 ½° Capricorn, is conjunct the position of Neptune (24 ½° Capricorn) at the raising of the youth of Nain and the raising of the daughter of Jairus from the dead. Mars (13° Aries) lines up with the position of the Sun at the transfiguration (14° Aries). Jupiter (27° Cancer) is conjunct where Mercury was at the death of Mary of Nazareth (27 ½° Cancer). Saturn's position at 13° Leo recalls the Sun at the death of Mary of Nazareth (12 ½ Leo). Neptune, at 5 ½° Pisces, is within 2° of Jupiter's position (3 ½° Pisces) at the changing of water into wine at Cana. Pluto (14 ½° Aries) is aligned with where the Sun was at the crucifixion (14° Aries). The only planet left out of this accounting—Uranus—stood at 15° 16' Taurus at Rudolf Steiner's birth, in conjunction with the Royal Star Aldebaran (15° Taurus). Though each of these planetary positions carries impulses that manifest uniquely within the destiny of the great initiate Rudolf Steiner, one senses that the sidereal natal horoscope proclaims the birth of an individual whose mission was intimately bound to the mission of Christ. Surely, as the first great witness—indeed, the prophet—of Christ's return in the etheric in the

---

the *Journal for Star Wisdom* (formerly *Christian Star Calendar*), published annually by SteinerBooks. It combines monthly ephemerides with commentaries on the significance of certain days relative to the geocentric and heliocentric planetary movements attending the events in the life of Jesus Christ.

twentieth century, Rudolf Steiner fulfilled a task as solemn and historic as that of John the Baptist during Christ's life.[38]

Turning to other great individualities, using the sidereal chart to compare with events from the life of Christ, one finds, for example, that Leonardo DaVinci was born with the Sun at 16½° Aries, close to the position of the Sun at the resurrection (15½° Aries). Jesus of Nazareth, born with the Sun at 16° Sagittarius, had the star Nunki closest to the Sun at that time, Nunki marking the shaft of the archer's arrow. As modern astronomy has recently shown, the tip of the arrow points directly at 2° Sagittarius toward the Galactic Center (see the figure on page 92), the "Throne of God" from which emanates the Divine Love that animates the entire galaxy, and the place from which the Christ Being, the Son of God, descended to Earth from the Father. Ludwig von Beethoven, whose symphonies were transformative creative fire wrested from Heaven, was born with the Sun conjunct the Galactic Center, at 3° Sagittarius.

Our own sidereal horoscope is a map of what aspects of the Cosmic Christ we are destined to work with particularly. Identifying and then meditating on these aspects can be a deeply moving, healing experience. In Christ's own words: "Lo, I am with you always, to the end of time" (Matthew 28:20), and "Heaven and Earth will pass away, but my words will not pass away" (Matthew 24:35). As the words of Christ are of eternal significance, so too are his deeds, and by remembering these deeds by attuning to them as they are reflected in our own horoscopes, we connect ourselves with something grand and eternal. Each Christ event contains a rejuvenating power that can be applied in daily life to helping ourselves, others, and even the world situation.

On July 17, 2007, when thousands of people joined the "Fire the Grid" initiative launched by Shelley Yates—a Nova Scotia woman who had after an automobile accident lived through a near death experience along with her son—few participants were aware of the underlying astronomical reality for that date (this included Yates

---

38 In his *Star Wisdom & Rudolf Steiner*, David Tresemer artfully portrays a wide array of Steiner's "Star Brothers" and "Star Sisters"—individuals from centuries before, after, and during Rudolf Steiner's life—who share the same sidereal configuration for the Sun, which Tresemer terms the "Gate Image." (His research also investigates three other heavenly positions determined by the Sun location.) The biographies he considers are extremely helpful in discovering a qualitative, Christ-centered dimension to one's own biography.

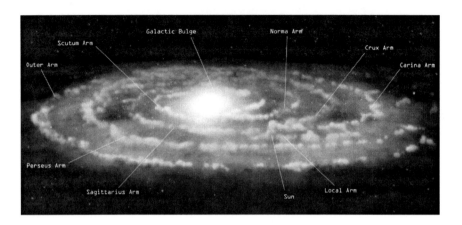

herself, until a week or two before the event). Pluto—as it had been on December 29, 2006, and would be again on October 27, 2007—was on July 17, 2007 conjunct the Galactic Center at 2° Sagittarius. Further, recalling the conjunction of Pluto with the Sun (9° Sagittarius) at the third temptation in the wilderness—the temptation of turning stones into bread—which took place on November 29, A.D. 29, the July 17, 2007 configuration clearly marked a moment when all of humanity faced a strenuous challenge, stimulated by the oppositional force of Pluto's dark aspect as Hades. Knowledge of the archetypal dimension of this event, as expressed in the life of Christ, undoubtedly would have aided the meditative effort, by clarifying both the stellar pattern and the issues at stake in humanity's path at this moment in world destiny.[39]

Mindful of this new gospel of the stars, one can—as in the instance of the "Fire the Grid" large-scale meditative endeavor—go beyond individual biography to the titanic currents of world history to discover striking patterns of significance, and these can serve as guideposts as events continue to unfold. That the Christ events are not just past history, but a living, contemporary reality, may be seen from contemplating current episodes of world historical importance in their sidereal astronomical context. In the *Christian Star Calendar*

---

39 For further consideration of the contemporary challenge of the third temptation in the wilderness, see Powell and Dann, *Christ & the Maya Calendar*. See also, Powell, *Chronicle of the Living Christ* (pp. 424–432) and *Hermetic Astrology*, vol. 2, chapter 9, "The Second Coming and the New Age." Powell's article "Pluto and the Galactic Center," *Christian Star Calendar 2007* (pp. 7–18) takes up the issue of the dual aspect of *Hades* (Darkness) vs. *Phanes* (Light) in relation to the working of Pluto (online at https://sophiafoundation.org/articles/).

for January 19, 1991, it was stated that: "the Sun enters into conjunction with Saturn and with the Moon's North Node. This latter event reminds us of the temptation in the wilderness." Just two days before this, on January 17, coincident with the opposition between the Moon and Jupiter, "Operation Desert Storm"—the first Gulf War—began. On the evening of the Sabbath, Friday, October 21, A.D. 29, at the start of the forty days of Christ's temptation in the desert, the Moon stood in opposition to Jupiter. "Operation Desert Storm" continued for forty-one days, until the proclamation of a cease-fire on February 27, 1991. Seen against the background of the forty days of temptation of Christ Jesus in the desert, one can see in these forty-one days of the Gulf War a modern apocalyptic drama. (The US-led Iraq War—bearing the deceptive double-speak euphemism "Operation Iraqi Freedom"—was prematurely declared "accomplished" by President George W. Bush on May 1, 2003; having begun on March 20, this was also a period of forty-one days.)

At the beginning of Operation Desert Storm on January 17, 1991, Jupiter (15 ½° Cancer) was in conjunction with the star cluster Praesape (the Beehive) at 12 ½° Cancer, and at the start of the Iraq War on March 20, 2003, Jupiter was at 13 ½ Cancer, even more closely conjunct Praesape than at the start of the first Gulf War. The Babylonians considered Praesape the place of exaltation for Jupiter. Clearly, not only do the sites of exaltation denote the most potent working of a planet's benevolent beings; they also denote the locations in the zodiac where adversarial beings will challenge those workings. Another event from 1991 that can be seen in this light is the three-day coup by communist hardliners in Moscow that began on August 18/19, 1991, just as the Sun (in conjunction with Jupiter) entered sidereal Leo. For three days President Gorbachev was confined to his Crimean vacation retreat at Foros on the Black Sea. As stated in the *Christian Star Calendar 1991*:

> Prior to the Sun reaching conjunction with Regulus (the heart of the Lion) there are on August 21st and 22nd inferior conjunctions of Mercury and Venus with the Sun, close to the degree where the Sun was at the raising of Lazarus (3° Leo).

The breakdown of the coup and the release of Mikhail Gorbachev occurred on Wednesday, August 21, when the Sun was at 3° Leo.

During the three days of President Gorbachev's confinement, it was as if the seeds of the new political order that were yearning for sunlight and growth were suddenly entombed, only to blossom forth more vigorously after the overcoming of the death-like grip exerted by the old order through the coup. Recalling the words of Jesus concerning Lazarus's illness—"This illness is not unto death; it is for the glory of God, so that the Son of God may be glorified by means of it." (John 11:4)—the historical record clearly shows that the coup was not a death blow to the coming to birth of a new Russia. Rather, overcoming it was "for the glory of God," in the sense of its being a step on the path toward the emergence of a future *community of Philadelphia* (Revelation 3:7), which will one day spring from the ground of East European culture.[40]

Three thousand years ago, the Babylonian temple astronomers who watched the night sky so fastidiously for planetary omens conceived of the auspices they received as "world-shaking," and yet that "world" was a tightly circumscribed one, restricted to their villages and the surrounding valleys and hills. So it was for many millennia, in villages the world over, where any floods, famines, or wars prophesied by the planets and stars were ones that went unfelt and unrecorded a few valleys or mountain ranges away. Today the planets and stars look down upon an Earth knit from pole to pole and hemisphere to hemisphere into a truly global community, where no corner of the planet escapes the deeds—and misdeeds—of modern industrial humanity. That a new gospel of the stars should arise at this moment in world history, when humanity yearns more than ever to speak to and be spoken to by the stars, is truly world destiny. Seth's long lost stone pillar—the sidereal zodiac of equal constellations—stands before us, but it is mute unless we bring our most heartfelt and well-prepared questions to bear upon it.

---

40 Andreev, *The Rose of the World* discusses this coming community of Philadelphia in the Age of Aquarius, which he refers to as the "Rose of the World." See also Powell and Dann, *Christ & the Maya Calendar*, chapter 9.

CHAPTER FIVE

CHRIST AND THE STARRY HEAVENS

Yonder goes Cygnus, the Swan, flying southward,—
Sign of the Cross and of Christ unto me.
    —T. BERRY SMITH, from "Come Learn of the Stars"[1]

THE ASTROLOGICAL SIGNIFICANCE OF THE ENTIRE CELESTIAL SPHERE

As indicated in chapter 4, "The New Gospel in the Stars," a significant aspect of the astrological revolution is the growing awareness of the cosmic nature of Christ. To many readers the previous chapter's juxtaposition of Astrology and Christianity may seem quite strange. However, we need only recall the biblical account of the three magi who learned about the birth of the Messiah from the stars to see how there has always been an astrological dimension to the story of Christ. The tale of the Magi originally led to an exploration of astrology in connection with the Star of the Magi, which in turn led to a vast panoramic spectrum of new astrological wisdom.[2] This new astrological star wisdom shares with Cosmic Christianity a focus upon the cosmos—a very different realm than that of traditional Christian theology.

It was precisely through research into the cosmic dimension of Christ that one of the most significant breakthroughs came with regard to research into the mysteries of the stars. This breakthrough demonstrates the truly cosmic nature of Christ in relation to the stars in the heavens. The initial discoveries of the significance of the sidereal zodiac occurred early in 1970.[3] Then, 33 ⅓ years later, on May

---

1 From Allen, *Star Names: Their Lore and Meaning*, p. 195.

2 Powell, *Christian Hermetic Astrology* and *Chronicle of the Living Christ*.

3 We are indebted to the Irish astrologer Cyril Fagan for pointing to the ancient sidereal zodiac in *Astrological Origins* and *Zodiacs Old and New*. In the former, Fagan gives dates for the passage of the vernal point through the signs of the sidereal zodiac—dates approximating those in *Hermetic Astrology*, vol. 1, which (as described there) are in accordance with Rudolf Steiner's dating of the cultural epochs. In 1982, when Willi Sucher noticed these dates, he commented, "These

7, 2003, there came a remarkable expansion in consciousness from the sidereal zodiac to include the *entire celestial sphere of fixed stars* (33 ⅓ years being the rhythm of Christ's life from birth to the resurrection). This signified a quantum leap with respect to the astrological worldview, as will appear in the following. In this expansion of consciousness, the nature of each sidereal sign is perceived as a constellation, or a kind of "group effect," of each star belonging to that sign. Beyond the stars comprising each zodiacal sign/constellation, *all the stars* of the constellations above and below the zodiac also have an effect. In other words, the entire celestial sphere is the real domain of astrology; every star in the heavens has significance for human beings and for life here on the Earth. It will take some time to assimilate the extraordinary consequences of this discovery for astrology. The following is an attempt to communicate the deeper implications of the expansion of consciousness, astrologically, to include the starry heavens in their entirety—a step into galactic consciousness. Paradoxically it is through an understanding of the cosmic dimension of Christ that conclusive proof is offered of the *astrological significance of the entire celestial sphere.*

THE ASTROLOGICAL SIGNIFICANCE OF MEGA STARS

One aspect of this breakthrough is the discovery of the significance of *mega stars*, which is a term for extremely luminous stars—stars with a luminosity at least 10,000 times that of our Sun.[4] In order to

---

are the correct dates." Coming from a great teacher of star wisdom, this is very important for us to hear and provides encouraging support for validating the use of the equal-division sidereal zodiac in the new star wisdom of astrosophy (see Powell, *History of the Zodiac*).

4 The famous Bayer catalog of stars (1603) by Johann Bayer assigns *Greek letters* to the brightest stars visible in each constellation, usually in descending order of apparent brightness (though Bayer was not always consistent in this). In the early 1700s, John Flamsteed assigned *numbers* to the bright stars in each constellation according to right ascension. Because one eventually runs out of Greek letters, the Flamsteed numbers proved useful, for there is virtually no limit to the number of stars that can be assigned a number. The Flamsteed catalog (which includes the stars in the Bayer catalog) is more or less sufficient for exploring the visible cosmos, but more and more stars in our galaxy have now been cataloged with the development of ever more powerful telescopes. For the purpose of exploring the sidereal influences at work in our *cosmos* (the local region of the galaxy known as the Orion Arm); see figure on page 105.

illustrate the notion of mega stars, let us consider the star Deneb, which marks the tail of the Swan (or the head of the Northern Cross) and which can be seen on high during summer nights in the middle of the Milky Way. Deneb is a first magnitude star (apparent magnitude +1.2) which, however, appears less bright than its neighbor Vega in the constellation of the Lyre. Both the Swan and the Lyre were sacred to Apollo, and both Deneb and Vega are of great significance in relation to our solar system. As described in chapter 4, Deneb and Vega mark two points of the *summer triangle*, whose third point is marked by Altair in the constellation of the Eagle. Whereas Vega is the fifth brightest star that we can see in our cosmos, Deneb is the nineteenth brightest in terms of apparent magnitude. Sirius, of course, is the brightest star we can see, in terms of apparent magnitude. However, neither Vega nor Sirius is a mega star, whereas Deneb is. How may this be understood?

Our grasp of the surrounding cosmos is changed immediately when we consider the *distance* of stars from our solar system. These distances are so vast that a special cosmic unit (*light year*) was devised for measurement—a light year being the distance that light travels during the course of one year. To gain an understanding of the enormous distances involved, we need only consider that Sirius—8 ½ light years away (amounting to some fifty trillion miles or eighty trillion kilometers)—is a *close neighbor* to our Sun in comparison with the greater distances of almost all other stars (only the triple star system Alpha Centauri and Barnard's star, Wolf's star, and Lalande's star are closer to our Sun than Sirius).[5] It is because Sirius is so close, in comparison with other stars, that it appears so bright. If we were to place Sirius alongside our Sun, how bright would it appear in comparison with our Sun?

This leads us to the concept of *luminosity*, which measures a star's intrinsic brightness. Generally the luminosity of our Sun is set at the value one (L=1). By way of comparison, then, the luminosity of Sirius is 24 (L=24). In other words Sirius, if it were to be placed alongside our Sun, would appear twenty-four times brighter. From our perspective, our Sun is an extremely bright star. However, if the Earth were revolving around Sirius—in other words, if Sirius were our sun—it would be seen by us as twenty-four times brighter. If we imagine a

5 http://en.wikipedia.org/wiki/List_of_nearest_stars.

second sun alongside our Sun, then a third sun, a fourth sun, a fifth sun, up to a twenty-fourth sun, all grouped together as twenty-four suns, we can begin to imagine the luminosity of Sirius, which would blaze down upon us with the light of twenty-four of our Suns.

Vega at twenty-five light years is *three* times the distance of Sirius. If Vega would appear to us to be just as bright as Sirius then, because the intensity of light decreases proportionately to the *square* of the distance, it would follow that the intrinsic brightness (luminosity) of Vega would be about *nine* times (3 x 3) that of Sirius. However, Vega—as the fifth brightest star in terms of apparent magnitude—appears *less bright* to us than Sirius. In fact, the luminosity of Vega (L=50) is a little more than *twice* that of Sirius. Vega's luminosity is fifty, so that if the Earth were revolving around the star Vega as our Sun, Vega would blaze down upon us with a light fifty times brighter than that of our Sun.

Having specified luminosity, we are now in a position to understand why Deneb is a mega star. Deneb is over 3,200 light years distant from our solar system and has a luminosity of about 250,000. In other words, Deneb is shining with a light 250,000 times more powerful than our Sun, twenty-five times the luminosity of the "least" luminous mega star (L = 10,000 being the minimum luminosity for a star to qualify as a mega star).

Deneb well illustrates the significance of mega stars. Looking up at Deneb, we see that it is 60° north of the zodiac—this is its latitude. If we trace an arc down from the *ecliptic pole* through Deneb, it intersects the sidereal zodiac at 10½° Aquarius—this is Deneb's longitude. According to the astrological research referred to in the previous chapter, which provides the foundation for the yearly *Journal for Star Wisdom* (formerly *Christian Star Calendar*),[6] at the feeding of the 5,000 the Sun was at 10½° Aquarius.[7] Let us consider this in light of a statement from Rudolf Steiner:

> In Palestine during the time that Jesus of Nazareth walked on Earth as Christ Jesus—during the three years of his life, from his thirtieth to his thirty-third year—the entire being of the Cosmic Christ was acting uninterruptedly upon him, and was working into him. The Christ stood always under the influence of

6 Powell (ed.), *Journal for Star Wisdom* (yearly).

7 Powell, *Chronicle of the Living Christ*, pp. 275–276; see p. 170 for the horoscope of this event. The feeding of the 5,000 is described in John 6:1–14.

the entire cosmos; he made no step without this working of the cosmic forces into and in him.... It was always in accordance with the collective being of the whole universe with whom the Earth is in harmony, that all which Christ Jesus did took place.[8]

From these words it is clear that it was not mere coincidence that there was a *conjunction* between the Sun and the mega star Deneb at the feeding of the 5,000, and that the cosmic forces streaming from Deneb were transmitted via our Sun and were received and transmitted further by Christ at the time of the miracle of the multiplication of bread and fish. Here the word "conjunction" means a conjunction in *longitude*, both at 10½° Aquarius. Even though the Sun and Deneb were 60° apart in terms of latitude, there was still a conjunction in longitude, with the Sun crossing the *Deneb meridian* at the time of the miracle.

Just as there are meridians—lines of energy flow—in the human being, these meridians exist also in the greater cosmos of the macrocosm. As may be understood from the law of correspondences (*as above, so below*), if there are meridians in the human being, they must also exist "above" in the cosmos. We can picture an energy flow streaming from each star and intersecting the zodiac, the place of intersection indicating the point of influx where energy flows from the cosmos into our solar system. For Deneb, this point of influx is 10½° Aquarius. Thus, whenever the Sun or any planet in our solar system crosses the Deneb meridian at 10½° Aquarius, the Deneb energy flows in to unite with that planet or with our Sun. (Here, the word *energy* is represents Divine Energy, or Divine Love, radiating from the stars.)

The fact that at the feeding of the 5,000 Deneb was 60° *north* of the Sun is not so relevant. Why? The key concept here, as mentioned above, is the meridian running through the star and then intersecting the ecliptic. The ecliptic (the apparent path of the Sun through the zodiac) can be regarded as the *heart meridian* of the cosmos—the point of entry of stellar influences streaming in from outside our solar system. The important point at the feeding of the 5,000 was that the Sun was crossing the Deneb meridian, since the Sun and Deneb were in conjunction at 10½° Aquarius in terms of sidereal longitude. Focusing upon the meridians as *energy lines* flowing through every star, the *entire celestial sphere* becomes astrologically significant.

---

8 Steiner, *Spiritual Guidance of the Individual and Humanity*, p. 28.

This discovery signifies a broadening—in relation to the original Babylonian and Egyptian astronomy/astrology based on the ancient sidereal zodiac—to include the entire celestial sphere. For the Egyptians and the Babylonians the sidereal zodiac provided the natural frame of reference for observing the passage of the *planets* (meaning "wandering stars") against the background of the *fixed stars*. It is thanks to the clairvoyance of the Babylonian astronomer/priests, through the guidance in the sixth century B.C. of the great Persian initiate Zaratas (Greek: Zoroaster), that the background of the fixed stars was divided into twelve equal constellations/signs of the zodiac, each 30° long, with Aldebaran at 15° Taurus and Antares at 15° Scorpio—this being the original definition of the zodiac.[9] Each of the stars in the twelve signs was assigned a degree in longitude in the zodiac—Spica, for example, near the end of Virgo, was found to have a zodiacal longitude of 29° Virgo.

Thanks to the star-gazing Babylonians the *exaltations* of the planets were discovered, these being generally identified with stars or star clusters in the zodiac.[10] For example, the Babylonians found that the Moon's most powerful location (exaltation) in the entire zodiac was when the Moon was in conjunction with the star cluster of the Pleiades in the neck of the Bull (5° Taurus). However, the Babylonian tradition which located the positions of the planetary exaltations was not very exact, and so in modern astrology the Moon's exaltation is said to be 3° Taurus when in fact it is 5° Taurus, in conjunction with the Pleiades (the Seven Sisters). Cuneiform tablet VAT 7851 shows the Moon at exaltation in conjunction with the Pleiades in Taurus. Likewise, the Babylonians discovered Jupiter's exaltation to be in conjunction with the star cluster of Praesepe in Cancer (12 ½° Cancer). Again, the astrological tradition that Jupiter's exaltation is 15° Cancer is only approximate, because Jupiter's exaltation point is 12 ½° Cancer, in conjunction with Praesepe (the Beehive).

The clairvoyance of the Babylonians, focused upon the passage of the planets against the background of the fixed stars, led to the discovery of the exaltations as the most potent stellar locations of the

9 Powell, *History of the Zodiac.*

10 Ibid., p. 84, fn.3, p. 116, fn.4. Cf. also Robert Powell, *Hermetic Astrology,* vol. 1, pp. 225–230, which discusses the astrological tradition of planetary exaltations that Babylonians called *qaqqar nisirti* ("places of secret revelation").

planets in the zodiac. The ancient teaching of the exaltations, relating to stars or star clusters within the zodiacal belt, has been fundamental in the history of astrology. Now, with the development toward a new astrological star wisdom encompassing the galaxy, our consciousness is expanded to see the Sun, Moon, and planets not just in relation to the constellational background of the signs of the sidereal zodiac, but to include all the stars in the heavens, the entire celestial sphere.

This is part of the arising of a galactic level of consciousness, which lies at the heart of a new astrological star wisdom. Could it be the Cosmic Christ who is behind this awakening of consciousness to the galaxy? The awakening to this galactic level of consciousness signifies a step for humanity comparable to the new consciousness that came about through the Copernican revolution, when the old geocentric solar system gave way to the new heliocentric one. The revolution at that time was at the level of the cosmos, rather than at the level of the galaxy. Here the word *cosmos* is used in the Greek sense of the word to encompass the entire visible universe, including all stars visible to the naked eye. The revolution that is taking place in our time is the step from cosmos to galaxy. Now that there is a consciousness of the shape and structure of our Milky Way Galaxy, we are enabled to inwardly behold that which lies beyond the confines of our local part of the galaxy. As will be discussed below, the cosmos coincides, by and large, with our local part of the galaxy, known as the Orion Arm. Galactic awareness signifies an expansion of consciousness to include the whole of the Milky Way Galaxy, not just the Orion Arm on which our Sun is located (see diagram on page 105 and figure of our Milky Way Galaxy on page 140).

DENEB: OUR BRIGHT GUIDING STAR IN THE ORION ARM

The star Deneb is of special significance. On the one hand it is the most luminous first magnitude star in our cosmos—our local part of the galaxy, known as the Orion Arm. (According to the Wikipedia "List of Most Luminous Stars" Deneb's luminosity is given as 250,000 and it is listed as the thirty-second most luminous star in our galaxy.) On the other hand it is—for our Sun and most of the other stars/Suns that we can see—the *guiding star* of the Orion Arm. What is meant by this?

When we contemplate the constellation of Orion, we are gazing back toward the center of the Orion Arm (hence the name). However, when we behold Deneb, we are looking forward in the Orion Arm to a star that is at an enormous distance away, located near the front of the Orion Arm (defining "front" to be that part of the Orion Arm that is leading as we spiral around the galactic center).[11] In this sense, as our Sun together with all the other stars/suns revolves around the galactic center, Deneb as the "front star" (of the bright stars visible to the naked eye) is leading the way, and a great multitude of the other stars in the Orion Arm are following. Nevertheless, there are many stars ahead of Deneb in our spiral arm, but they are not generally visible to the naked eye. One striking exception is a star located in the direction of the constellation of Cassiopeia. This star, Rho Cassiopeiae, is a yellow hypergiant about 8,150 light years away, with a luminosity of 550,000.[12] Since Deneb is about 3,200 light years away, Rho Cassiopeiae is approximately 5,000 light years further ahead of Deneb within our spiral arm. Since the apparent magnitude of this star Rho Cassiopeia is +4.5 (this is the present value, which fluctuates as it is a variable star), one needs keen eyesight to see this star, whereas Deneb stands out clearly as a bright star towards which everyone can readily find an orientation in thinking of the motion of our Sun and the other stars/Suns around the Milky Way. Looking up to the starry heavens, therefore, Deneb is our most prominent guiding star ahead of us in our spiral arm. Moreover, Deneb more or less exactly marks the place in the heavens of the Vertex—the direction of rotation of our Sun around the galactic center.[13] When we gaze at Deneb, we are looking exactly in the direction in which our Sun is moving as it orbits around the galactic center, and in this sense, too, Deneb is our guiding star.

---

11 The use of the word *near* is relative. In real terms, Deneb is very near the front of the Orion Arm. It is nearer the front than our Sun. However, in fact, the Orion Arm extends many thousands of light years beyond Deneb. For example, as indicated in the discussion concerning this star, the star Rho Cassiopeiae is some 5,000 light years further ahead of Deneb in our spiral arm.

12 http://en.wikipedia.org/wiki/Rho_Cassiopeiae. Rho Cassiopeiae is listed as the twentieth brightest star in the Milky Way Galaxy—http://en.wikipedia.org/wiki/List_of_most_luminous_stars. The luminosity value of 550,000 for Rho Cassiopeiae given in the "List of Most Luminous Stars" is the bolometric value.

13 Keller, *Kosmos Himmelsjahr 2000*, p. 139. See also the figure on page 106.

Deneb, seen by the Greeks as marking the tail of the Swan, is at the head of the Northern Cross. It is remarkable to consider that the cross is the symbol of Christ, and that—in the sense of "as above, so below"—his central miracles (the feeding of the 5,000 and the walking on the water) were aligned via the Sun with Deneb at the head of the cross, and the miracle he performed shortly before these two (the healing of the paralyzed man at the pool of Bethesda) was aligned via the Sun with Sadr—the star marking the breast of the Swan, located at the center of the Northern Cross. Here we gain a glimpse into the mysteries of Cosmic Christianity and we can begin to truly understand that Christ was a cosmic being who had a relationship with the stars in the heavens—not just the stars in our cosmos, our local part of the galaxy known as the Orion Arm, but also with the stars beyond, in the greater galaxy, as shown by the alignment via the Sun, at the miracle of the healing of the nobleman's son, with the mega star Rho Leonis, located on the inside edge of the Perseus Arm (according to the distance measurement found by the Hipparcos satellite). The conjunction of the Sun with the mega star Rho Leonis at the miracle of the healing of the nobleman's son is discussed below.

This discovery shows that true astrology is a science that takes into account the entire celestial sphere and not just the stars composing the signs of the zodiac. It is the step from solar to galactic consciousness. This signifies an enormous expansion of Babylonian astrology, which focuses primarily on passage of the Sun, Moon, and the five visible planets against the background of fixed stars that make up the twelve signs of the zodiac. Similarly, mega stars represent an extension from the exaltations discovered by the Babylonians. Whereas the exaltations were discovered to be stars or stellar clusters lying within the zodiacal belt, the meridians which run through the mega stars circle around the entire celestial globe. For the new astrological star wisdom all that needs to be known, essentially, is the mega stars' longitudes in the sidereal zodiac. These are known thanks to the star catalog included in Peter Treadgold's program *Astrofire*, which lists the longitude, latitude, apparent magnitude, absolute magnitude, type, class, distance, and luminosity of more than 4,000 stars. Thus, information about the mega stars can be derived from *Astrofire*. The *Astrofire* star catalog, in turn, is based on the Hipparcos catalog, which is one of the most accurate of all star catalogs, whose measurements were made by the Hipparcos satellite between 1989 and 1993.

In the *Astrofire* star catalog there are eighty mega stars with a luminosity exceeding 10,000, thus defining (potentially) eighty powerful meridians scattered around the zodiac—"potentially" because some of these mega stars lie on the same meridian or very close to the same meridian. Of these eighty stars, as mentioned above, fifty-six of them are identified by number or Greek letter and are thus to be found in the Bayer-Flamsteed star catalog, whereas twenty-four of them are unnamed, unnumbered, and unlettered; yet these are mega stars belonging to our galaxy and are therefore included (in the group *Mega*) in Peter Treadgold's *Astrofire* program.

To take an example, let us consider the star *Mega* 39, signifying that in the Hipparcos catalog it is the thirty-ninth most luminous star. *Mega* 39 is located in the southern hemisphere constellation of Centaurus the Centaur.[14] It is 56° south of the ecliptic and at the time of Christ had a longitude in the sidereal zodiac of 0°45′ Libra. According to Hipparcos it is just under 6,000 light years away and has a luminosity of over 77,000. This distance would place it in the Sagittarius–Carina Arm of our galaxy, like the grand mega star, Eta Carinae (luminosity around 5,000,000), which for a time was thought to be the most luminous star in our galaxy. At 10 a.m. on September 23 in the year 29, at the moment of the baptism of Jesus in the River Jordan, when Christ descended into incarnation in Jesus, the Sun at 0°50′ Libra was located on the meridian of *Mega* 39.[15] Thus, there was a conjunction of the Sun with *Mega* 39 at the baptism in the Jordan, where the divine energy evidently flowing from the extraordinarily luminous star *Mega* 39 was transmitted to our Sun and from our Sun to Jesus Christ—remembering Rudolf Steiner's words quoted above about the perfect concordance between Christ's life and the "collective being of the whole universe." From this and many other examples, the significance of mega stars becomes evident. There are numerous examples of conjunctions of the

---

14 *Mega* 39 in the *Astrofire* star catalog is listed in the Hipparcos catalog as HIP 54463 and in the Henry Draper catalog as HD 96918. Although it is visible to the naked eye, with an apparent magnitude of +4.0, it was not included in the Bayer-Flamsteed catalog presumably because of its southerly latitude (56° south).

15 Powell, *Chronicle of the Living Christ*, pp. 199–200; see p. 161 for the horoscope of this event. The baptism of Jesus is described in Matthew 3: 13–17.

Sun with mega stars at the miraculous events in the life of Christ, indicating the remarkable significance of mega stars. Of course, there still remains much astrological research to be done to investigate the individual nature and influence of these most luminous stars.

The research that has been carried out thus far—discussed below in relation to their significance at Christ's healing miracles—indicates that certain mega stars are astrologically highly significant. By way of analogy, the longitudes at which the meridians of these mega stars intersect the ecliptic can be compared with the stars or star clusters marking the zodiacal locations of the astrological exaltations discovered by the Babylonians. These mega stars can thus be thought of effectively as indicating a new set of *exaltation points*. The discovery of the significance of certain mega stars, as demonstrated in relation to the Christ events, shows on the one hand that Christ is connected with the entire starry heavens and on the other hand that the domain of astrology includes the entire celestial sphere—truly an astrological revolution.

MEGA STARS IN RELATION TO THE HEALING MIRACLES

Research into the planetary configurations during the life of Christ—inspired by the words from Rudolf Steiner quoted earlier that, "*It was always in accordance with the collective being of the whole universe with whom the Earth is in harmony, that all which Christ Jesus did took place*"—reveals that the most important stellar meridians in the life of Christ are those running through certain mega stars. We have already seen the example of the Sun at 10½° Aquarius on the Deneb meridian at the miracle of the feeding of the 5,000. It should also be noted that, since the miracle of the walking on the water occurred that same night, the Sun at this miracle (at 11° Aquarius) was still very close to the Deneb meridian also at this miracle. In fact, taking account of Deneb's proper motion, at the time of Christ the longitude of Deneb was closer to 11° Aquarius, whereas at the present time it is 10½° Aquarius.[16]

Ten days prior to the miracles of the feeding of the 5,000 and the walking on the water, Christ had healed a paralyzed man at the pool of Bethesda in Jerusalem. At this miracle, which took place on

---

16 Ibid., p. 276; see p. 171 for the horoscope of this event. The miracle of the walking on the water is described in Matthew 14:25–33.

January 19 in the year 31,[17] the Sun was at 0½° Aquarius on the Sadr meridian which, at the time of Christ, was located at 0½° Aquarius (owing to Sadr's proper motion it is now closer to 0° Aquarius). Like Deneb, Sadr is in the constellation of Cygnus the Swan, also known as the Northern Cross. Sadr means "breast", and this star, which marks the breast of the Swan (the central star of the Northern Cross), is also a mega star, since its luminosity, according to the Hipparcos catalog, is 24,388 and it is located at a distance of 1523 light years

At noon on December 28 in the year 29,[18] when the changing of water into wine at the wedding at Cana took place, the Sun was at 8° 19' Capricorn in conjunction with a very luminous star at 8° 18' Capricorn—a star that is indicated to be even more luminous than Deneb.[19] This star in the constellation of Capricorn, just 11° north of the ecliptic, with an apparent magnitude of +6.4, is scarcely visible to the naked eye, as the value +6.5 denotes the usual limit for naked eye visibility. Whereas Deneb is the most luminous star of the first magnitude in our local part of the galaxy, known as the Orion Arm, this unnamed star in the direction of Capricorn is at such a distance that its true distance has not yet been confirmed. Thus, neither the distance nor the great luminosity of this star has been reliably determined at the present time. Nevertheless, it is very striking that at the first of Christ's miracles, the changing of water to wine at the wedding at Cana, the Sun was exactly aligned with this mega star identified by Hipparcos as one of the most luminous stars in our galaxy.

Another example of a very luminous star that was aligned with one of Christ's miracles is that of 68 Cygni in the constellation of the Swan. This star, which is located a little to the east of Deneb, and slightly above Deneb, is an (as yet) undetermined number of light years away. It is certainly a mega star, although its exact luminosity

---

17 Ibid., p. 273; see p. 169 for the horoscope of this event. The healing of the paralyzed man at the pool of Bethesda is described in John 5:1–15.

18 Ibid., p. 213; see p. 164 for the horoscope of this event. The miracle of transforming water into wine at the wedding at Cana is described in John 2:4–11.

19 The Hipparcos catalog and the Wikipedia "List of Stars in Capricornus" (http://en.wikipedia.org/wiki/List_of_stars_in_Capricornus) indicate the luminosity of this star at almost 2,700,000, but this seems to be contradicted by the fact that this star is not included in the Wikipedia "List of Most Luminous Stars." Only future observations will be able to confirm if the Hipparcos catalog's high luminosity value of this star holds true or if it needs to be modified.

has not yet been confirmed.[20] At the time of Christ the longitude of 68 Cygni was almost exactly 20° Aquarius, and the latitude 55 ½° north of the ecliptic. Crossing the meridian of 68 Cygni, the Sun was at 20° Aquarius on February 7 in the year 30, when Christ raised a girl from the dead. This girl was born into an Essene family, whom Christ Jesus visited at their home in Phasael, six weeks after the wedding at Cana. At that time she was about sixteen years old, and her father's name was Jairus. Jesus warned those present not to speak of what they had witnessed, and this event—which took place less than five months into his 3 ½-year ministry—was therefore not recorded in the Gospels.[21] It is remarkable that this raising from the dead took place when the Sun was aligned with a star which the Hipparcos satellite identified as one of the most luminous stars in our galaxy.

Almost sixth months after having raised this sixteen-year-old Essene girl from the dead, Christ Jesus performed a miracle that was recorded in the Gospel of John—the miracle of the healing of the nobleman's son. The boy was the adopted son of a high-ranking official in Capernaum, who sent the boy's physical father (who was in his service) to Christ to ask him to come and heal the boy. Christ Jesus, who at the time was teaching in Cana, upon hearing the pleas of the father, healed the boy from a distance. This took place at 1:00 p.m. on August 3, 30.[22] At this event the Sun was at 11° Leo, aligned with the mega star Rho Leonis at 11 ½° Leo, which according to the Hipparcos catalog has a luminosity of 78,000 and is located 5,719 light years away—placing this star in the Perseus Arm of our galaxy, on the inside of this arm (the part of the Perseus Arm closest to our Orion Arm). As noted earlier, this indicates that Christ worked with stars beyond our local part of the galaxy, the Orion Arm, and thus Christ's

---

20 The enormous distance given in the Hipparcos catalog seems to be beyond the bounds of possibility. Regarding luminosity: in the Hipparcos catalog this star is indicated to be the fifth most luminous star of all the stars measured by the Hipparcos satellite, with a luminosity of over 3,300,000. This extremely high value seems to be contradicted by the fact that this star is not included in the Wikipedia "List of Most Luminous Stars" referred to above. Only future observations will be able to confirm whether or not the Hipparcos catalog's high luminosity value of this star holds true or whether it needs to be modified.

21 Powell, *Chronicle of the Living Christ*, p. 219; and *Astrofire* computer program for the horoscope of this event.

22 Ibid., p. 239; see p. 165 for the horoscope of this event. The healing of the nobleman's son is described in John 4:46–54.

consciousness was truly galactic, embracing all the stars in our galaxy. Becoming conscious of this, human consciousness expands to the galactic level, and this denotes an astrological revolution comparable to the expansion of consciousness from the geocentric to the heliocentric level that arose with the Copernican revolution.

While several more examples could be given, let us consider one further example—the last and greatest of Christ's miracles, the raising of Lazarus from the dead. This took place early on the morning of July 26 in the year 32, when the Sun was at 3° 04′ Leo, exactly aligned with the mega star Eta Leonis at 3° 04′ Leo.[23] This is the star above Regulus in the "sickle" of Leo. It appears much less bright than the first magnitude Regulus at 5° Leo, which has a luminosity 140 times that of our Sun. The apparent brightness of Regulus because of its relative proximity (67 light years) to our solar system. Eta Leonis, on the other hand, which is 2131 light years away, has a luminosity of 15,087, according to Hipparcos. When looking up at this star just above Regulus, and slightly to the west of Regulus, one can think of it as the "star of the raising of Lazarus." In the same way, one can think of Sadr as the "star of the healing of the paralyzed man" and Deneb as both the "star of the feeding of the 5,000" and the "star of the walking on the water."

A consideration of the mega stars relating to Christ's healing miracles, viewed within the horoscopes of historical and contemporary individuals, opens up an entirely new avenue of astrological research. Frederick Chopin's natal Sun is conjunct the meridian of Deneb. Does the magic of Chopin's music have anything to do with an inspiring spiritual stream[24] that he received from Deneb and incorporated into his music? Could it be that the greatness of Abraham Lincoln had to do with a stream of inspiration he received from the star Sadr, with which the Sun conjoined at his birth? Did the mega stars play a role in the unfolding of the destinies of the individuals listed opposite?

---

23 Ibid., pp. 316–317; see p. 173 for the horoscope of this event. The raising of Lazarus from the dead is described in John 11: 1–44.

24 The conjunction of the Sun with the galactic center (2° Sagittarius) at Beethoven's birth indicates the source of Beethoven's inspiration in his activity as a composer. Beethoven himself spoke of receiving the inspiration for his compositions from beyond the stars, from the Ultimate Source of existence— perhaps an allusion by this great composer to the galactic center—also known as the Central Sun, the Divine Heart at the center of our galaxy from which the entire Milky Way Galaxy was born (see Powell and Dann, *Christ and the Maya Calendar*, appendix 1, "The Central Sun").

MEGA STAR	SIDEREAL LONGITUDE	HEALING MIRACLE IN CHRIST'S LIFE	HISTORICAL PERSONALITIES
Eta Leonis	3° Leo	Raising of Lazarus from the dead	Robert Redford Emperor Franz Joseph I of Austria King Friedrich Wilhelm I of Prussia
Rho Leonis	11 ½° Leo	Healing of the nobleman's son	Antoine Lavoisier Michael Jackson Johann von Herder
Mega star in Libra	0 ½° Libra	Baptism of Jesus in the River Jordan	King Henry III Emperor Augustus King Richard III
Mega star in Capricorn	8° Capicorn	Changing of water into wine at the wedding at Cana	Joan of Arc James Watt Auguste Comte
Sadr (Gamma Cygni)	0° Aquarius	Healing of the paralyzed man at the pool of Bethesda	King Henry VII Charles Darwin Abraham Lincoln
Deneb (Alpha Cygni)	10 ½° Aquarius / 11° Aquarius	Feeding of the 5,000 /Walking on the water	Cardinal Newman Heinrich Hertz Frederick Chopin

Here we have come full circle to return to the ancient star wisdom that was oriented—by way of star-gazing—to the stars in the heavens, but from a new perspective, with a view to learning how the starry heavens play into human destiny according to the inner power and strength of the stars, paying particular attention to the most powerful stars—the mega stars. The mood of this new star wisdom to which the astrological revolution is leading is conveyed in the following words of Rudolf Steiner, bearing in mind that *mega* means *great:* "Christ's Light from great stars streams into my heart" (see full meditation at the end of this chapter).

THE ASTROLOGICAL REVOLUTION

There are many aspects to the astrological revolution discussed in this book, one of them being the inclusion of the entire celestial sphere, as discussed in the foregoing. To conclude this chapter, therefore, let us contemplate a shift toward galactic consciousness that would include

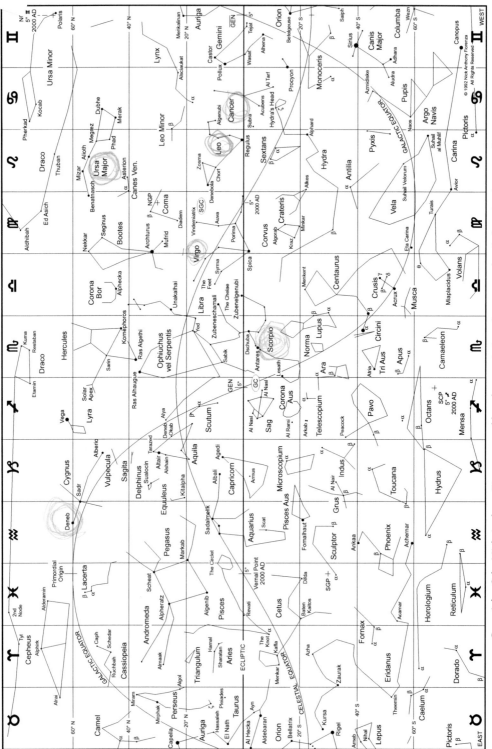

all the stars in the heavens as astrologically significant. Having said "all," in practice it is a matter of a selection of stars. One person who has worked with such an approach, based on the sidereal zodiac, is Nick Anthony Fiorenza, who has done much valuable research into the meaning of a large selection of stars. He has also developed a most helpful tool, a map of the heavens as seen from the vantage point of the sidereal zodiac (see opposite[25]). Using this figure, it is possible to follow the Sun's passage day by day through the sidereal zodiac and picture the Sun's conjunctions with various stars and constellations above and below the ecliptic/zodiacal belt, as it progresses along its path. (The apparent path of the Sun along the ecliptic running through the middle of the zodiacal belt is determined by the Earth's orbit around the Sun, which gives rise to this apparent movement.)

In relation to the figure, the ecliptic is the horizontal axis (0° latitude) through the middle of the twelve signs, or constellations, of the sidereal zodiac, whereby the astronomical definition of the zodiacal belt extends 8° north and 8° south of the ecliptic. Above the central axis of the ecliptic/zodiacal belt are the constellations of the northern sky (N latitude) and below the ecliptic/zodiacal belt are the constellations of the southern sky (S latitude). The orientation of the figure is from the perspective of a viewer in the northern hemisphere, who sees the zodiacal constellations proceeding in a counterclockwise direction—from right to left: Gemini (♊), Cancer (♋), Leo (♌), Virgo (♍), Libra (♎), Scorpio (♏), Sagittarius (♐), Capricorn (♑), Aquarius (♒), Pisces (♓), Aries (♈), Taurus (♉). A southern hemisphere view necessitates turning the figure upside down, whereby the viewer beholds the constellations upside down and sees the zodiacal signs/constellations proceeding in a clockwise direction—from left to right. For ease of reference, the northern hemisphere perspective, as presented by the sidereal map, is adopted in the following discussion.

---

25 In this sidereal zodiac (like a Mercator projection map, in which the lands of extreme north and south are enlarged out of proportion), the constellations are enlarged, especially above and below the 60° longitudes. It shows the entire sky and stars that align with each sidereal sign. The celestial equator moves westward about 1° per 72 years with respect to the fixed stars and sidereal signs. The vernal point, currently at 5° Pisces, must precess 90° before it aligns with the galactic equatorial node (GEN) at 5° sidereal Sagittarius. At that time, the north celestial pole (now at 5° sidereal Gemini) will lie closest to the galactic plane (at the primordial origin just above Lacerta), completing one great world cycle.

The Sun is pictured moving through the signs of the sidereal zodiac from right to left, starting in the figure with the sign of Gemini. On June 19/20 the Sun comes into conjunction with the red supergiant Betelgeuse—a mega star (luminosity about 100,000).[26] Moreover, the sidereal longitude of Betelgeuse is 4° Gemini. As the Sun travels approximately 1° through the zodiac each day, and since the Sun enters Gemini on June 15/16, it reaches 4° Gemini (conjunction with Betelgeuse) four days later, on June 19/20. Betelgeuse marks the right shoulder of the giant Orion and is a star associated with military might and prowess: "The star is indicative of great fortune, martial honors, and kingly attributes."[27] It is worth noting that Saturn was conjoined with Betelgeuse at the outbreak of World War I on August 1, 1914, and was again in conjunction with this red super-giant on D-Day (June 6, 1944), which was a decisive battle and turning point during World War II.[28]

Just one day after the Sun's conjunction with Betelgeuse at 4° Gemini, the summer solstice (winter solstice in the southern hemisphere) takes place—at the present time when the Sun is at 5° Gemini.

High up above Betelgeuse is the Pole Star, Polaris, which lies on the same meridian (4° Gemini) as Betelgeuse. Thus, at the same time as the Sun crosses the Betelgeuse meridian, receiving the energy flow of Betelgeuse from "below" (Betelgeuse's latitude is 16° S), it is also crossing the Polaris meridian, receiving the energy flow of Polaris from "above" (Polaris's latitude is 66° N). The luminosity of Polaris is about 2,200 and this star is about 430 light years away. Because of the simultaneous conjunction of the Sun with Betelgeuse and Polaris, both lying on the same meridian (4° Gemini), but 82° apart, it is a question

---

26 The precise luminosity of Betelgeuse is difficult to ascertain, as it is a variable star that fluctuates in size and brightness. It is one of the largest stars known, with a diameter of about a thousand times that of our Sun, which would mean that—in the place of our Sun—it would extend in size between the orbits of Mars and Jupiter.

27 "The Astrological Influences of the Star Betelgeuze," *Constellations of Words,* http://www.constellationsofwords.com/stars/Betelgeuse.html.

28 This research finding relating to Saturn's conjunction with Betelgeuse indicates that it is not only the conjunction of the Sun with other Suns/stars that is significant, but also that the conjunction of the planets with stars is important for astrology. Indeed, further research along these lines confirms Rudolf Steiner's statement (see appendix I) that the conjunctions of planets with stars is fundamental to astrology.

of distinguishing the influences of these two stars in any given situation where 4° Gemini is involved in astrological considerations. For example, at the birth of Franklin D. Roosevelt on January 30, 1882 Mars was at 4° Gemini, in conjunction with Betelgeuse and Polaris. Roosevelt was President for twelve years and led the United States during the Great Depression, a time of severe economic crisis. During this time he was a kind of "Pole star" for the American people, leading them through the crisis. This would speak for the influence of Mars in conjunction with Polaris, toward which the Earth's axis is oriented. Though to a lesser degree, the influence of Mars conjunct Betelgeuse was playing in as well, as is evident from the resolute fortitude demonstrated by the president in this difficult time. FDR's tenure as President during World War II seems to demonstrate both the influence of Mars in conjunction with Betelgeuse and the influence of Mars in conjunction with Polaris, whose expression can be seen in the President's firm quality of leadership. It is also interesting that when Jesus pronounced woe upon the Pharisees, on March 24 in the year 33, Mars was in conjunction with the Betelgeuse–Polaris meridian at 4° Gemini. This powerful speech (see Matthew 23:13–36) would also seem to have to do more with Mars being conjunct Betelgeuse.

Another striking example of two prominent stars lying on the same meridian (more or less) are Spica (29° Virgo) and Arcturus (29 ½° Virgo). Their astrological influences are commingled. At the present time the Sun crosses the Spica meridian around October 17 and the Arcturus meridian half a day later. A half day later, the Sun enters Libra, where it was located at the baptism of Jesus in the River Jordan (0 ½° Libra). Indeed, in relation to the life of Jesus Christ, every step he took was "in accordance with the collective being of the whole universe," as indicated by Rudolf Steiner. Thus the life of Christ offers an archetype to help us understand the influences of Spica and Arcturus. On the day prior to the baptism in the Jordan, Jesus had a most significant conversation with the Virgin Mary.[29] The Sun (representing Christ) was conjunct Spica (representing the Virgin Mary). It is noteworthy that in ancient astrology Spica had to do with wise women priestesses: "Spica makes people become the interpreters of sacred things, high, supreme, honored and respected priests or philosophers or the inspired interpreters of some mysteries and, especially...in female genitures, it

---

29 Powell, *Chronicle of the Living Christ*, pp. 107–109.

makes the natives priestesses of Demeter, who is the mother of the gods, or of Core or of Isis, as well as women who are the interpreters of sacred things or experts in mysteries or in initiation rites...and who are helped by the gods very much."[30]

Spica, well within the zodiacal belt (extending 8° above and below the ecliptic), lies just 2° south of the ecliptic. On the other hand, Arcturus in the constellation of Boötes (the Ploughman) is located 31° north of the ecliptic. In the course of his conversation with the Virgin Mary, the inner decision was taken by Jesus to go to the place of baptism, to receive the baptism of John the Baptist. By making this decision, the influence of Arcturus evidently began to make itself felt. Arcturus, which the ancient Britons thought of as the star of King Arthur,[31] can be seen as the inspiration of a heroic deed: Jesus offering himself to Christ in an act of sacrifice and bringing hope for the future. It was John the Baptist who facilitated the deed of baptism, whereupon he proclaimed: "Behold the Lamb of God!" (John 1:29). Can this pronouncement by John be seen as an earthly correspondence to the influence of Arcturus pouring down from above through the Sun? This is an influence connected with joy,[32] in this case the joy of the coming of the Messiah, the Christ.

THE PRIMARY PHENOMENON

Without going into too much detail, the primary phenomenon to be noted is that the Sun is influenced on its path along the ecliptic not only by stars *within* the zodiacal belt, but also by stars *above and below* the zodiacal belt. The primary phenomenon, since the Sun is a star among stars, is that the Sun is literally "in" a zodiacal constellation, its rays uniting with the rays of all the other Suns/stars within that constellation, when from the perspective of the Earth the Sun is located against the background of a particular zodiacal constellation. To illustrate this, let us consider again the sign/constellation of Gemini as an example.

---

30 At www.cieloeterra.it/eng/eng.testi.379/eng.379.html.

31 Tradition "links the name *Arthur* to *Arcturus*, the brightest star in the constellation Boötes" (http://en.wikipedia.org/wiki/King_Arthur).

32 Prehistoric navigators between the Polynesian islands referred to Arcturus as *Hōkūleʻa*, "Star of Joy" (http://en.wikipedia.org/wiki/Arcturus).

Having entered Gemini on June 15/16, the Sun is "in" Gemini until it passes beyond the stars Castor (25 ½° Gemini) and Pollux (28 ½° Gemini) marking the heads of the Twins. The Sun enters Cancer on July 16/17 and is then "in" Cancer, uniting its rays with all the Suns/stars in the starry region of Cancer. At the time when the Sun is "in" Gemini from mid-June to mid-July, it is also receiving influences from stars in the constellations above and below Gemini (see figure, page 158, and see more detailed figure in appendix 3):

Ursa Minor (the Lesser Bear), Lynx (the Lynx), and Auriga (the Charioteer)—above;

 Orion (the Giant), Monoceros (the Unicorn), Canis Major (the Greater Dog), Columba (the Dove), and the tip of the oar of Argo Navis (the Ship Argo) marked by the star Canopus—below.

Here it is noteworthy that the two brightest stars in the heavens, Sirius (19 ½° Gemini) and Canopus (20° Gemini) are also (more or less) on the same meridian, which at the present time the Sun crosses each year around July 6/7—Sirius being located 39 ½° south and Canopus 76° south of the ecliptic. As a matter of fact, two presidents of the United States—Calvin Coolidge (born July 4, 1872) and George W. Bush (born July 6, 1946) were each born with the Sun between 19 ½° Gemini and 20° Gemini, aligned with the Sirius–Canopus axis.

Clearly there is much research remaining to be done in terms of expanding consciousness toward a more galactic perspective embracing all the stars/constellations in the heavens. The foregoing is intended to draw attention to this primary phenomenon of the Sun's passage each year through the twelve zodiacal signs, or constellations, along the ecliptic, simultaneously receiving also from the extra-zodiacal constellations above and below the ecliptic.[33] This is the kernel of the astrological revolution as an expression of this special time of humanity's opening to galactic consciousness in connection with the year 2012.[34]

---

33 Paul and Powell, *Cosmic Dances of the Zodiac* gives an overview of the ancient 36 extra-zodiacal constellations above and below the twelve zodiacal signs/constellations, where these 36 constellations according to ancient tradition correspond to the 36 decans (10° sectors of the zodiac, three to each sign of the sidereal zodiac).

34 Powell and Dann, *Christ and the Maya Calendar,* discuss the special significance of the times associated with the year 2012. See also Powell, "World Pentecost," *Journal for Star Wisdom 2010,* pp. 53–65.

To summarize: The essence of the astrological revolution is the expansion of consciousness from the Sun's path through the twelve zodiacal signs/constellations to include the entire celestial sphere—all the extra-zodiacal constellations above and below the zodiac—ultimately embracing all the stars of the entire galaxy. Then, for example, when the Sun is at 10½° Aquarius—clearly "in" the constellation of Aquarius—it is at the same time *in conjunction with Deneb*, the tail of the Swan (or head of the Northern Cross), 60° north of the ecliptic. Whereas the influence of Aquarius at this moment in time (presently, each year around February 24) is obvious by virtue of the Sun's blending with all the other Suns/stars in the constellation of Aquarius located at this degree, our Sun is also receiving the energy flow along the entire meridian running through 10½° Aquarius extending all the way up to the north pole of the ecliptic and all the way down to the south pole of the ecliptic.

Contemplation of the significance of the mega stars in the life of Christ—such as the Sun's conjunction with the mega star Deneb at the feeding of the 5,000 and the walking on the water—reveals the truth of the foregoing exposition concerning the essence of the astrological revolution. This truth is embedded in the meditation referred to above—a meditation which serves to uplift the human spirit to the galactic level of existence—bearing in mind that the word *mega* means *great*: "Christ's Light from great stars streams into my heart." These words are a potent mantra for the astrological revolution and serve as a powerful focus of orientation on the path of initiation into the mysteries of the starry heavens.

The following meditation is from Rudolf Steiner:

> *EVENINGS:* Review the course of the day.
> Then imagine:
>   the setting Moon
>   and within [the Moon] the Cross with Roses.
> [Then meditate on the words:]
>   **"Christ's Light from great stars streams into my heart."**
>
> *MORNINGS:* Imagine a blue flower
>   growing larger and larger.
> Then remain standing in front of the flower.
> [And meditate on the words:]
>   **"May Christ's Life Force grow in my soul."**

Immerse oneself totally in the flower.
Let this ebb away again
   and [then] inner peace for some minutes.[35]

Rudolf Steiner's significance for the astrological revolution cannot be overemphasized. This meditation is just one example of the many meditations connecting the human being to the stars. Embedded throughout his books and lectures are astrological gems that expand in a remarkable way on the framework of traditional astrology and on our present understanding of the world, as well as on the relationship between human beings and the planets and the zodiac. These jewels of cosmic knowledge form the core of the great revolution leading from astrology to Astrosophy. For both authors of this book, the study of Steiner's pioneering spiritual science has served to awaken increasing awe and wonder for the mysteries of creation concealed in the starry heavens.

The magnitude of Rudolf Steiner's contribution to help lift human consciousness through his systematic unveiling of cosmic mysteries may not be fully appreciated for several centuries. However, just as the Copernican revolution caused a major paradigm shift for Western humanity, so the assimilation of spiritual science, going far beyond the materialistic science of our time, will bring about a far-reaching paradigm shift away from materialism, eventually leading to an awakening of galactic consciousness.

As a contribution to helping this revolutionary shift come about, Steiner also pioneered a cosmic alphabet of movement and gestures, which he called "eurythmy" (Greek = beautiful, harmonious movement). Eurythmy has been taken up as a practice that enables a living experience of the planets and zodiacal signs through *choreocosmos* (Greek = cosmic dance), described in books by Lacquanna Paul and Robert Powell, *Cosmic Dances of the Zodiac* and *Cosmic Dances of the Planets*. Choreocosmos is just one development of the many that are arising from spiritual science and expanding consciousness to cosmic awareness, thus facilitating the astrological revolution.

---

35 Steiner, *Seelenübungen: Band I. Übungen mit Wort- und Sinnbild-Meditationen zur methodischen Entwicklung höherer Erkenntniskräfte, 1904–1924* ("Soul-Exercises: vol. 1: Exercises with Word and Image Meditations for the Methodological Development of Higher Powers of Knowledge, 1904–1924"; Dornach: Rudolf Steiner Verlag, 1997), p. 324.

Notes Concerning Horoscopes

Table of Astrological Symbols

Planets		Zodiacal Signs	
⊕	Earth	♈	Aries (Ram) AR
☉	Sun	♉	Taurus (Bull) TA
☽	Moon	♊	Gemini (Twins) GE
☿	Mercury	♋	Cancer (Crab) CN
♀	Venus	♌	Leo (Lion) LE
♂	Mars	♍	Virgo (Virgin) VI
♃	Jupiter	♎	Libra (Scales) LI
♄	Saturn	♏	Scorpio (Scorpion) SC
♅	Uranus	♐	Sagittarius (Archer) SG
♆	Neptune	♑	Capricorn (Goat) CP
♇	Pluto	♒	Aquarius (Waterbearer) AQ
		♓	Pisces (Fishes) PI

Categories:

The horoscopes in this book fall into two categories:

    1: *individual horoscopes*—for events or for the conception,
       birth, and death of individuals.
    2: *comparison horoscopes*—various comparison horoscopes.

In the case of the comparison horoscopes (2), each includes an inner circle and an outer circle. The inner circle is generally the later horoscope, chronologically, while the outer circle is the earlier one. The chronological order of the comparison charts is organized in relation to the inner circle.

CONCERNING THE ZODIAC

It should be noted that—unless otherwise stated—all zodiacal longitudes indicated in the text and in the horoscopes are in terms of the sidereal zodiac, which should be distinguished from the tropical zodiac in widespread use in contemporary astrology in the West. The Greek astronomer Claudius Ptolemy introduced the tropical zodiac into astrology in the middle of the second century A.D.. Prior to this the sidereal zodiac was in use. Such was the influence of Ptolemy upon the western astrological tradition that the tropical zodiac became substituted for the sidereal zodiac used by the Babylonians, Egyptians, and early Greek astrologers. Yet Ptolemy did not influence the astrological tradition in India, and so the sidereal zodiac is still used to this day by Hindu astrologers.

The sidereal zodiac originated with the Babylonians in the sixth to fifth centuries B.C. and was defined by them in relation to certain bright stars. For example, Aldebaran ("the Bull's eye") is located in the middle of the sidereal sign/constellation of the Bull at 15° Taurus, and Antares ("the Scorpion's heart) is in the middle of the sidereal sign/constellation of the Scorpion at 15° Scorpio. The sidereal signs, each thirty degrees long, coincide closely with the twelve astronomical zodiacal constellations of the same name. The signs of the tropical zodiac (since they are defined in relation to the vernal point) now have little or no relationship to the corresponding zodiacal constellations. This is because the vernal point, the zodiacal location of the Sun on March 20/21, shifts slowly backward through the sidereal zodiac at a rate of one degree in seventy-two years ("the precession of the equinoxes").

When Ptolemy introduced the tropical zodiac into astrology, there was an almost exact coincidence between the tropical and the sidereal zodiac, because the vernal point, defined as 0° Aries in the tropical zodiac, was 1° Aries in the sidereal zodiac in the middle of the second century A.D. Thus, there was only 1° difference between the two zodiacs. Consequently, it made little difference to Ptolemy and his contemporaries whether they should use the tropical zodiac or the sidereal zodiac. Now, however, because of precession the vernal point has shifted back from 1° Aries to 5° Pisces, there is a 25° difference, leaving virtually no correspondence between the two. Without going into further detail concerning the complex issue of the zodiac, as shown in the *Hermetic Astrology* trilogy, it was the sidereal (according to the stars) zodiac that was used by the three Magi, who were the last representatives of the true star wisdom in antiquity.

A comprehensive study of the history of the zodiac and how it came to be defined in the first place is the subject of the doctoral research published in Robert Powell's *History of the Zodiac*.

CONCERNING THE ASTROLOGICAL CHARTS

Each chart indicates the positions in the zodiac of the Sun, Moon, Moon's nodes and planets and also the Ascendant, the Midheaven, and the other astrological house cusps. The information relating to the Ascendant, the Midheaven, and the other astrological house cusps is relevant *only in cases where the time is known,* and can therefore be ignored if the substitute (average) time of midday is used. The data is based on accurate computer calculations of the planetary positions, geocentric and heliocentric, at the time of the event or at the epoch/conception (Ø), birth (✳) and death (†) of the person under consideration. These planetary positions are accurate if the time is known[1] and are only approximate if the substitute (average) time of noon is used. The approximate planetary positions are acceptable in all cases, with the exception of the Moon and heliocentric/hermetic Mercury, since the Moon's position can be up to 7 ½° different if the event took place around midnight, and it can be up to 3° 10′ different in the case of h-Mercury—both values exceeding the usual three degree range of tolerance for planetary alignments (conjunction or opposition).

Planetary positions are listed in the zodiac to degree and minute; all dates are given in terms of the Julian or the Gregorian calendar according to which was in use at the time, and all times are given in the twenty-four-hour system either as local standard time or as zone standard time. (See bibliography of works by Robert Powell for information concerning the astronomical basis of these charts).

---

1 This statement should be qualified in terms of the degree of accuracy with which the time is known.

The authors offer grateful acknowledgment to Peter Treadgold for his *Astrofire* computer program (see details at the end of the bibliography), with which the charts and comparison charts for this body of research were produced. For those interested in working with or carrying out research in the field of Astrosophy or hermetic astrology, the *Astrofire* computer program is ideal, enabling the production of charts similar to the horoscopes in this book and in the *Journal for Star Wisdom,* as well as in the works of Willi Sucher and others.

APPENDIX 1
A NEW SCIENCE OF THE STARS
AND A NEW SCIENCE OF DESTINY

We see here how great the difficulties are when one wishes to approach the wisdom of the stars rightly and righteously. Indeed the true approach to the wisdom of the stars, which we need to penetrate the facts of karma, is only possible in the light of a true insight.... It will show you once more, how through the whole reality of modern time there has come forth a certain stream of spiritual life that makes it very difficult to approach with an open mind the science of the stars, and the science, too, of karma.—RUDOLF STEINER[1]

According to these words, there exists a star wisdom (a "science of the stars") that one needs for a true understanding of karma, and that linked to this is a "science of karma." This book presents some of the research undertaken during the course of many years. This book goes beyond the two volumes of *Hermetic Astrology*, which contained the first two rules of astrological reincarnation research. Heinz Herbert Schöffler referred to the first rule in his book *Rudolf Steiner und die Astrologie* ("Rudolf Steiner and Astrology").

> The mathematician, eurythmy therapist, and astrologer Robert Powell has discovered a rule that stands out significantly from various positions in so far as this discovery can be reconstructed...let us call this rule "Powell's rule.[2]

The first rule is discussed in chapter 2 of this book. It relates to the angular relationship between the Sun and Saturn at death in one incarnation and how this angle—sometimes in a metamorphosed form—repeats itself at birth in the following incarnation.

---

1 Steiner, *Karmic Relationships*, vol. 4, p. 111.

2 Schöffler, *Rudolf Steiner und die Astrologie*, pp. 106–107.

The second rule is extremely important for grasping the new science of the stars as a science of reincarnation and karma, calling for an in-depth look, one that is a catalyst for an astrological revolution. What does the second astrological reincarnation rule state?

The sidereal zodiacal position(s) of h-Mercury and/or h-Venus at birth in one incarnation tend(s) to align with the sidereal zodiacal position(s) of h-Mercury and/or h-Venus at death in the preceding incarnation. (Note that the designation "h" signifies heliocentric/ hermetic, so that the second rule refers to the heliocentric/hermetic positions of Mercury and Venus in the sidereal zodiac.)

Since the content of the second rule implies a totally different basis from that of present-day Western astrology, the new science of the stars requires that we look first at this basis before going on to consider the second rule itself.

THE ZODIAC: AN OUTLINE

The basic thing we need to consider is the zodiac itself, and what it is. Originating from the Greek language, zodiac meant "animal circle" as it referred to the circle of twelve constellations with animal names such as the Ram, the Bull, and so on. The question is: Why were these twelve constellations considered to be so significant that they were singled out from all the other stellar constellations? To answer this question we need to look back to the origins of astronomy and astrology with the Babylonians.

Stargazing was a common practice for the Babylonians, particularly the Babylonian priesthood.[3] They looked up at the night sky and saw the stars and star groupings (constellations) as the abode of divine beings. The constellations were observed as groups of stars always remaining in the same positions toward each other. Hence the term "fixed stars" was used because they believed these stars never change their position in relation to one another, therefore appearing to be fixed upon the globe of the heavens.

---

3 Other peoples practiced star gazing as well, but the Babylonians were the first to do it systematically so that a science (astronomy) could be founded. The Babylonians were the first to define the zodiac and other basic elements of astronomy.

In their observations of the night sky the Babylonians noticed five stars that move in relation to the background of the fixed stars. They connected these five stars with five gods belonging to the Babylonian pantheon: Ninib, Marduk, Nergal, Nebo and Ishtar. In addition to the five wandering stars, or the five planets visible to the naked eye, the movements of the Sun and Moon were also observed against the background of the fixed stars. (In the case of the Sun, this movement was deduced.) The Sun and Moon as moving heavenly bodies were counted together with the five planets to make a total of seven planets.

It was observed that these seven planets always move within a belt through the same groupings of fixed stars, and that there are twelve such groupings (constellations). This is the reason these twelve constellations assumed such importance—they provide the stellar background for the movements of the Sun, Moon, and five visible planets. The twelve constellations seem to form a circle around the sphere of the heavens, and were usually identified as forming various animal shapes. In the Greek zodiac, or "animal circle" these twelve constellations were identified with names we know well: Aries the Ram, Taurus the Bull, Gemini the Twins, Cancer the Crab, Leo the Lion, Virgo the Virgin, Libra the Scales, Scorpio the Scorpion, Sagittarius the Archer, Capricorn the Goat, Aquarius the Waterbearer, and Pisces the Fishes. As the planetary movements were observed against the background of this animal circle of twelve constellations, simple "rules of motion" of the planets were derived, enabling the planetary movements to be compared. This signified the beginning of a very rudimentary computational astronomy that went hand in hand with observational astronomy (the "stargazing" of the Babylonians).

The first historical reference to a scientific division of the twelve constellations is to be found in two lunar texts stemming from 475 B.C. and excavated from Babylon. In these texts the constellations are divided into twelve 30° signs.[4] This is the original, or *sidereal* ("pertaining to the stars"), zodiac. There is abundant evidence that this sidereal zodiac is the authentic astrological zodiac, including the evidence provided by the astrological reincarnation research presented in this book—in particular, the second rule of astrological reincarnation.

---

4 For more on the history of these Babylonian texts, the reader is referred to Powell's foundational work, *History of the Zodiac*.

It is postulated in the following quotation that the Babylonians still had a clairvoyant perception (vision) of the world. If this postulate is correct, we may deduce that they could perceive the spiritual beings at work from the zodiacal constellations and that it was their task—out of a clairvoyant perception of spiritual reality—to define the extent of influence of the spiritual beings working through the zodiacal constellations.

> We must learn to have respect for the profound knowledge of the heavens possessed by the Babylonians, and for their great mission, which lay in drawing forth from what was known to humankind through vision of the spiritual world, from the laws of measure prevailing in the heavens, everything that must be incorporated into civilization for the needs of outer, practical life.[5]

If we accept the validity of this statement, we may conclude: "Through vision of the spiritual world, from the laws of measure prevailing in the heavens," the Babylonians determined the division of the zodiacal constellations into twelve 30° signs, as "something that must be incorporated into civilization for the needs of outer, practical life."

In contrast to the Babylonians, evidently the Greek astronomers, including Ptolemy, no longer had a clairvoyant perception of the heavens. Therefore Ptolemy's description of the zodiacal constellations as being unequal in length was based on sense perception alone. A most striking example of Ptolemy's divergence from the ancient clairvoyant perception is provided by the discrepancy between the Babylonian portrayal of Virgo/Libra and that to be found in Ptolemy's *Almagest*. The Babylonians saw Virgo and Libra as being equal length, each 30° long. The bright star Spica is located toward the end of the sign of Virgo at 29°. The Babylonians saw the Virgin as a figure standing upright, holding the sheaf of wheat in her right hand, the tip of the sheaf being marked by Spica. With her left hand she reaches out toward the tail of the Lion. This is also the precise image that the Egyptians had of the Virgin, as may be seen from the zodiac of Denderah at the Louvre Museum.[6]

---

5 Steiner, *Occult History*, p. 67 (translation revised).

6 Vetter. *Das Geburtshoroskop der Welt: Ägyptische Geburstskon-stellation der Welt und die Kulturepochen*, pp. 38–39. See also Neugebauer and Parker,

The zodiac of Denderah, showing the standing Virgin

Ptolemy's Virgin, on the other hand, is not upright but reclining, which is how she is depicted on modern astronomical star maps, all of which—at least, with respect to the classical 48 constellations cataloged in the *Almagest*—derive ultimately from Ptolemy. It can be said that Ptolemy thus "dethroned" the Virgin. As the Virgin is said to represent the heavenly wisdom (Sophia), the dethroning of the Virgin signifies the loss of the divine wisdom that was accessible through the ancient clairvoyance. Moreover, Ptolemy's Virgin is not only lying down, but has her legs and feet extending halfway into the Babylonian sign of Libra. In this way Ptolemy displaced the figure of the Balance Holder from the heavens, who was seen holding the scales in his right hand, as depicted also in various Egyptian portrayals of the zodiac.[7] In Christian iconography St. Michael is the Balance Holder. With the loss of the ancient clairvoyance, not only was Divine Sophia (represented by Virgo) no longer accessible to human consciousness, but also "St. Michael" was banished from the zodiac, leaving only the

7 Neugebauer and Parker, Ibid, Plate 43 (Esna B).

Scales that he holds. This explains the peculiar situation that whereas the remaining zodiacal signs are all animal or human figures, only the Scales is a sign of something inanimate (mechanical). With the Babylonians and Egyptians the Scales was a sign to which a human figure belonged—that of "Michael" (or rather his pre-Christian equivalent)—who was seen holding the Scales. In turning back to the Babylonian sidereal zodiac, the Balance Holder "Michael" is restored to his proper position in the heavens—alongside the Virgin (Divine Sophia), whom he protects.

Thus, hermetic (sidereal) astrology reinstates the Balance Holder "Michael" to the circle of twelve zodiacal signs—to his sign of Libra. This is important in view of Rudolf Steiner's words (quoted incompletely on page 170): "The true approach to the wisdom of the stars, which we need to penetrate the facts of karma, is only possible in the light of a true insight into the dominion of Michael. It is only possible at Michael's side."[8]

The practice of casting horoscopes at an individual's birth originated with the Babylonians, the oldest known horoscope being dated to April 29, 410 B.C. (from Babylon).[9] This horoscope, like all subsequent horoscopes cast in antiquity, was in terms of the geocentric planetary positions in the sidereal zodiac. This was the case with all Babylonian, Egyptian, Greek, Roman, and Hindu (Vedic) horoscopes. In India horoscopes are cast to the present day in the sidereal zodiac, so that Hindu (Vedic) astrology has remained true to the original Babylonian astrology (albeit with minor deviations[10]). Why has Western astrology adopted the tropical zodiac rather than the original sidereal zodiac?

THE TROPICAL CALENDAR

The tropical zodiac is defined in relation to the vernal point as the location of the Sun on March 21 (or March 20) each year. It is helpful to consider how the tropical zodiac originated. In fact, the tropical zodiac was originally not a zodiac at all. Rather, it was a

---

8 Steiner, *Karmic Relationships*, vol. 4, p. 111.

9 Abraham Sachs, "Babylonian Horoscopes," *Journal of Cuneiform Studies 6*, 1952, pp. 49–65.

10 Powell and Treadgold, "The Indian Zodiac," *The Sidereal Zodiac*, pp. 16–20.

calendar of the cycle of the year. So what was the basis of the tropical calendar?

The Greek astronomer Euctemon, living in Athens around 430 B.C., orginally defined the tropical calendar by counting twelve months, each 30 or 31 days long, beginning with day 1 of the month of Aries coinciding with the day of the vernal equinox.[11] The month of Aries contained 31 days, followed by the month of Taurus that also had 31 days. That was followed by the month of Gemini, again with 31 days. This meant that Day 1 of the month of Cancer coincided with the day of the summer solstice (see figure following, in which Euctemon's calendar is presented in a modernized form).

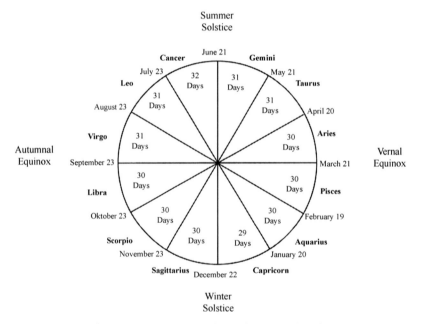

From this figure we can see that the month of Cancer and the remaining months, each with 30 days (except for the months of Aquarius and Pisces having 31 days), kept step with the cycle of the year, so that day 1 of the month of Libra coincided with the day of the autumnal equinox, and day 1 of the month of Capricorn with the day of the winter solstice. It is important to note that whereas the sidereal zodiac is defined spatially in relation to the animal circle of

---

11 W. K. Pritchett and B. L. van der Waerden, "Thucydidean Time-Reckoning and Euctemon's Seasonal Calendar," *Bulletin de Correspondence Hellénique,* 85, 1961, pp. 17–52.

the zodiacal constellations surrounding us in space, the tropical calendar is defined in relation to the temporal phenomenon of the cycle of the seasons. The basis for this definition is the Sun's movement up and down in relation to the Earth's equator. This movement is called "declination," which measures (in degrees and minutes) how far the Sun is North or South of the equator.

THE TROPICAL CALENDAR
AND THE SUN'S MOVEMENT IN DECLINATION

Thus, from the perspective of the Northern Hemisphere (which applies throughout the following description) the Sun at the vernal equinox is at 0° declination, i.e. exactly on the equator, proceeding from South to North. At the summer solstice the Sun reaches its maximum angular distance North of the equator, approximately 23 ½° North. This declination defines the Tropic of Cancer. At midday on the day of the summer solstice, someone on the Tropic of Cancer—23 ½° North of the equator—will find that the Sun is directly overhead, and consequently this person's shadow disappears. The first three months of the tropical calendar (Aries, Taurus, and Gemini) are defined by the Sun's declination in the following way: Aries (0 to 11 ½° North), Taurus (11 ½ to 20° North), and Gemini (20 to 23 ½° North); however, the values in degrees are approximate. That is, the month of Aries (March 21–April 20) is defined by the Sun's ascent from the equator until it reaches 11 ½° North; the month of Taurus (April 20–May 21) coincides with the Sun's further ascent from 11 ½ to 20° North; and the month of Gemini (May 21–June 21) corresponds to the Sun's further passage from 20 to 23 ½° North. The first three months (Aries, Taurus, Gemini) in the tropical calendar constitute spring in the Northern Hemisphere (see figure next page).

From the figure we can see that the next three months (Cancer, Leo, Virgo) of the tropical calendar constitute summer in the Northern Hemisphere. In terms of the Sun's movement in declination, these three months are defined by the Sun's descent from maximum northerly declination back to the equator in such a way that the month of Cancer (June 21–July 23) mirrors the month of Gemini (23 ½ to 20° North), the month of Leo (July 23 to August 23) mirrors the month

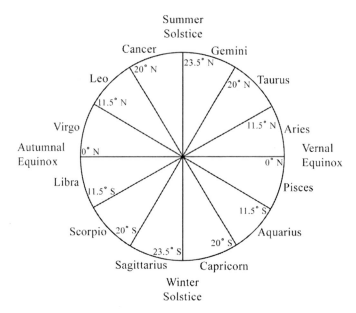

Sun's motion in declination in relation to the twelve solar months
of the tropical calendar in the cycle of the year

of Taurus (20 to 11 ½° North), and the month of Virgo (August 23 to September 23) mirrors the month of Aries (11 ½ to 0°).

Looking again at the above figure, the next three months (Libra, Scorpio, Sagittarius) of the tropical calendar constitute autumn in the Northern Hemisphere. In relation to the Sun's movement in declination, the month of Libra (September 23 to October 23) is defined by the Sun's descent from the equator until it reaches 11 ½° South; the month of Scorpio (October 23 to November 23) coincides with the Sun's further descent from 11 ½ to 20° South; and the month of Sagittarius (November 23 to December 22) corresponds to the Sun's further passage from 20 to 23 ½° South.

Finally, the above figure shows us that the last three months (Capricorn, Aquarius, Pisces) of the tropical calendar constitute winter in the Northern Hemisphere. In terms of the Sun's movement in declination, these three months are defined by the Sun's ascent from maximum southerly declination back to the equator in such a way that the month of Capricorn (December 22 to January 20) mirrors the month of Sagittarius (23 ½ to 20° South), the month of Aquarius

(January 20 to February 19) mirrors the month of Scorpio (20 to 11 ½° South), and the month of Pisces (February 19 to March 21) mirrors the month of Libra (11 ½ to 0°).

The foregoing description reveals something of the mysterious relationship of the four seasons to the Sun's movement in declination. There are several points to be understood here. The first is that the Sun's movement in declination is completely independent of its position in the zodiac. In other words, when the Sun is at 0° (at the time of the vernal equinox) it is always the start of spring (beginning of the month of Aries) regardless whether the vernal point (the Sun's location in the zodiac) is in Taurus (as in the third cultural epoch, that of the Egyptian and Babylonian civilizations), or whether it is in Aries (as in the fourth cultural epoch, the Greco-Roman civilization), or whether in Pisces (as in the fifth cultural epoch, that of present-day European civilization). This shows that the occurrence of the seasons is determined solely by the Sun's relationship to the equator—as measured by its declination—and has nothing to do with the location of the Sun in the zodiac.

The second point to note is that the Sun's movement up and down in declination was known and described in the hermetic astrology of antiquity as the Sun's "steps" (Greek: *Bathmoi*). The foregoing description shows twelve major "steps" for the Sun during the course of the year, both up and down. In the hermetic astrology of antiquity an even more detailed description of the Sun's movement in declination was given in terms of twenty-four "steps."[12]

Intrinsic to the hermetic mode of thought is the principle of correspondences expressed in essence by the saying attributed to Hermes Trismegistus of ancient Egypt: "As above, so below." Thus it was quite natural to establish a correspondence between the Sun's "steps" during the cycle of the year and the signs of the sidereal zodiac. This correspondence, however, entails looking at the cycle of twelve steps rather than twenty-four steps.

Evidently Euctemon was thinking in terms of correspondences when he called the twelve months of the tropical calendar by the names of the twelve signs of the zodiac. In so doing he drew a parallel between the time division of the year into twelve months and the spatial division of the encircling zodiacal belt of twelve constellations. All that was

---

12 Powell, *Hermetic Astrology*, vol. 1, pp. 22–28.

necessary to establish a correspondence was to determine which month of the tropical calendar was the first month of the yearly cycle, and to place that in correspondence with Aries as the first sign of the zodiac.

Before elucidating why the month extending from March 21 to April 20 can be thought of as the first month of the year, it is helpful to consider why the sign/constellation of Aries is considered to be first in the circle of living creatures. This has to do with the astrological correspondence between the twelve zodiacal constellations and the various parts of the human body. This correspondence was shown in ancient times by depicting a human form in a circle, with the feet touching the head, wrapped around the twelve constellations. Since the constellation of Leo corresponds to the heart, the star Regulus (the "Lion's heart" at 5° Leo) is shown at the place of the heart in this human form.[13] Moreover, the head is shown in the constellation of Aries and the feet in the constellation of Pisces. Since the head is the natural starting point in delineating twelve parts of the body from the head down to the feet, correspondingly, it is natural to think of Aries as the first sign of the zodiac.

THE REVERSAL OF THE TROPICAL CALENDAR
IN THE SOUTHERN HEMISPHERE

When considering the cycle of the year in the Northern Hemisphere, the vernal equinox is a time when the activity of growth starts to become noticeable in Nature. Also the days start to become longer than the nights. For this reason the month from March 21 to April 20 is naturally thought of as the first month of the year in the tropical calendar. Having specified this as the first month, clearly it corresponds to Aries and thus may be called the "month of Aries" in the tropical calendar. The next month (April 20 to May 21) then corresponds to the zodiacal sign of Taurus and the month from May 21 to June 22 corresponds to Gemini, and so on. Later we shall return to consider the significance of the tropical calendar in relation to the birth of the human being. However, the question still remains of what the real significance of the tropical calendar is for the cycle of Nature.

Briefly, it can be said that all of Nature is drawn up with the increasing light and warmth of the Sun as it ascends above the equator

---

13 Pingree, *The Yavanajataka of Sphujidhavaja*, vol. 1, p. 148.

during the first quarter comprising the months of Aries, Taurus, and Gemini. Then in each subsequent quarter there is a corresponding response in Nature to the Sun's light and warmth. Considering the Earth as a whole, at the same time spring is taking place through these three ascending steps in declination of the Sun in the Northern Hemisphere, autumn is underway through the three descending steps of the Sun in declination in the Southern Hemisphere. So in the Southern Hemisphere the month of Libra is occuring in Nature during the month of Aries in the Northern Hemisphere. Similarly, in the Southern Hemisphere it is the month of Scorpio while it is the month of Taurus in the Northern Hemisphere, thus indicating a reversal in the tropical calendar between the Northern and the Southern Hemispheres. The table shows a full tabulation of the months of the tropical calendar in the Northern Hemisphere and the reversal of the tropical calendar in the Southern Hemisphere.

THE ASTROLOGICAL MONTHS OF THE TROPICAL ZODIAC

CYCLE OF THE YEAR	STEPS OF THE SUN	NORTHERN HEMISPHERE	DATES	SOUTHERN HEMISPHERE
From vernal equinox to summer solstice	From 0° Dec. to 23 ½° N	Aries Taurus Gemini	Mar. 21—Apr. 20 Apr. 20—May 21 May 21—June 21	Libra Scorpio Sagittarius
From summer solstice to autumnal equinox	From 23 ½° N to 0° Dec.	Cancer Leo Virgo	June 21—July 23 July 23—Aug. 23 Aug. 23—Sep. 23	Capricorn Aquarius Pisces
From autumnal equinox to winter solstice	From 0° Dec. to 23 ½° S	Libra Scorpio Sagittarius	Sep. 23—Oct. 23 Oct. 23—Nov. 22 Nov. 22—Dec. 22	Aries Taurus Gemini
From winter solstice to vernal equinox	From 23 ½° S to 0° Dec.	Capricorn Aquarius Pisces	Dec. 22—Jan. 20 Jan. 20—Feb. 19 Feb. 19—Mar. 21	Cancer Leo Virgo

(Dates may vary by one day, from year to year.)

THE TROPICAL ZODIAC AS A SPATIAL PROJECTION
OF THE TROPICAL CALENDAR

Now we will address the question of how the tropical zodiac came into being and how it came to be used in Western astrology in place of the sidereal zodiac. The tropical zodiac was defined from the tropical calendar by way of transformation from a time division to a spatial construction. The vernal and autumnal equinoxes, and the summer and winter solstices, are events in time, and are the most significant turning points in the cycle of the year. As we have seen, they specify day 1 in the months of Aries and Libra, and Cancer and Capricorn, in the tropical calendar, and they delineate the start of the four quarters in the cycle of the year: spring and autumn, summer and winter. The twelve months of the tropical calendar came about by way of trisecting the four quarters as time periods. You may ask how this procedure can be transformed from the temporal to the spatial?

Quite simply, if the spatial location of the Sun is determined at the vernal and autumnal equinoxes, and at the summer and winter solstices, a virtual cross in space is formed. The 90° arcs between the four corners of the cross can each be trisected to form three 30° arcs. In principle, the starting point of each 30° arc denotes the spatial location of the Sun on day 1 of each of the twelve months of the tropical calendar. In this way the time division of the tropical calendar became transformed into the spatial division of the tropical zodiac. But why would anyone want to do this?

If we look at the astrological textbook of Claudius Ptolemy, the *Tetrabiblos,* written in Alexandria around A.D. 150, it becomes apparent that he was a gifted astronomer interested in astrology more from an academic standpoint than as a practicing astrologer. Thus, the *Tetrabiblos* contains no horoscopes, and there is no evidence that Ptolemy ever cast a horoscope. The practice of casting horoscopes had spread from Babylon to Egypt, Greece, and Rome during the centuries prior to the Christian era, and was transmitted to India at about the time of Ptolemy. At that time all horoscopes were cast "Babylonian style" in terms of the sidereal zodiac. However, in the course of time, it seems that knowledge of the definition of the sidereal zodiac was lost. As far as we can tell, Ptolemy did not know exactly how the twelve 30° signs of the zodiac were defined. It is nevertheless clear from the following passage that he regarded the zodiacal signs as sidereal:

> The sign of Taurus as a whole is indicative of both temperatures and is somewhat hot; but taken part by part, its leading portion, particularly near the Pleiades, is marked by earthquakes, winds, and mists; its middle moist and cold, and its following portion, near the Hyades, fiery and productive of thunder and lightning.[14]

In the sidereal zodiac the Pleiades are located at 5° Taurus and the primary star of the Hyades, Aldebaran, is at 15° Taurus. The above passage by Ptolemy makes sense in terms of the sidereal zodiac but is nonsense in terms of the tropical zodiac where Aldebaran's longitude is 10° in the sign of Gemini at the present time. However, it was Ptolemy himself who introduced the tropical zodiac into astrology.[15] In the *Tetrabiblos* he wrote: "Although there is no natural beginning of the zodiac, since it is a circle, they assume that the sign that begins with the vernal equinox, that of Aries, is the starting point of them all."[16] At the time he wrote this (circa A.D. 150), the vernal point was located at 1° of the sign of Aries in the sidereal zodiac, making it quite accurate (to within a degree) to say that the sign of Aries "begins with the vernal equinox." But owing to the precession of the equinoxes, the vernal point has now drifted back, since Ptolemy, from 1° Aries to 5° Pisces, signifying that the sign of Aries no longer begins with the vernal equinox (March 21) but about twenty-five days later (April 15). Twenty-five days is the length of time required by the Sun to traverse from 5° Pisces to 0° Aries in the sidereal zodiac at a rate of approximately 1° per day. Ptolemy, if he were alive today, would undoubtedly be the first to say that in our present time the sign of Aries begins around mid-April and not with the vernal equinox.

Ptolemy was not wrong in defining the sign of Aries to begin with the vernal point, considering that at his time the vernal point was at 1° Aries. However, by putting this down in writing he essentially created a new astrological zodiac. Let's look now at the steps involved in the creation of this new (tropical) zodiac.

---

14 Ptolemy, *Tetrabiblos* II.11, pp. 201–203.

15 John North, *The Fontana History of Astronomy and Cosmology*, p. 67.

16 Ptolemy, *Tetrobiblos* I.10, pp. 59–61.

THE SUBSTITUTION OF THE TROPICAL ZODIAC
FOR THE SIDEREAL ZODIAC

The first thing to bear in mind is that the tropical zodiac is a projection into space of the tropical calendar. At the time of Ptolemy this projection more or less coincided with the spatial, constellational division of the sidereal zodiac of the Babylonians. Initially, astrologers paid no attention to Ptolemy's new astrological creation of the tropical zodiac. This has been demonstrated in studies of Greek horoscopes spanning the first to the fifth centuries A.D., compiled by Otto Neugebauer in his work *Greek Horoscopes*. Neugebauer remarked that the Greek horoscopes were sidereal, using a similar reference to the Babylonian sidereal zodiac.[17] This conclusion has been confirmed by Nick Kollerstrom's independent analysis of those Greek horoscopes together with a number of Babylonian horoscopes, leading to the conclusion that

A single frame of reference for the sidereal zodiac was used by both Babylonian and Greek astrologers, enduring over eight centuries, before being forgotten in the Dark Ages....These charts show that even in the centuries after Ptolemy, the astrologers writing in Greek continued to use a sidereal reference. The charts are mainly from Alexandria, indicating that even in Ptolemy's city the sidereal tradition endured.[18]

With the expansion of Christianity in the West, the practice of astrology in the Christian world declined, effectively disappearing by the sixth century A.D.. The last sidereal horoscopes from *Greek Horoscopes* were dated to the years 497 and 516.[19] Soon after this, astrology—as the practice of casting horoscopes—was taken up in the Arab world with the first Arabic horoscope dating to the year

---

17 Neugebauer and Van Hoesen, *Greek Horoscopes*, p. 172.

18 Kollerstrom, "The Star Zodiac of Antiquity," *Culture and Cosmos*, vol. 1, no. 2 (1997), p. 15. See also Kollerstrom, "On the Measurement of Celestial Longitude in Antiquity," *Optics and Astronomy*, pp. 145–159.

19 *Greek Horoscopes*, op. cit., p. 158. The horoscope cast for someone born in the year 497 is definitely sidereal. Unfortunately, the horoscope cast for someone born in 516 is too inexact to be able to say definitely one way or the other. At the most one can say that this horoscope is more likely sidereal when the planetary longitudes are compared with both the sidereal and the tropical longitudes computed according to modern astronomy.

531.[20] As in the case of the horoscope from the year 516, it is difficult to determine whether that horoscope from the year 531 is tropical or sidereal.[21] At any rate, the "Horoscope of Islam" (see page 195) dated to the year 621 is definitely tropical.[22] It may well be the world's first tropical horoscope, revealing the first astrological implementation of the tropical zodiac put forth by Ptolemy in the *Tetrabiblos*. Indeed, when the *Tetrabiblos* was translated from the Greek, it became almost a "bible" of astrology for the Arab world. Consequently the sidereal zodiac was forgotten. Sidereal astrology also disappeared from the Christian world of the West. At the same time a new kind of astrology based on the tropical zodiac and the work of Ptolemy began to grow and flourish in the Arabic-speaking world. This new astrology was then introduced into the Christian Western world from about 1140 onward through translations from the Arabic into Latin.[23] In this way the tropical astrology of the Arabs became established in place of the ancient sidereal astrology that had flourished for some nine hundred years (410 B.C. is the date of the world's oldest horoscope found so far, and A.D. 497 or A.D. 516 is the date of the last sidereal horoscope in *Greek Horoscopes*).

The extraordinary thing is that hardly anyone in the West seems to know that there had been any other kind of astrology than that of the Arabs based on the tropical zodiac. And it was not until the twentieth century that knowledge of the existence of the Babylonian sidereal zodiac reemerged in the West through the excavation and deciphering of cuneiform texts. The sidereal zodiac provides the foundation underlying the astrological revolution.

If we accept the validity of the second astrological reincarnation rule described above, it is evident that the astrology of the Babylonian and the Egyptians based on the sidereal zodiac is still valid. However, it is important to note that Elisabeth Vreede, Günther Wachsmuth, and Willi Sucher, among others, used the unequal-division constellations of the astronomical zodiac rather than the equal-division (30°) signs of the sidereal zodiac. They could not do otherwise because

---

20 Nicholas Campion, *An Introduction to the History of Astrology*, p. 29.

21 This horoscope is for the coronation of the Sassasian King Khosro on August 18, 531.

22 *Greek Horoscopes*, op. cit., p. 159.

23 Jim Tester, *A History of Western Astrology*, p. 147.

they had no knowledge of the Babylonian sidereal zodiac. They knew only the astronomical zodiac, based on Ptolemy's description, which is composed of unequal constellations. It is significant to note that an accurate comparison from death in one incarnation to birth in the next incarnation is possible only with the Babylonian sidereal zodiac and its division into 30° signs. Using the unequal division constellations of the astronomical zodiac—without any division into degrees—does not allow for an accurate comparison.

THE VALIDITY OF PLANETARY RULERSHIPS
OF THE SIGNS AND THE DECANS

It remains a mystery why neither Elisabeth Vreede nor Günther Wachsmuth questioned the unequal divisions of the constellations of the astronomical zodiac. As stated earlier, given Rudolf Steiner's dating of equal-length cultural epochs, each 2,160 years long, arising in connection with the retrograde movement of the vernal point through the zodiacal constellations, it follows that the spiritual influence of the constellations would also be *equal* in length. In this case the equal-length constellations, each 30° long, are called "signs." These are evidently the signs of the sidereal zodiac that Rudolf Steiner is referring to in the following:

> When the sun entered the sign of Cancer at the vernal equinox, the first post-Atlantean civilization began. It could actually be called "the Cancer civilization," as long as we do not misunderstand the expression. In other words, when the sun rose in the spring, it stood in the sign of Cancer.... Every constellation of the Zodiac is related to a particular planet and must be regarded as belonging to that planet.... Cancer is considered to be particularly connected to the moon. Since the forces of the moon work in a very particular way when its stands in Cancer, one says that the moon has its house, its home in Cancer. Its forces reside there, and there they are particularly developed.... Then the sun entered the sign of Gemini, the Twins, at the vernal equinox.... Just as the moon has its house in Cancer, so Mercury has its house in Gemini.[24]

---

24 Steiner, *Ancient Myths and the New Isis Mystery*, pp. 81–83.

In this lecture, Rudolf Steiner refers not only to the signs of the sidereal zodiac, but also affirmatively answers the question as to whether the correspondences of the planets to certain constellations of the zodiac, which were valid during the Babylonian–Egyptian epoch, are still valid today. Steiner clearly points out that, in relation to the present time, each zodiacal constellation (sidereal sign) has a planet particularly related to it, and the correspondences he indicates—Moon/Cancer, Mercury/Gemini, Venus/Taurus, Mars/Aries, Jupiter/Pisces—are precisely those of traditional astrology.[25] Steiner then elaborates on an additional division of each zodiacal constellation (sidereal sign) into three 10° segments called decans, also relevant for the present time. Steiner does not specifically state in this lecture that the decans are 10° segments, but elsewhere he divides the cultural epochs (2,160 years) into three equal time divisions lasting 720 years, thus validating the classical astrological subdivision of the sidereal signs of the zodiac into decans.[26] The decans, as 10° segments of the signs of the sidereal zodiac, originated during the Hellenistic period of Egypt beginning with the conquest of Egypt by Alexander the Great, who in 332 B.C. founded the city of Alexandria.[27] The very use of decans in this sense implies equal constellation divisions. Not only does Rudolf Steiner validate the decans as such, but he also confirms the planetary rulerships of these decans as specified in Hellenistic Egypt. That is, just as each constellation (sidereal sign) of the zodiac, according to Rudolf Steiner and in agreement with astrological tradition, has a planetary ruler, so also each decan has a planetary ruler. Rudolf Steiner's designation of the planetary rulers of the decans—for example, Mars, Sun, Venus for the three decans of the sidereal sign of Aries; Mercury, Moon, Saturn for the three decans of the sidereal sign of Taurus, and so on—is in exact agreement with the Egyptian astrological tradition.[28] Moreover, it is clear from his lecture on the decans that Steiner views this correspondence as being valid today. In other words, "The assignment of certain planets...to

25 Ptolemy, *Tetrabiblos* I. 17 (trsl. pp. 79–83).

26 Steiner, *How Can Mankind Find the Christ Again?* p. 92.

27 Neugebauer and Parker, *Egyptian Astronomical Texts*, vol. 1, pp. 95–96 and vol. 3, p. 168.

28 *Liber Hermetis Trismegisti*, I (edited and with a commentary by Wilhelm Gundel, *Neue astrologische Texte des Hermes Trismegistos*, pp. 19–23).

definite constellations of the zodiac" is "still valid today, in the same way it was in the Babylonian/Egyptian epoch."

Two Levels: Sidereal Zodiac and Tropical Calendar

Let's consider the question of whether it makes sense to draw horoscopes as Günther Wachsmuth did, with the signs of the tropical zodiac in the inner circle surrounded outside by the constellations of the astronomical zodiac. Considering the equal-length astrological ages and corresponding cultural epochs, we can safely conclude that the unequal constellations of the astronomical zodiac need to be replaced by the equal-division sidereal signs. Based on the astrological reincarnation research presented in this book, it is evident that planetary positions at someone's birth often enter into significant alignments in the sidereal zodiac—both geocentric and heliocentric—with the sidereal planetary positions at death in the previous incarnation. This evidence positively and conclusively validates sidereal astrology. It would only make sense to include the signs of the tropical zodiac in the inner circle if the tropical zodiac were also valid. Indeed there are some researchers who maintain that the sidereal and the tropical zodiac are valid on different levels:

The visible constellations of the fixed stars are the astral world. One can even say, with certain reservations, that this fixed-star zodiac is an image of the astral body of the cosmos. World astrality, world soul forces, move the stars. It is in this sense that we take the zodiac of the constellations as an expression of the astral body of the cosmos. The signs of the ecliptic rest on the vernal point in which the Sun indicates in the heavens the commencement of spring. This is a zodiac associated with the seasons, with the yearly rhythms of life in nature. It is particularly obvious in the plant world, as a kind of image of the ether, or life forces, in the universe. Here too we can, with certain reservations, say that this zodiac of the ecliptic signs is an image of the ether body of the cosmos, particularly of the solar cosmos.[29]

---

29 Sucher, *Cosmic Christianity and the Changing Countenance of Cosmology*, p. 175.

This last statement by Willi Sucher offers a key. In speaking of the solar cosmos and the effect on the yearly rhythms of life in Nature as expressed in relation to the signs of the tropical zodiac, he is referring to the Sun's movement up and down in declination. This was spoken of earlier as the central factor in the determination of seasons in the Northern and Southern Hemispheres. So essentially he is speaking about the *tropical calendar,* which is the reverse in the Northern and Southern Hemispheres. The tropical calendar truly expresses "the yearly rhythms of life in Nature," i.e. the realm of the etheric or life forces. However, when a spatial projection of the Northern Hemisphere's tropical calendar was made by Greek astronomers—now called the tropical zodiac—the true nature of things was obscured. As pointed out earlier, the word zodiac ("animal circle") relates properly to the circle of zodiacal constellations surrounding us in space. In bringing this into connection with "world astrality, world soul forces," Willi Sucher drew a correspondence with the human astral body, and the fact that the astral body is the highest principle in the animal kingdom. The realm of the etheric, however, is a "time world." The interaction between the Sun and the Earth's etheric realms during the cycle of the year is well described by the *tropical calendar* (i.e. a time-based description) when this calendar is reversed in the Southern Hemisphere as an expression of the Sun's movement in declination from the Northern Hemisphere. However, the tropical *zodiac,* as a *spatial projection* of the Northern Hemisphere's tropical calendar, no longer describes the time phenomena of Nature's yearly cycle—at least not in the Southern Hemisphere.

It is necessary to dwell at length upon this clarification of the different levels of the sidereal and the tropical, because of the widespread confusion surrounding this subject. The very use of a two-leveled horoscope of "constellations" and "signs" is an expression of this misunderstanding. The fact is that in the astrology of the Babylonians, Egyptians, Greeks, and Romans—and to the present day in Hindu astrology—there is no distinction between "signs" and "constellations." The "signs" are simply 30° divisions of the zodiacal constellations. It may help to think of the sidereal signs being embedded in the zodiacal constellations. This is elaborated upon in chapter 8 of *Hermetic Astrology,* vol. 1, where it is shown that the zodiacal signs are actually pictorial representations of the outlines of the stellar configurations constituting the zodiacal signs.

However, it is a complete illusion to conceive of tropical signs as existing in space, as will become clear in the following. The tropical calendar is a spiritual reality, having to do with the Earth's etheric aura and its relationship to the Sun, as indicated above in the quotation by Willi Sucher. The Earth's etheric aura comprises a multitude of beings of Nature, called "elemental beings," and these beings respond to the Sun's movement in declination. The higher the Sun rises, the more the elemental beings are drawn up with the increasing light and warmth of the Sun. This phenomenon needs to be seen globally. As the elemental beings are attracted to the mid-summer Sun, simultaneously on the opposite side of the Earth they withdraw into the Earth and it is mid-winter, exactly mirroring the polarity in the declination movement of the Sun between the Northern and the Southern Hemispheres. The Sun's movement in declination is the primary spiritual reality underlying the passage of the seasons and the corresponding activity of the elemental beings. It is a reality pertaining to the Earth's etheric aura, into which the human being incarnates at birth.

Thus, the tropical calendar is a spiritual reality. Its spatial projection (the tropical zodiac) has given rise to the illusion that there are tropical signs of the zodiac existing "out there" in space. Many people will react inwardly to this assertion with the conviction that the tropical zodiac is not an illusion. To everyone who believes in the tropical zodiac, one can only say, "Go out and look at the stars." At the time of writing this, Jupiter and Saturn were visible each morning before sunrise in the constellation of Aries. How is it possible to maintain that at the same time as beholding Jupiter and Saturn in Aries, they are supposed to be in Taurus? Yet this is indeed what many people firmly believe. The reality underlying this belief, however, is the tropical calendar, which is a time division of the cycle of the year and became projected into space as a consequence of Ptolemy's description in the *Tetrabiblos*.

The result of weighing everything up is the following conclusion: Claudius Ptolemy had no intention of creating a new zodiac when he referred to the zodiacal sign of Aries as being measured from the vernal point. The vernal point at his time just happened to be almost exactly at the beginning of the sign of Aries (at 1° sidereal Aries), and this is why he said that the sign of Aries begins with the vernal point. Intrinsically he was referring to the *sidereal signs* of the zodiac, as is evident from his description referred to above (the Pleiades and the Hyades in the sign of Taurus). The Arab astrologers who took up the *Tetrabiblos* did not understand this. They took Ptolemy's words at face value, that the zodiac begins with the vernal point, and cast their horoscopes accordingly. After Arabic astrology was introduced into the West, from the mid-twelfth century onward, the knowledge that a substitute zodiac had been introduced in place of the authentic zodiac had disappeared. All the astrological concepts that originally applied to the sidereal zodiac became transferred to the tropical zodiac. For example, the tropical astrologer firmly believes that the Moon "rules" the tropical sign of Cancer. In fact, as Rudolf Steiner clearly states in the quotation referred to above, the Moon rules the *sidereal sign* of Cancer. If we were to go out and look at the night sky when the tropical astrological ephemeris indicates that the Moon is in Cancer, we would actually see the Moon in Gemini. These simple observations need to be thought about in all earnestness if we are not to live in illusion.

The authors of this book recommend star-gazing—looking up at the stars—to behold the reality in the starry heavens of the zodiac, meaning "animal circle." If one sees Jupiter and Saturn in Aries, they are not "in Taurus," as stated in the tropical ephemeris. And they are not simultaneously in Aries on the astral level and in Taurus on the etheric level, as some people believe. The truth that the Babylonians, Egyptians, Greeks, and Hindus knew long ago is that in looking up to the world of stars, the zodiacal constellations begin to reveal themselves in their true form as the realm of divine beings. In looking up to the stars we see the outer aspect of these divine beings. This is the spiritual reality underlying the sidereal zodiac.

SIGNS AND CONSTELLATIONS

Willi Sucher was a pioneer in the twentieth century of a new star wisdom, in turn encouraged by Elisabeth Vreede, who worked closely together with Rudolf Steiner. Günther Wachsmuth, mentioned earlier, was also someone close to Rudolf Steiner who was concerned with the development of a new astrology on a scientific basis. Those who are familiar with the works of these authors[30] may object that all of them, including Rudolf Steiner, utilized the tropical zodiac. Surely Rudolf Steiner could not have been mistaken? In Appendix 2 this question will be examined in depth, addressing all the relevant points.

With regard to Elisabeth Vreede, Günther Wachsmuth, and Willi Sucher, without knowing about the sidereal zodiac they could not do otherwise than to cast horoscopes in terms of the conventional tropical zodiac and then add in the zodiacal constellations around the outside. Each of them realized the importance of the sidereal frame of reference; however, not knowing of the equal-division constellations/signs of the sidereal zodiac, they were obliged to work with the unequal-division constellations of the astronomical zodiac. The only way to draw a horoscope showing the location of the planets in the constellations is first to draw the horoscope showing the planets in the signs of the tropical zodiac and then to draw the unequal constellations around the outside. The convention of speaking of "constellations" (unequal, astronomical) and "signs" (equal, tropical) arose in this way. If, however, the sidereal zodiac is employed, any talk of "signs" and "constellations" as separate entities is superfluous; in terms of the sidereal zodiac, the zodiacal constellations are equal-division sidereal signs. Moreover, because of the way sidereal signs are defined—each 30° long—they can be utilized to specify the locations of the planets in degrees and minutes within the signs. As with the tropical zodiac, therefore, the sidereal zodiac is a completely adequate horoscopic frame of reference, as evidenced by the horoscopes in this book.

---

30 See bibliography for relevant works by Elisabeth Vreede, Willi Sucher, and Günther Wachsmuth.

APPENDIX 2
FURTHER CONSIDERATIONS
CONCERNING THE TROPICAL ZODIAC

In appendix 1 we discussed the fact that the tropical zodiac appears to have originated with the Greek astronomer, Hipparchus (second century B.C.), who used it simply as an astronomical coordinate system. In this way the precession of the equinoxes was discovered. This term refers to the vernal point (where the Sun is located in the sidereal zodiac at the start of spring) shifting backward through the constellations of the zodiac. The tropical zodiac was also used by Ptolemy (second century A.D.) in a purely astronomical way as found in his textbook, the *Almagest.* Over and above this, however, Ptolemy introduced the tropical zodiac into his astrological textbook, the Tetrabiblos.

As a starting point Rafael Gil Brand's excellent research on the tropical zodiac (published in Ulrike Voltmer's book *How Free is the Human Being?*) concerns the origin of the tropical zodiac with Hipparchus. He writes:

> Hipparchus of Nicea (ca. 180–125 B.C.) is seen as the discoverer of the precession of the equinoxes.... The consequences that Hipparchus drew from his discovery are decisive for the history of astrology. Thus he defined the tropical zodiac, in which 0° Aries is defined to be the vernal point. All twelve signs of the zodiac represent equal sections on the path of the Sun, measured from this point.[1]

Although this is quite correct, there are three things to be noted here: (1) Hipparchus was an astronomer, not an astrologer. He defined the tropical zodiac as an astronomical coordinate system for measuring the positions of the fixed stars and thus discovered the precession of the equinoxes. It was only later, through Ptolemy's book *Tetrabiblos,* that this astronomical coordinate system was introduced into astrology. (2) What Rafael Gil Brand does not men-

---

1 Voltmer, *Wie frei ist der Mensch?*, pp. 161–165.

tion is Euctemon's tropical calendar, the predecessor of Hipparchus' coordinate system of the tropical zodiac. As described in Appendix 1, the tropical zodiac is a spatial projection of the tropical calendar (in the Northern Hemisphere). The tropical calendar was already introduced by Euctemon (ca. 430 B.C.) approximately three hundred years before Hipparchus defined the tropical zodiac in astronomical terms. (3) There is a possibility that the tropical zodiac as originally defined by Hipparchus was actually the sidereal zodiac. How may this be understood? G. P. Goold puts forth this view in his introduction to the *Astronomica* by the Roman author Manilius. It must be borne in mind that all Babylonian, Egyptian, Greek, Roman, and Hindu astrologers used the sidereal zodiac, and that the world's first tropical horoscope was probably the "Horoscope of Islam" for the year A.D. 621 (see horoscope opposite).

The sidereal zodiac was the only frame of reference used by astrologers in antiquity for casting horoscopes, and the question of the location of the vernal point in the sidereal zodiac engaged their attention. Prior to the discovery of the precession of the equinoxes, and before it was known that the vernal point moves in relation to the sidereal zodiac, various "systems" were used. For example, the Babylonians used two astronomical systems now referred to as System A and System B. In System A, the vernal point was located at 10° in the sign of Aries and in System B it was placed at 8° Aries. Commenting on these systems, the science historian B. L van der Waerden writes:

> In 1963 I made an attempt to estimate the accuracy of ancient Babylonian observations of the equinoxes and solstices. I found that about 400 B.C. or even earlier the summer solstice was known to within one or two days.... Kugler also investigated Tablet ACT 60 (old signature SH 93), which belongs to System A and in which the spring equinox was assumed at 10° of Aries. His conclusion was: "An analogous calculation for Tablet No. 93 would bring us back to 500 B.C. ± several years."[2]

Since the vernal point was at 0° Aries in A.D. 221,[3] and since it moves retrograde through the sidereal zodiac at a rate of 1° in 72 years, it is

---

2 B. L. van der Waerden, *Science Awakening, Volume II: The Birth of Astronomy*, p. 266.

3 Michelsen, *The American Sidereal Ephemeris*.

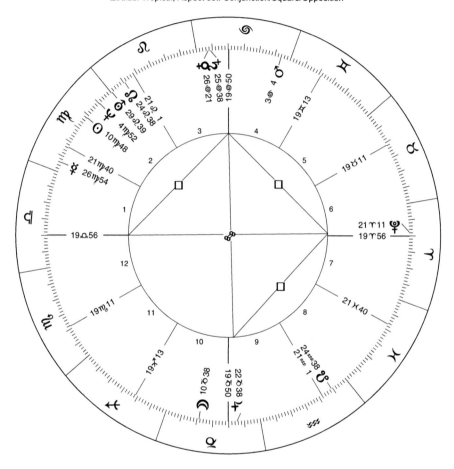

Horoscope of Islam - Geocentric
At Mecca, Saudi Arabia, Latitude 21N27', Longitude 39E49'
Date: Tuesday, 1/SEP/621, Julian
Time: 8:35, Local Time
Sidereal Time 7:25:55, House System: Placidus
Zodiac: Tropical, Aspect set: Conjunction/Square/Opposition

easy to see that the vernal point was located at 10° Aries at around 500 B.C., which is 720 years (10 x 72) prior to A.D. 221.

Van der Waerden also concluded that the Greek astronomers Meton and Euctemon drew their knowledge of the zodiac from the Babylonians, adopting System B:

These two astronomers observed the summer solstice in Athens in 432 B.C. (Ptolemy, *Almagest* III, 1). . . . Meton placed the equinoxes and solstices at 8° Aries, 8° Cancer, etc. (Columella, *De re rustica* IX, 14), exactly like the Babylonian System B calculations.[4]

Note that the vernal point was located at 8° Aries actually around 356 B.C., that is, 144 years (2 x 72) after 500 B.C., since it moved 2° from 10° to 8° of Aries in 144 years. Therefore Meton was approximately 1° in error, since the vernal point was at 9° Aries in about 428 B.C., midway between 500 B.C. and 356 B.C.

THE CREATION OF A MOVABLE, ARTIFICIAL ZODIAC

Now we can consider G.P. Goold's hypothesis that at the time of Hipparchus the vernal point was at 0° Aries. If Hipparchus did believe this, again—like Meton—he was in error, because, in fact, the vernal point did not reach 0° Aries until A.D. 221.[5] Therefore, at the time of Hipparchus (around 140 B.C.) the vernal point was actually at 5° Aries, since it shifted 5° in the 360 years (5 x 72) between 140 B.C. and A.D. 221. Nevertheless, according to G. P. Goold, there is evidence that Hipparchus believed that the vernal point was located at 0° Aries at his time. If this were indeed the case, it would account for the supposition that Hipparchus invented the tropical zodiac. All he did, however, was to assume wrongly that the vernal point in his day was located at 0° Aries. And just as Meton assumed that the vernal point was at 8° Aries three hundred years before Hipparchus, Ptolemy assumed that the vernal point was at 0° Aries three hundred years after him when it was actually at 1° Aries.

> It is the great glory of Hipparchus to have discovered the precessional shift, apparently by comparing his observations of Spica with those of Timocharis....Eudoxus, we are told (Hipparchus 2.1.18), placed the vernal point at 15° Aries, Aratus at the beginning of the sign [0° Aries]. Now since their chronological difference corresponds to a precessional shift of not much

4 Op. cit., p. 246.

5 Note that the date A.D. 215 is usually given as the start of the Age of Pisces, since it lies exactly 2,160 years prior to the start of the Age of Aquarius in A.D. 2375. An "average date," A.D. 215, is based on a uniform rate of motion of the vernal point of 1° in 72 years, thus 30° in 2,160 years (72 x 30 = 2160) However, because the rate of motion of the vernal point fluctuates slightly, A.D. 221 is a more astronomically precise date for the location of the vernal point at 0° Aries.

more than 1°, it is obvious that both are struggling to preserve conventions that do not fit the phenomena. Occasional references to 8° [Aries] may be related, as Neugebauer suggests, to the vernal point of System B of the Babylonian lunar theory; and 8° [Aries] or thereabouts may well have marked the [vernal] equinox when the zodiac as we know it was devised (the Romans—Caesar, Vitruvius, Columella, Pliny—generally adopted 8° [Aries]).... If in the time of Hipparchus the vernal equinox occurred at the first point of Aries [0° Aries], then in the time of Ptolemy it must have occurred at about 26° Pisces, and today it must occur at about 1° Pisces.[6]

Note that this last sentence, if it were to be formulated giving the actual positions of the vernal point at the time and in the present, should read: "At the time of Hipparchus the vernal equinox occurred at 5° Aries, then in the time of Ptolemy it must have occurred at about 1° Aries; and today it must occur at about 5° Pisces." Continuing with the words of G. P. Goold:

Today in fact the effect of precession has been to move every zodiacal sign 29° away from where, according to astrological doctrine, it ought to be. Oddly enough it is Ptolemy who has saved the day for astrologers. In *Tetrabiblos* I, 22 the astronomer virtually says that for astronomical purposes he will define the first point of Aries as the vernal equinox. If that moves, then the whole zodiac will just have to move with it. For astrological purposes men had better look to this movable, artificial zodiac. And so it has come to pass. When today's readers of almanacs are informed that the Sun travels through Aries from March 21 to April 20, the name Aries denotes not the group of stars so identified and marked in our star atlases, but 30° of the ecliptic measured off from the vernal equinox, a length of line constantly moving and today almost entirely contained in the astronomical constellation of Pisces.[7]

The vernal point is not at 29°, but rather it has shifted back approximately 25° from 0° Aries to its current location at about 5° Pisces. Nevertheless, G. P. Goold's statement still holds some validity, provided we

---

6 Manilius, *Astronomica*, lxxxii–lxxxiii [additions in brackets by RP].

7 Ibid., lxxxiii–lxxxiv.

modify 29° to 25°. If we follow his interpretation, there were various "systems" locating the vernal point at different degrees in the sidereal sign of Aries, and Hipparchus' "system" locating the vernal point at 0° Aries was one of them. Yet it was Ptolemy who "absolutized" Hipparchus' system by unwittingly fixing the vernal point permanently at 0° Aries. According to Goold this signified the creation of a "movable, artificial zodiac," known to us as the "tropical" zodiac. Whether we accept G. P. Goold's interpretation or not, it is clear that Ptolemy's system changed things completely. Previous to Ptolemy it was quite natural to ask what degree the vernal point was located in the (sidereal) zodiac? The word *sidereal* is in parentheses because as long as the sidereal zodiac was the *only* zodiac, there was no need to designate it "sidereal"; it was simply the zodiac. By fixing the vernal point at 0° Aries, the sidereal zodiac became "eclipsed." Now that it is coming back into view, especially with the beginning of the new millennium, it is again possible to ask in what degree of the (sidereal) zodiac the vernal point is located. The answer now, at the start of the new millennium, is 5° Pisces. (According to the *American Sidereal Ephemeris*, 2001–2025, the vernal point will be at exactly 5° Pisces in the year 2018.[8])

THE TEXTBOOK OF MANILIUS IS PURELY SIDEREAL

Rafael Gil Brand refers to the Greek author Geminos and the Roman author Manilius:

> Marcus Manilius lived at the beginning of the first century A.D. and described in his *Astrology* [*Astronomica*—RP]—an astronomical–astrological textbook in poetic form—the tropical zodiac. Among the many passages confirming this, the following two may be mentioned briefly: "Cancer is loth to end the day, winter to renew it" (Manilius, III, 229–230). "For the Ram deducts as many hours from the nights as the Fisches had previously taken away on their own account" (ibid., 469–470). These passages say basically the same as the previously mentioned quote by Geminos that the equinoxes and solstices, respectively, form the boundaries between the signs Fishes–Ram, Twins–Crab, etc. The poetic textbook is full of quotes that prove the

---

8 Michelsen, *The American Sidereal Ephemeris, 2001–2025*.

significance of the equinoxes and solstices for the definition of the zodiac.[9]

Unfortunately this is not the case, as the entire poetic textbook refers to the constellations of the sidereal zodiac:

> Resplendent in his golden fleece the Ram leads the way and looks back with wonder at the backward rising of the Bull, who with lowered face and brow summons the Twins; these the Crab follows, the Lion the Crab, and the Virgin the Lion. Then the Balance, having matched daylight with the length of night, draws on the Scorpion, ablaze with his glittering constellation, at whose tail the man with the body of a horse aims with taut bow a winged shaft, ever in act to shoot. Next comes Capricorn, curled up with his cramped asterism, and after him from urn upturned the Waterman pours forth the wanted stream for the Fishes that swim eagerly into it; and these as they bring up the rear of the signs are joined by the Ram (*Astronomica* I, 263–264). These then are the constellations that decorate the sky with even spread (ibid., 532). How great is the space occupied by the vault of the heavens and how great the territory within which the twelve signs of the zodiac move (*Astronomica* I, 539)...distribute 30° to each sign (*Astronomica* III, 439). In this way you must seek among the fast-rotating stars the rising point of the heavens (ibid., 503). Some ascribe these powers [the equinoxes and solstices] to the 8°; some hold that they belong to the tenth; nor was an authority lacking to give to the first degree the decisive influence and the control of the days (ibid., 680–682).[10]

In his introduction to *Astronomica,* G. P. Goold comments: "Whereas Manilius mostly locates the actual tropic degree [of the equinoxes and solstices] at the beginning of a tropic sign, here he places it within the sign and specifically in the eighth or tenth degree. Indeed, his last line, referring to the authority who assigned the tropic to the first degree, even suggests eccentricity on that person's part."[11]

---

9 Brand, op. cit., p. 163. In the meantime, Rafael Gil Brand has become a leading proponent of sidereal astrology in Germany.

10 Manilius, *Astronomica*, op. cit.

11 Ibid., p. lxxxi (comment in brackets by R.P.).

Was this authority Hipparchus? In any case it is clear that Manilius was not using the tropical zodiac as such since he refers implicitly to System A (vernal point at 10° Aries) and System B (vernal point at 8° Aries), as well as to Hipparchus' system (vernal point at 0° Aries). At the most he was using the latter system, which, however, became fixed as the tropical zodiac as such only by Ptolemy, more than a century after Manilius. If readers have doubts about this, a single glance at the *Astronomica* by Manilius will suffice to demonstrate that the entire work is sidereal, based on a definition of the sidereal zodiac very close to the original Babylonian definition. Consider the following sentence for example: "As he emerges in his backward rising with head hanging down, the Bull brings forth in his sixth degree the Pleiades" (*Astronomica* V, 140–142). In the Babylonian sidereal zodiac the Pleiades are located at 5° Taurus. Therefore, either Manilius was 1° in error in his specification of the longitude of the Pleiades in Taurus, or he was using the Hindu sidereal zodiac, which is shifted 1° from the original Babylonian zodiac.[12] (At present the Pleiades, marking the neck of the Bull in the sidereal zodiac, are located at 0° Gemini in the tropical zodiac.)

A NEW CONSCIOUSNESS OF THE BABYLONIAN SIDEREAL ZODIAC

Rafael Gil Brand is one of the few astrologers who have researched the history of the zodiac. Therefore he knows of the existence of the Babylonian (Chaldean) sidereal zodiac, of which most astrologers are not aware. It is more or less correct when he writes:

> Many horoscopes from that time have come down to us that have been cast according to the sidereal zodiac. There are studies (Neugebauer, *Greek Horoscopes*) that show that with these horoscopes there is a constant average difference from the tropical positions in favor of the sidereal. Apart from the fact that the computation of planetary positions was not so accurate then, planetary tables were often used that had been computed in Chaldean style, sidereally.... One can assume that the centuries after Hipparchus—approximately from the first century B.C. to the fifth century A.D.—were a time of transition during which,

---

12 Powell and Treadgold, *The Sidereal Zodiac*, pp. 16–20.

according to the author and according to the tables at his disposal, the tropical or the sidereal zodiac was used.[13]

This last statement is a plausible hypothesis, i.e. that there was a period of transition (first century B.C. to fifth century A.D.) during which either the tropical or the sidereal zodiac was used, according to the astrologer who cast the horoscope. However, as mentioned in appendix 1, Otto Neugebauer determined that the Greek horoscopes were sidereal.[14] Neugebauer's finding was confirmed by Nick Kollerstrom, who pointed out that the world's first tropical horoscope was probably the Arabic "Horoscope of Islam" for the year A.D. 621.[15]

What conclusion then does Rafael Gil Brand draw from his research?

Claudius Ptolemy can be seen as the most important proponent and defender of the tropical zodiac..., which has been used in classical Western astrology since then. This astrology places the "native," the individual, at the center of its considerations much more definitely than Babylonian astrology did. This is also an achievement of the Greek spirit, and in the Mystery of Christos, the human being who became God, adored by the astrologers from the orient at his birth, this acquired a new, spiritual dimension.[16]

The implication is that Rafael Gil Brand sees tropical astrology as an achievement of the Greek spirit and that this had something to do with the Mystery of Christ's Incarnation. In light of the research referred to above, tropical astrology was practiced by Arab astrologers who used it for casting horoscopes, but it was not generally used by Greek astrologers. Moreover, the three magi who came to pay homage to the child Jesus were followers of the Babylonian tradition using the sidereal zodiac.[17]

Nevertheless, it is accurate to say that the tropical zodiac was an achievement of Greek astronomers, notably Hipparchus and Ptolemy,

---

13 Rafael Gil Brand, op cit, p. 164.

14 Neugebauer and van Hoesen, *Greek Horoscopes*, p. 172.

15 See p. 195 for the "Horoscope of Islam."

16 Ibid, pp. 164–169.

17 Powell, *Christian Hermetic Astrology*, p. 28–40.

and that through Ptolemy the tropical zodiac became introduced into astrology and was taken up centuries later by Arab astrologers.

Before returning to consider the belief that the introduction of the tropical zodiac had something to do with the Incarnation of Christ, we need to understand that the most important research presented in this book is the rediscovery and return to consciousness of the original, sidereal zodiac of the Babylonians. And the simplest and most direct way for knowledge of the sidereal zodiac to come about is to refer to the current location of the vernal point in the zodiac.

At the present time the vernal point is close to 5° Pisces in the sidereal zodiac and is shifting back through Pisces at a rate of about 1° in 72 years. As previously stated, it will reach 0° Pisces and enter Aquarius in the year 2375. It takes 2160 years (30 x 72) to retrograde through one sign of 30°. Hence it was at 0° Aries, entering Pisces, in about A.D. 215, given as an "average date" (A.D. 220/221 was the astronomically exact date). Seventy-two years prior to that—around the middle of the second century—the vernal point was at 1° Aries when Ptolemy was active as an astronomer in Alexandria. Going back another 288 years (4 x 72) we arrive at the time of Hipparchus, around 140 B.C., when the vernal point was at 5° Aries. That was just under 2160 years ago = the time for the vernal point to shift from 5° Aries to 5° Pisces, a total of 30° at a rate of 1° every 72 years (30 x 72 = 2160).

AN ASTROLOGICAL "DOUBLE THINK"

Most Western astrologers are unaware that the Babylonian sidereal zodiac was the original zodiac, and therefore have little conception of the actual extent of the zodiacal ages. They do know, however, that the location of the vernal point in the constellations is significant in specifying those zodiacal ages. Since all astronomical star maps depict the vernal point in the constellation of Pisces, most astrologers are aware that we are living in the Age of Pisces with the Age of Aquarius soon to begin. This will take place when the vernal point shifts into the constellation of Aquarius. So today's astrologers clearly attribute significance to the vernal point's position against the background of the fixed stars, accepting the influence of the sidereal zodiac, at least with regard to the position of the vernal point.

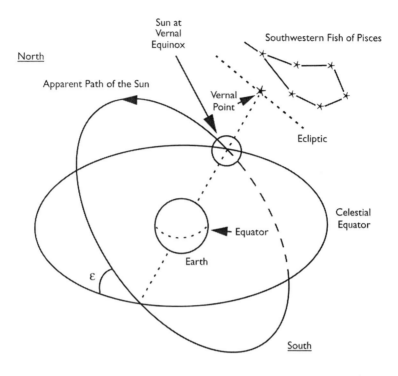

Definitions
Celestial equator = projection of earth's equator.
Ecliptic = projection of the apparent path of the sun.
ε, the obliquity of the ecliptic = angle between celestial equator and ecliptic ($\varepsilon = 23\frac{1}{2}°$).
Vernal point = projection onto ecliptic of extended earth–sun line at moment of vernal equinox. At present the vernal point is located in the southwestern Fish of Pisces.

The present location of the vernal point

This makes for a curious kind of "double think" prevailing among tropical astrologers. As an illustration, consider the movement of Jupiter, which was visible in the constellation of Pisces in the evening sky during February 1999. Jupiter entered into a remarkably close conjunction with Venus on February 23, 1999, the two brilliant planets appearing next to one another close to the tail of the Southwestern Fish, and about 2° from the vernal point located beneath the Southwestern Fish (see figure above).

In fact, Jupiter was in exact conjunction with the vernal point at 5¼° sidereal Pisces on the night of February 12/13, 1999. Consulting a tropical ephemeris for February 13, 1999 we find Jupiter's longitude to be 0° Aries, since the vernal point denotes the start of the sign of Aries in the tropical zodiac. The curious kind of "double think" prevailing among tropical astrologers is to acknowledge that the vernal point is located in Pisces, giving rise to the Age of Pisces, and at the same time to think, as in this example, that Jupiter, when it is in conjunction with the vernal point, is in Aries. How can it be that the two—the vernal point and Jupiter—are both located at exactly the same place in the heavens, and yet the one is said to be in Pisces and the other in Aries? (This example applies, of course, to any planet, when it is located at the vernal point.)

THE TROPICAL CALENDAR AND THE PRACTICE OF THE VIRTUES

Tropical astrologers will often say that it is evident that the sign of Aries begins on March 21, when the Sun is in conjunction with the vernal point, because this is the beginning of spring. However, this argument does not hold for the Southern Hemisphere! The truth of the matter is that in terms of the tropical calendar, the month of Aries begins in the Northern Hemisphere on March 21 but on this day in the Southern Hemisphere the month of Libra commences. Yet this applies only to the "mood" of Nature, and correspondingly to the world of elemental beings, and is not of major astrological significance for human beings, as may be seen from the following consideration. Let us suppose two people are born on March 21, and thus have the same sidereal horoscope of birth. However, one is born in the Northern and one in the Southern Hemisphere. In terms of the tropical calendar, one is born at the start of the month of Aries and the other at the start of the month of Libra. Does this affect their character or psychological constitution?

Those who are convinced that the tropical zodiac is astrologically effective will answer "yes." But what if these two people are both born in the same town right on the equator, with the equator running through the middle of the town in such a way that one is born to the north of the equator and the other to the south? Would it make any sense to speak of one born "in Aries" and the other "in Libra"? And what if one was born at the North Pole and the other at the South Pole? By considering the extreme situations it becomes clear that the tropical calendar certainly applies to Nature, but only in the temperate zones. Its relevance to human beings is indirect and only via Nature, in so far as the human being is a part of Nature. This does not diminish the importance of the tropical calendar; it simply puts it into perspective. It does indeed have a significance, as we shall see in relation to an indication given by Rudolf Steiner:[18]

THE TWELVE (MONTHLY) VIRTUES
To be meditated upon and to be taken into consideration in life

APRIL	Devotion: Reverence	becomes force of sacrifice
MAY	Equilibrium: (Inner) Balance	becomes progress
JUNE	Perseverance: Endurance (Persistence, Steadfastness)	becomes faithfulness
JULY	Unselfishness: Selflessness	becomes catharsis
AUGUST	Compassion: "Suffering with"	becomes freedom
SEPTEMBER	Courtesy: Politeness	becomes tact of the heart
OCTOBER	Contentment: Peaceful satisfaction	becomes equanimity
NOVEMBER	Patience: Forbearance	becomes insight
DECEMBER	Control of speech: Control of thought (Control of speech—to be master of one's tongue, "Guard your tongue")	becomes feeling for truth
JANUARY	Courage: Boldness	becomes power of redemption
FEBRUARY	Discretion: Prudence (Keeping silent)	becomes meditative force
MARCH	Magnanimity: Generosity	becomes love

Always begin the exercise on the twenty-first of the previous month.
For example, April, March 21–April 20.

---

18 Steiner, *Anweisungen für eine esoterische Schulung*, ("Guidance in Esoteric Training"), p. 31.

This indication by Rudolf Steiner concerning twelve virtues to be practiced during the course of the year clearly relates to the months of the tropical calendar as they apply in the Northern Hemisphere, with the month of Aries extending from March 21 to April 20, and so on. During the month of Aries the virtue of devotion is to be practiced, and devotion becomes the force of self-sacrifice. This signifies that as human beings we are part of Nature, and we can best practice the Aries virtue when the "mood" of Aries prevails in Nature. It's a matter of harmonizing with and even adding something to Nature—a quality that only we, as human beings, are able to transmit—which is morality.

Note that Rudolf Steiner's indication was given for spiritually striving people living (for the most part) in Europe. We can be certain that had he lived in Australia or somewhere else in the Southern Hemisphere, he would have taken into account the reversal of the tropical calendar for the Southern Hemisphere when giving his indication concerning the practice of these virtues. For example, he would have indicated the Libra virtue of contentment as the virtue to be practiced from March 21 to April 20. So it is evident that Rudolf Steiner did ascribe significance to the tropical calendar; otherwise he would not have given this indication concerning the monthly practice of the virtues in the way that he did. But before jumping to the conclusion that he endorsed the tropical zodiac, we need to consider the following statement made in the introduction to his *Calendar 1912–1913*:

> The following calendar, in the flow of monthly images, demonstrates the fact that the gaze, as it turns to the rising Sun, simultaneously discovers a constellation—here expressed in a symbolic image. In the course of the year, this relationship changes, so that all twelve zodiacal signs enter consideration.
>
> The position of the Sun may be related to a zodiacal image for about a month. After the year has run its course, the same positions more or less repeat themselves. The designation "approximately" is justified, because as time moves forward, a shift occurs in the positions. Centuries ago, for example, one's gaze at the rising Sun in March fell on the constellation Aries, while at the present, during the same time period, it falls on Pisces. [19]

---

19 Steiner, *Calendar 1912–1913*, p. 18.

In the German text Rudolf Steiner refers to *Tierkreiszeichen* (zodiacal sign) interchangeably with the word *Sternbild* (constellation). This interchangeability applies to the equal-division sidereal zodiac. However, it does not apply to the astronomical zodiac of unequal-division constellations. Therefore Rudolf Steiner implicitly referred to the sidereal zodiac in the Introduction to this calendar. Explicitly, however, he used unequal-division zodiacal constellations in line with astronomical tradition, although the constellations he indicated differ somewhat from those of modern astronomy in terms of their length. Had Rudolf Steiner known of the equal-division sidereal zodiac in terms of its astronomical definition, he would probably have used it in the Calendar.

Another interesting point with regard to the above quotation is Rudolf Steiner's expression of the "gaze" directed toward the Sun at sunrise, which falls at the same time on the particular constellation where the Sun is to be found—for example, the way it falls on the constellation of Pisces in March. Of course we know that it is not possible to actually see the background of the constellation in which the Sun is to be found except during a total solar eclipse. So the "gaze" that Steiner is speaking of can only be a clairvoyant gaze. It was Rudolf Steiner's clairvoyance that enabled him to see the Sun in Pisces around March 21. In former times (during the Age of Aries from 1946 B.C. to A.D. 221), clairvoyants saw the Sun in Aries around March 21. The fact that it is really a matter of clairvoyance or soul experience is expressed in the following: "The more complex soul experience 'In springtime I feel the power of the Sun increasing and the Earth preparing itself for new growth' can be expressed in the words, 'The rising Sun is seen in the direction of Pisces.'"[20]

In the *Calendar 1912–1913*, Rudolf Steiner indicated the passage of the Sun through Pisces between March 9 and April 13. This immediately qualifies his statement about seeing the Sun in Pisces during March. It does not apply to the first part of March, but only to the rest of that month. Here the tropical zodiac, which begins with the sign of Aries on March 21, is clearly not intended. The clairvoyant—in this case Rudolf Steiner—sees the Sun in Pisces, not in Aries, during the latter half of March. This statement is a vindication of the clairvoyance of the Babylonians, who specified the sidereal zodiac on the basis of their clairvoyant perception. Nevertheless, the

---

20 Ibid., p. 6.

Calendar 1912–1913, while basically depicting the passage of the Sun through the signs/constellations of the sidereal zodiac, deviates somewhat from the latter in terms of dates indicated by Steiner. For example, the passage through Pisces in the sidereal zodiac is from March 15 to April 15 (see figure on page 7) and not between March 9 and April 13. Even if we allow a shift of one day due to precession, the fact that the vernal point has moved about 1¼° for the passage of the Sun through Pisces since 1912, this would change the dates given by Rudolf Steiner by only one day from March 10 to April 14 in our present time.[21] How do we account for this discrepancy? To begin with, we can consider the following excerpt from a letter by Joachim Schulz, an astronomer who researched the zodiacal divisions indicated by Rudolf Steiner. As the deceased astronomer Joachim Schultz knew, apparently from Dr. Elisabeth Vreede,

> The principal correspondence of the monthly images to various length time intervals in the course of the year and corresponding to the present situation of the constellations (vernal point in Pisces and no longer in Aries)" stemmed from Rudolf Steiner. "Here a conscious step differing from the usual astrological signs of equal length is taken. On the other hand he had not drawn exact boundaries of the segments himself, and when he was later asked about this, he said that these should be fitted to the astronomical positions of the constellations and, where necessary, were to be corrected.[22]

It is interesting that, while Rudolf Steiner's *Calendar 1912–1913* gave the passage of the Sun through unequal-length zodiacal constellations, the Moon's passage was indicated through the signs of the

---

21 The Sun travels around the zodiac in one year of 365¼ days. Since the zodiac comprises 360°, the Sun's rate of progress is approximately 1° per day. Hence, when the vernal point shifts back 1° in the zodiac, as it does after 72 years, the Sun requires an extra day to return to conjunction with the same fixed star. This explains the change of dates from March 9 to March 10 and April 13 to April 14 since Rudolf Steiner's day.

22 According to a letter about the *Calendar*, dated May 11, 1949, from Joachim Schultz to the engineer Andree Kassel. The *Sternkalender* yearly (since 1929 at the Goetheanum through the initiative of Dr. Elisabeth Vreede) consciously connects onto the *Calendar 1912–1913* by giving all indications in terms of the visible constellations in the heavens. See Hella Wiesberger, "Das Kalendarium," *Beiträge zur Rudolf Steiner Gesamtausgabe*, Nr. 37/38, Dornach, 1972, p. 32.

tropical zodiac. This could again be interpreted as an endorsement of the tropical zodiac. Concerning this, Hella Wiesberger writes:

> Rudolf Steiner indicated the *Calendar of the Moon* precisely in the manuscript for the Calendar of Names. However, unlike the Calendar of the Sun, it is not in terms of the constellations, but is oriented to the signs, agreeing with the ephemerides for the years 1912/1913. The reason for this must have been solely lack of time; for Rudolf Steiner had only a few weeks for the work on the Calendar, during which he was able to do this work alongside his constant lecture journeys.[23]

Her explanation was that Rudolf Steiner did not have time to work out the Moon's passage through the constellations, which is why he simply drew upon the available tropical ephemerides for the Moon. Lack of time also played a role in his drawing up only an approximate passage of the Sun through the constellations. According to Joachim Schultz, Steiner requested that in future the exact astronomical divisions of the zodiac be respected. Rudolf Steiner evidently estimated the extent of zodiacal constellations as they are usually depicted in star maps. Thus the divisions he gave were only approximate, and this was the reason he pointed out that they should be corrected where necessary, and adjusted to the constellations of the astronomical zodiac.

The fact that Rudolf Steiner's indications for the passage of the Sun through the zodiacal constellations agree neither with the unequal divisions of the astronomical zodiac, nor with the equal divisions of the sidereal zodiac, was made clear when Elisabeth Vreede began to bring out the *Sternkalender* from 1929 onward. She adjusted Rudolf Steiner's indications to comply more closely with the unequal divisions of the astronomical zodiac. Although her estimates of these divisions were more accurate, they were by no means precise. In the *Sternkalender* 1972/73, Suso Vetter amended the divisions once again, but the slight modifications he made were also imprecise. Subsequently Peter Treadgold computed the precise divisions as defined by the International Astronomical Union in 1928, and these were published in the book *The Sidereal Zodiac*.[24] A comparison of the precise divisions defined by the International Astronomical Union with those of the *Sternk-*

---

23 Ibid, p. 32.

24 Powell and Treadgold, *The Sidereal Zodiac*, table 1, p. 32.

alender reveals divergences in some of the boundaries (Virgo–Libra, Libra–Scorpio, Scorpio–Sagittarius) amounting to as much as 2° or 3°.

If Rudolf Steiner had had more time to meet the publication deadline for the *Calendar 1912–1913*, he could have devoted more time to the "zodiac question" and thus arrived at equal-division constellations identical or similar to those of the Babylonian sidereal zodiac. At least, this would have been consistent with his indication of equal-length cultural epochs of 2160 years long, implying equal-division zodiacal constellations. Evidently he was unaware that the Babylonian sidereal zodiac with equal-division zodiacal constellations had been rediscovered around 1900. But it's obvious that he was aware his estimates were inaccurate, otherwise he would not have requested them to be adjusted in the future.

RUDOLF STEINER'S INTERPRETATION OF TROPICAL HOROSCOPES

Three decades of investigation have led to the conclusion that wherever Rudolf Steiner refers to signs of the zodiac, he invariably means sidereal signs, even though he never articulated this explicitly. The *Calendar 1912–1913* and his many statements concerning the spiritual cosmos manifesting through the starry heavens point to the validity of the sidereal zodiac. There are two exceptions, however. In the *Curative Education* lectures, he asked Elisabeth Vreede to draw up the horoscopes of two children with albinism for him to interpret. The horoscopes were tropical, of course, since Elisabeth Vreede evidently did not know that there was any other way to cast horoscopes. When presented with the horoscopes, Rudolf Steiner interpreted them at face value. Evidently there were some errors in the horoscopes, since Steiner's interpretation does not correspond exactly to them. This is highly significant in relation to the tropical/sidereal zodiac question, so we need to explore this in some detail. For this purpose both the tropical and sidereal horoscopes of the two children are presented on the following pages. Now let us consider Rudolf Steiner's interpretation.

> Take first this horoscope (of the elder sister). It will probably have struck you that you find here in this region, Uranus together with Venus and Mars.[25]

---

25 Steiner, *Education for Special Needs*, pp. 195–196.

In fact, when we look at the first horoscope, we see that Venus and Uranus were 11 ½° apart, Venus and Mars were 65° apart, and Mars and Uranus were 76 ½° apart.

> Here, then, are Mars, Venus and Uranus.... Mars, which has Venus and Uranus in its vicinity, stands itself in strong opposition to the Moon.

Again, looking at the horoscope it would appear that Saturn is in the vicinity of Mars, since Saturn is just 11° away from Mars, while Venus is 65° away and Uranus is 76 ½° from Mars. Yet Saturn is not mentioned. Astrologically speaking, it is correct to say that Mars is in opposition to the Moon since they are 174° apart (180° being an exact opposition).

> And now I would ask you to pay careful attention also to the fact that the Moon is at the same time standing before Libra. This means, the Moon has comparatively little support from the zodiac; it wavers and hesitates; it is even something of a weakling in this hour; and its influence is still further reduced through the fact that Mars (which pulls along with it the luciferic influence) stands in opposition to it.

The curious thing is that in both the tropical and the sidereal horoscopes the Moon is in Virgo, not in Libra (tropical horoscope, page 212; sidereal horoscope, page 213).

Did Elisabeth Vreede make a computational error in casting the horoscope? If this were the case, it would show that Steiner took the horoscope as it was without viewing it clairvoyantly. Otherwise he would have discovered this error. This is a very important point as it relativizes the significance of the fact that it was a tropical horoscope for which Rudolf Steiner gave this interpretation. Moreover, his interpretation, in so far as it is primarily concerned with the relationships between the planets, would have been the same had it been a sidereal horoscope that he was looking at. The only mention of a zodiacal background—Moon in Libra—turns out to be erroneous since the Moon was in Virgo in both the tropical and sidereal horoscopes. Now we will look at Steiner's interpretation of the second horoscope: "Let us turn to the horoscope of the younger child. Again, here are Venus and Uranus and Mars near together,

Birth of Older Albino girl - Geocentric
At Jena, Latitude 50N56', Longitude 11E35'
Date: Monday, 6/DEC/1909, Gregorian
Time: 4: 0, Time Zone CET
Sidereal Time 8:43:23, House System: Placidus
Zodiac: Tropical, Aspect set: Conjunction/Square/Opposition

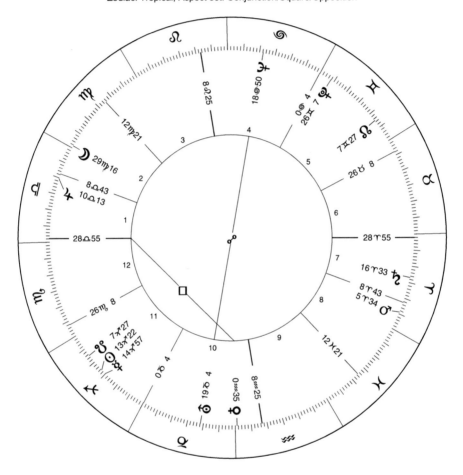

the three of them covering between them no more than this section
of the heavens."

In fact, the distance between Venus and Uranus is 45° and
between Venus and Mars it is 44°. The distance between Mars and
Uranus is 89°, or one quarter of the zodiac, which is what Rudolf
Steiner must have been referring to when he speaks of "the three of
them covering between them no more than this section of the heavens." Later he speaks of Mars, "which latter drags Uranus and Venus
along with it." Curiously he does not mention Mercury, which is

Birth of Older Albino girl - Geocentric
At Jena, Latitude 50N56', Longitude 11E35'
Date: Monday, 6/DEC/1909, Gregorian
Time: 4: 0, Time Zone CET
Sidereal Time 8:43:23, Vernal Point 6 ♓31' 2", House System: Placidus
Zodiac: Sidereal SVP, Aspect set: Conjunction/Square/Opposition

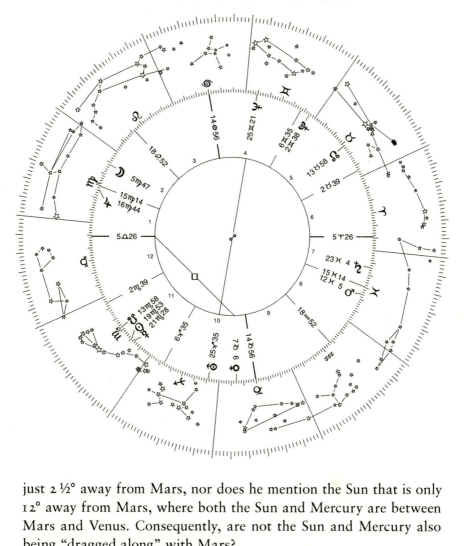

just 2½° away from Mars, nor does he mention the Sun that is only 12° away from Mars, where both the Sun and Mercury are between Mars and Venus. Consequently, are not the Sun and Mercury also being "dragged along" with Mars?

One thing that arises in raising this question is that perhaps Rudolf Steiner intuitively grasped the significance of Venus, Mars and Uranus in the case of albinism, with Mars "dominating" Venus and Uranus. Perhaps his intuitive grasp of this overrides whatever else leaps out when looking at these horoscopes—for example, the fact that Mars

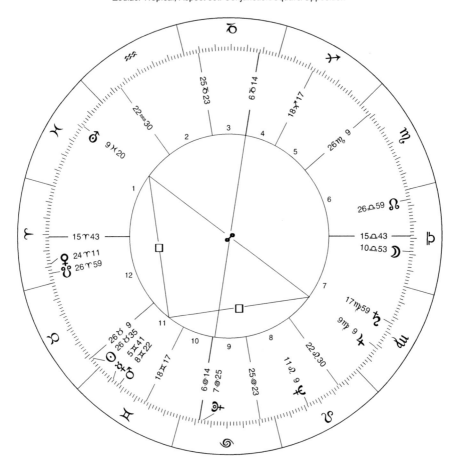

Birth of Younger Albino girl - Geocentric
At Jena, Latitude 50N56', Longitude 11E35'
Date: Wednesday, 18/MAY/1921, Gregorian
Time: 3: 0, Time Zone CET
Sidereal Time 18:27:12, House System: Placidus
Zodiac: Tropical, Aspect set: Conjunction/Square/Opposition

and Mercury are in close conjunction in the second horoscope, or that
Mars and Jupiter are in opposition in the first horoscope.

Evidently there was another component to this intuitive grasp if
our hypothesis is correct. We can look at the opposition of the Moon
to Mars with the Moon being in Libra. So holding open this hypothesis let's consider the further interpretation of the second horoscope.

Rudolf Steiner continued: "In this second horoscope, Mars, Venus
and Uranus are in close proximity, exactly as before; but when we
examine more nearly the position of Mars, we find it is not, as before,

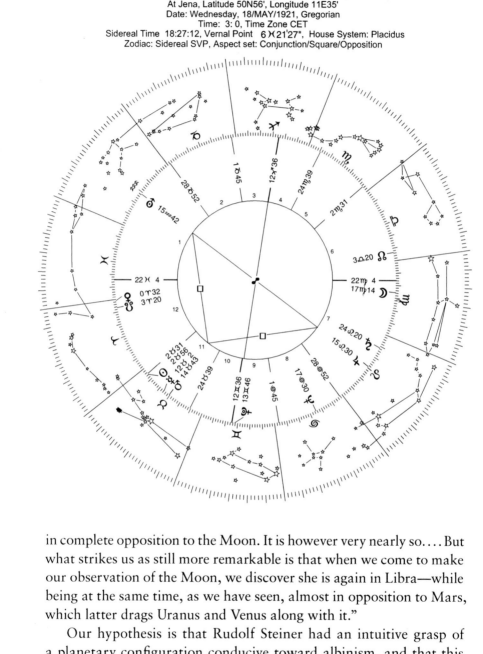

Birth of Younger Albino girl - Geocentric
At Jena, Latitude 50N56', Longitude 11E35'
Date: Wednesday, 18/MAY/1921, Gregorian
Time: 3: 0, Time Zone CET
Sidereal Time 18:27:12, Vernal Point 6℃21'27", House System: Placidus
Zodiac: Sidereal SVP, Aspect set: Conjunction/Square/Opposition

in complete opposition to the Moon. It is however very nearly so.... But what strikes us as still more remarkable is that when we come to make our observation of the Moon, we discover she is again in Libra—while being at the same time, as we have seen, almost in opposition to Mars, which latter drags Uranus and Venus along with it."

Our hypothesis is that Rudolf Steiner had an intuitive grasp of a planetary configuration conducive toward albinism, and that this planetary configuration comprised, "Mars, Venus and Uranus in close proximity" with Mars in opposition to the Moon in Libra. If our hypothesis is correct, this is what he saw inwardly coloring the reality of his perception of the two horoscopes. For, in the second horoscope, while the Moon is to be seen in tropical Libra, it is not in opposition to Mars. Rather, it is in trine to Mars since the angle between the Moon and Mars is 122½°. (Note that 120° is an exact trine, and 180° an exact opposition.) And in neither of the horoscopes are Mars, Venus and Uranus in close proximity to one another. Really close proximity (0° separation) would signify an exact conjunction, and the normal orb of distance allowed for a conjunction is 8° or 10° (or at the most 15°). Astrologically speaking, one would not use the expression "close proximity" for two planets 76½° or 89° separation, and one would not say "there is an approximation to opposition" in the case of a trine aspect.

Thus, endeavoring to understand Rudolf Steiner's interpretation of these two horoscopes, it would seem fairly irrelevant that they were tropical horoscopes. If the above hypothesis is correct, he took the horoscopes in his hands and had an intuitive grasp of an ideal (not really existing) configuration, the projection of which he saw inwardly while looking at the two horoscopes. This intuitive grasp enabled him—out of his genius—to provide an extraordinary therapy for the two sisters suffering from albinism. Rudolf Steiner worked in this case in the sense of medical astrology—his concern being to arrive at a therapy based on his diagnosis from the horoscopes. So it would seem that his intuitive grasp of the horoscopes was not dependent on their being tropical horoscopes. Indeed, the diagnosis may have been considerably enhanced had he had the sidereal horoscopes in his hands. Unfortunately we do not know this or even what he would have said to the tropical/sidereal zodiac question.

MERCURY IN THE BALANCE

Another statement by Rudolf Steiner much quoted in favor of the tropical zodiac as a spiritual reality is the following, which he wrote on the document placed in the Foundation Stone of the first Goetheanum in Dornach, Switzerland:

> Laid by the "Johannes-Bau-Verein" ... on the twentieth day of the month of September 1880 years after the Mystery of Golgotha,

that is, 1913 since the Birth of Christ, when Mercury as evening star stood in the Balance [Libra].[26]

Looking at the horoscope, cast for September 20, 1913 at 6:30 p.m. Central European Time (following page), at the laying of the Foundation Stone of the building known as the "first Goetheanum," we see that Mercury was setting in the West at that moment. Since Mercury was "ahead" of the Sun in the zodiac, it was the "evening star," whereas Venus, which was "behind" the Sun in the zodiac, was the "morning star" and would have been visible in the sky before sunrise, weather permitting. Mercury, however, was certainly not visible as evening star since it was too close—only 3 ½° from the Sun.

In the sidereal zodiac we see that Mercury was located at 7° Virgo, whereas in the tropical zodiac it was at 0½° Libra, in conjunction with the autumnal point at 0° Libra. (The autumnal point, diametrically opposite the vernal point at 0° tropical Aries, denotes the location of the Sun at the time of the autumn equinox. Since the vernal point in 1913 was at 6½° Pisces, the autumnal point was opposite at 6½° Virgo in the sidereal zodiac.) Here it is interesting to consider the following remarks made in a debate between two people in England concerning this location of Mercury in conjunction with the point of the autumn equinox:

> Mercury stood in the sign of the Scales [Libra], in the tropical zodiac of the astrologers, and not in the astronomical constellation. It appears that on this important occasion the position of Mercury in tropical [astrological] terms was more significant than in astronomical or sidereal terms.[27]

In response to this comment by John Salter, Margaret Jonas writes:

> With reference to John Salter's comments on Rudolf Steiner's use of the "tropical" zodiac at the laying of the Foundation Stone of the first Goetheanum, when he said that Mercury stood in the sign of the Scales, the point is:... it is not so much that Mercury was "in Libra" but that it had reached the exact position in the zodiac that the Sun would reach at the autumn

---

26 Vreede, *Astronomy and Spiritual Science*, p. 132.

27 Salter, "The Tropical Zodiac," *Anthroposophy Today*, vol. 7 (1989), p. 48.

Laying of Foundation Stone of 1st Goetheanum - Geocentric (Tropical/Sidereal)
At Dornach, Latitude 47N29', Longitude 7E37'
Date: Saturday, 20/SEP/1913, Gregorian
Time: 18:30, Time Zone CET
Sidereal Time 17:56:27, Vernal Point 0♈ 0' 0", House System: Placidus
Zodiac: Sidereal SVP, Aspect set: Conjunction/Square/Opposition

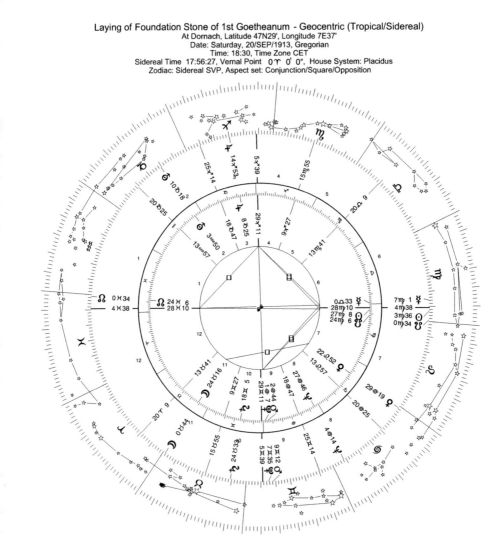

Inner circle: tropical; Outer circle: sidereal

equinox, when the Sun expresses a "state of balance" in that light and dark are of equal length.[28]

Since the autumnal point is in Virgo in the sidereal zodiac, Mercury was in Virgo but it was at the point of balance denoted by the autumn equinox. This, according to Margaret Jonas, is the signifi-

---

28 Margaret Jonas, "Mercury and the First Goetheanum," *Anthroposophy Today*, vol. 8 (1989), p. 49.

cance of Rudolf Steiner's expression "Mercury as evening star stood in the Balance." This statement by Steiner cannot be interpreted as an endorsement of the tropical zodiac, but it can be taken as an indication of the significance of the four points: vernal point, summer solstice point, autumnal point, and winter solstice point. Thus these four points, whose present locations in the sidereal zodiac are 5° Pisces, 5° Gemini, 5° Virgo, and 5° Sagittarius are of special significance. They represent "turning points" (summer and winter solstices) or "points of balance" (spring and autumnal equinoxes) on the path of the Sun as it spirals through the galaxy with the whole solar system.

Although 5° Virgo is the present autumnal turning point or point of balance on the path of the Sun, it was closer to 6⅓° Virgo when Rudolf Steiner looked at the horoscopes of the two children with albinism. Steiner spoke of the Moon being "in the Balance" for the first horoscope, while in fact the Moon was in Virgo in both the tropical and sidereal horoscopes. Yet it was close to the "balance point" (autumnal point) since it was at 5 ¾° Virgo, very close to 6⅓° Virgo. Here the expression "in the Balance" reminds us of his statement, "Mercury as evening star stood in the Balance," applying to when Mercury was at the autumnal point. So even though the Moon was actually in Virgo in the first horoscope, Rudolf Steiner again used the expression "in the Balance" since the Moon was in conjunction, to within 1°, with the autumnal point.

Rudolf Steiner used the same expression—"Moon in the Balance"—with regard to the second child's horoscope. Looking at this horoscope, the Moon was at 17° Virgo in the sidereal horoscope and at 11° Libra, i.e. 11° from the autumnal point, in the tropical horoscope. This could be regarded as a "loose conjunction" with the autumnal point. In this case, even though the Moon was actually in Virgo in the sidereal zodiac, the expression "Moon in the Balance" could again be justified in view of the Moon's proximity to the autumnal point.

FURTHER INDICATIONS REGARDING THE SIDEREAL ZODIAC

There are further indications by Rudolf Steiner that draw attention to the validity of the sidereal zodiac. One is from his lectures on bees:

> You know that on March 23, the Sun enters the Sign of the Fishes. I have told you before that the spring equinox is now in

this Sign of the Fishes. The Sun remains in this Sign till April 20, then it passes on into the Sign of the Ram.... Thus, it is quite different if the Sun sends its rays to the earth at the beginning of May, or at the end of May. In the beginning of May the full force of the Ram is working; by the end of the month the Sun is already in the Sign of the Bull.[29]

Here it is a question of whether Rudolf Steiner meant to say March 21, rather than March 23. In conventional Western tropical astrology the Sun enters the sign of Aries on March 21. Rudolf Steiner remarks that he had already pointed out before that "the spring equinox is now in this sign of the Fishes." For example, in the Introduction to his *Calendar 1912–1913*, he writes:

Just as one can express the simple experience, "I experience the darkness of night yielding to the light" through the words "The Sun rises," so the complex soul experience "I feel the earth—appropriate to spring—preparing for new growth and the power of the Sun increasing" may be expressed by saying, "The rising Sun may be seen in the direction of Pisces."[30]

When Rudolf Steiner says "The rising Sun [in springtime] is seen in the direction of Pisces," he can be referring only to clairvoyant sight, since the position of the Sun against the background of the zodiacal constellations can be seen on only the rare occasion of a total solar eclipse. In other words, he is talking about a clairvoyant perception of the Sun in Pisces at the beginning of spring. This perception ("soul experience") changes from month to month as the Sun progresses through the constellations/signs of the sidereal zodiac. Rudolf Steiner indicates this point in the following, where he uses the expressions "zodiacal constellations" and "signs of the zodiac" interchangeably. This makes sense only in terms of the sidereal zodiac where the signs are 30° (equal length) zodiacal constellations:

The following calendar, in the flow of monthly images, demonstrates the fact that the gaze, as it turns to the rising Sun, simultaneously discovers a constellation—here expressed in a symbolic

---

29 Steiner, *Bees*, pp. 62–63.

30 Steiner, *Calendar 1912–1913*, p. 18.

image. In the course of the year, this relationship changes, so that all twelve zodiacal signs enter consideration.

The position of the Sun may be related to a zodiacal image for about a month. After the year has run its course, the same positions more or less repeat themselves. The designation "approximately" is justified, because as time moves forward, a shift occurs in the positions. Centuries ago, for example, one's gaze at the rising Sun in March fell on the constellation Aries, while at the present, during the same time period, it falls on Pisces. [31]

Steiner states clearly here that clairvoyant sight beholds the progression of the Sun through the constellations/signs of the sidereal zodiac during the course of the year. He also says that now, in our time, it is a decisive *soul experience* that the Sun in March at the beginning of spring is in the constellation (sidereal sign) of Pisces. In the earlier Age of Aries, it was a soul experience of the Sun in the constellation/sign of Aries.

Returning to the quote from Steiner's lecture on bees, we may note that there is a contradiction in his words unless he meant March 21 instead of March 23. The spring equinox takes place on March 20 or 21, and if—as he states—the spring equinox is now in the Sign of the Fishes, which is the sidereal sign of Pisces, this means that the Sun cannot be entering the sidereal sign of Pisces on March 23. In terms of the Babylonian sidereal zodiac, the Sun enters Pisces on March 15, and enters Aries on April 15. But when the vernal point passes into the sign of Aquarius in A.D. 2375, the date of the Sun's entry into the sidereal sign of Pisces will be five days later, on March 20, and similarly the entry into sidereal Aries will be five days later, on April 20. Therefore, we may assume that Rudolf Steiner's statement about the dates of the passage of the Sun through the signs of the sidereal zodiac was based on a projection to a time shortly after the start of the Aquarian Age. (Around A.D. 2600, when the vernal point will be at 28° Aquarius, the Sun will enter the sidereal sign of Pisces on March 23.) Since the vernal point at the present time is at 5° in the sign of Pisces, it still has 5° to travel to enter Aquarius in A.D. 2375, moving at a rate of 1° in seventy-two years. Moreover, since the Sun travels about 1° through the zodiacal signs each day, this means that currently it enters Aries five days earlier, that is, on April 15 and not on April 20. Likewise, the Sun

---

31 Steiner, *Calendar 1912–1913*, p. 18.

enters Pisces on March 15, not on March 20/21. In fact, the Sun enters
a new sidereal sign on approximately the fifteenth of each month (see
figure on page 7 for exact dates.) It seems clear that Rudolf Steiner had
this in mind when he referred to the period January 15 to February 15
in his *Agriculture Course,* this being (approximately) the period of the
Sun's passage through the sign of Capricorn:

> The mineral substances must emancipate themselves from what
> is working immediately above the surface of the Earth, if they
> wish to be exposed to the most distant cosmic forces. And in
> our cosmic age they can most easily do so—they can most eas-
> ily emancipate themselves from the Earth's immediate neighbor-
> hood and come under the influence of the most distant cosmic
> forces down inside the Earth—in the period between January
> 15 and February 15; in this winter season. The time will come
> when such things are recognized as exact indications. This is
> the season when the strongest formative forces of crystallization,
> the strongest forces of form, can be developed for the mineral
> substances within the Earth. It is in the middle of the winter.
> The interior of the Earth then has the property of being least
> dependent on itself—on its own mineral masses; it comes under
> the influence of the crystal-forming forces that are there in the
> wide spaces of the cosmos.[32]

Here Rudolf Steiner draws attention to the period January 15 to
February 15 saying that the time will come when this will be recognized as an *exact indication.* This time has now come with the rediscovery of the original sidereal zodiac, in which the Sun travels through
the sign of Capricorn during (approximately) this period. Saturn is the
ruling planet of Capricorn according to astrological tradition, and it
is also acknowledged to be the planet of crystallization. This indicates
that when the Sun is passing through the sign of Capricorn the "stron-
gest formative forces of crystallization" are at work within the Earth,
according to Rudolf Steiner. The point here is that only against the
background of the sidereal zodiac is it possible to grasp the meaning
of Rudolf Steiner's words. Recognizing this, it is evident that his clairvoyant observation of the Sun's passage through the zodiacal signs
exactly confirms the Babylonian sidereal zodiac!

---

32 Steiner, *Agriculture,* p. 33.

PLANTING BY THE MOON IN THE SIDEREAL SIGNS

If there are still doubts that when Rudolf Steiner was speaking of the signs of the zodiac he meant the *sidereal signs,* let us consider the following statement: "The sowing, the scattering of the seed, can be very much affected by the passage of the Moon through a zodiacal sign."[33] This statement is the foundation for the lunar calendar used in the biodynamic agricultural movement as a calendar for sowing and planting.

Briefly, the biodynamic agricultural movement arose in the 1920s as the pioneering organic farming movement of the twentieth century. It was based on Rudolf Steiner's indications in the *Agriculture Course.* The statement by Steiner on the effect on the plant world of the Moon's passage through the zodiacal signs led to research into the effect of the Moon's position at the time of sowing upon plant growth. Various researchers came to the conclusion, on the basis of empirical research, that it is the Moon's passage through the *zodiacal constellations* that has a significant impact upon the growth and quality of plants sown when the Moon is in a certain constellation. But because biodynamic farmers were not aware of the equal-division *signs* of the sidereal zodiac (recalling that Rudolf Steiner explicitly says, "the passage of the Moon through a *zodiacal sign*"), they used—and continue to use—a calendar based on the *unequal-division constellations* of the astronomical zodiac. Since there is a high degree of overlap between the equal-division sidereal signs and the unequal-division astronomical constellations, biodynamic farmers have generally achieved good results. Nevertheless, the research of Nick Kollerstrom and others shows that biodynamic farmers would achieve still better results if they were to use the signs of the sidereal zodiac, which would actually be in accordance with Rudolf Steiner's indication referred to above.

Nick Kollerstrom investigated various sets of research findings concerning planting by the Moon. He compared three options for the specification of the Moon's position at the time of planting: the tropical zodiac, the sidereal zodiac, and the astronomical zodiac. He found a *poor* correlation of plant growth with the Moon in the signs of the tropical zodiac, a *good* correlation in terms of the constellations of the astronomical zodiac, and an *excellent* correlation in terms of the signs of the sidereal zodiac. As he points out:

---

33 Steiner, *Bees*, p. 47.

Just as investigation of lunar influence on plants is a recent phenomenon, so also is the rediscovery of the sidereal zodiac, in the West. Traditional gardening manuals have used the tropical zodiac without question, largely because it was the only one known to them. With the steady accumulation of evidence supporting the sidereal zodiac framework, the practice of lunar planting can now be established on a firm foundation.... The present calendar is based on the sidereal zodiac as being the *correct and optimal reference* that does really work in an organic gardening setup.[34]

Gathering findings over several decades, Nick Kollerstrom's research findings confirm conclusively that Rudolf Steiner's reference to the significance of the Moon's passage through the *zodiacal signs* can refer only to the sidereal signs of the zodiac, and not to the tropical signs or unequal-division astronomical constellations. In fact, in the *Agricultural Course,* Rudolf Steiner is quite explicit in his interchangeable use of the words "zodiacal signs" and "constellations." This is exclusively the case with the *signs* of the sidereal zodiac, which are also *equal-division constellations*, and the following statements are relevant to this:

You must obtain this skin of the field mouse at a time when Venus is in the sign of Scorpio.... We need ideas that reckon with the surrounding sphere of the fixed stars, notably the fixed stars of the zodiac.... It is necessary to perform this operation when the Sun is in the sign of Taurus.... This, you see, is precisely the opposite of the constellation in which Venus must be.... The Sun is not really the same when in the course of a year or a day it shines onto the Earth from Taurus, or from Cancer, or the other constellations....

Question: Did you mean the astronomical Venus...?
Answer: Yes, what we call the "evening star."
Question: What "constellation of Venus with Scorpio?"
Answer: Wherever Venus is visible in the sky with the Scorpio constellation in the background.[35]

---

34 Kollerstrom, *Planting by the Moon, A Gardner's Calendar*, p. 51. This is a yearly calendar. (The quote is from the 1999 issue—emphasis by R.P.)

35 Steiner, *Agriculture Course*, pp. 113–115, 123.

To begin with, Rudolf Steiner spoke of Venus in the *sign* of Scorpio, and then he specified this in terms of the *constellation* of Scorpio. In other words, he is referring to the sidereal sign of Scorpio = equal-division constellation of Scorpio. The same applies to his remark about the Sun in the sign of Taurus. He then goes on to speak of the Sun shining from this or that *constellation,* and he also specifies the constellation of Scorpio as being opposite to the *sign* of Taurus. This is the case only when the Sun is in the sidereal sign of Taurus. One may only hope that these remarks, and the findings of Nick Kollerstrom, will be taken seriously by the agricultural movement with regard to the question of which zodiacal division is the optimal one in terms of the influence of the Moon upon plant growth.

At the end of this book is an announcement about the *Journal for Star Wisdom.* Readers of the *Journal for Star Wisdom* will know that on its monthly ephemeris pages the precise times of entry (ingress) of the Moon, Sun, and planets into the sidereal signs of the zodiac are given each month geocentrically, as well as heliocentrically (for the planets). The times of ingress of the Moon—approximately every 2½ days—into a new zodiacal sign are given in Greenwich Mean Time (GMT), which can be converted easily to any other time zone. Once the simple time conversion is made from GMT to one's local time zone, the results may be applied to planting a garden or crops, as indicated in appendix 4: "Planting by the Moon."

In addition to its application for biodynamic agriculture, the sidereal zodiac, as described in the course of this book, offers a solid foundation for the astrological revolution, for a new and conscious astrology based on empirical laws—astrology as a true science of reincarnation and karma.

APPENDIX 3

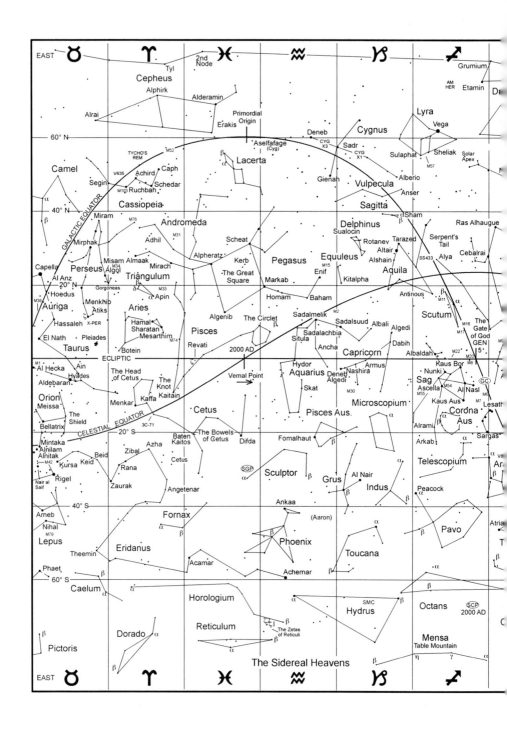

The Sidereal Heavens

MAP OF THE SIDEREAL ZODIAC

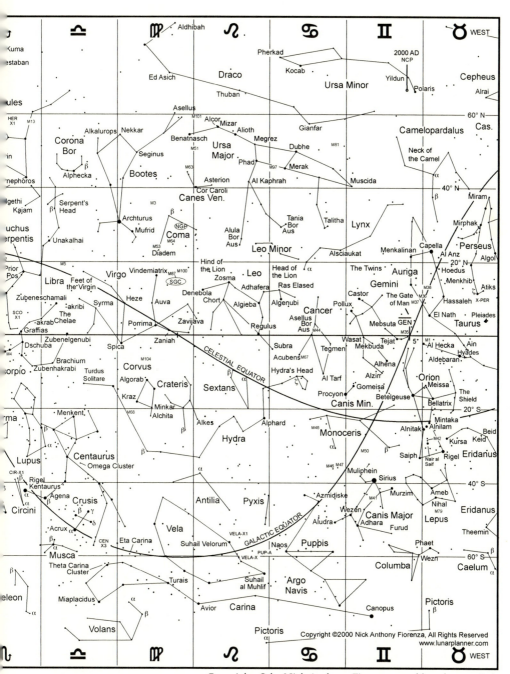

227

APPENDIX 4
PLANTING BY THE MOON

Although both the Sun and Moon powerfully influence plant life, the solar rhythm is too slow to use in planting schedules. On the other hand, agricultural practice frequently uses lunar calendars. Some planting calendars indicate the Moon's highest and lowest positions in the night sky, which correspond to the Sun's summer and winter solstice points—the Sun's highest position being at mid-summer and lowest at mid-winter.

With the lunar calendar, we can observe that the twelve lunar months trace the rhythm of the phases of the Moon against the background of the twelve constellations, with an additional month "intercalated" in years with thirteen lunar months. Each lunar month comprises four lunar weeks, corresponding to the Moon phases.

Rainfall and weather changes seem to correlate with the lunar weeks. In particular, new Moon and full Moon tend to precipitate rainfall, especially in the period of three to five days after the new or full Moon. Therefore, farmers often plan their planting schedules before the new or full Moon to take advantage of the anticipated rainfall.

The practice of biodynamic farming came about through the inspiration of Rudolf Steiner in 1924 to honor the spiritual dimension that brings wisdom to sowing crops.[1] His ideas have spawned a body of research over the years. For example, in observing the fourfold nature of plants, Maria Thun uses the knowledge that all plants can be classified into the four types: Root types (potatoes, carrots, turnips, and so on), leaf types (cabbages, lettuce), flower types (cauliflower, broccoli, etc.), and fruit–seed types (such as beans, peas, and tomatoes).

Günther Wachsmuth, a scientist who worked closely together with Rudolf Steiner, was the first to postulate that, since one of the four elements predominate in each of the signs of zodiac, the four types of plants might benefit from a planting schedule corresponding to their predominating element. Maria Thun tested this hypothesis with positive results. This table summarizes those relationships.

---

1   Steiner, *What is Biodynamics?*

Moon sign	Element	Best crops to plant
Taurus, Virgo, Capicorn	earth	root type
Cancer, Scorpio, Pisces	water	leaf type
Gemini, Libra, Aquarius	air	flower type
Aries, Leo, Sagittarius	fire	fruit–seed type

In 27⅓ days the Moon passes through each of the twelve constellations (sidereal signs) of the zodiac, spending a little over two days in each zodiacal division. Hence, the farmer who wisely waits for the planting of each type of plant until the Moon is in an appropriate part of the heavens can readily harness the influence exerted by the Moon. This method of planting by the Moon, according to the Moon's constellational background (as indicated in the table), has been popularized by Maria Thun, who produces a yearly calendar based on the Moon's passage through the constellations, indicating the best dates on which to sow each type of plants.[2]

Independent research by Lili Kolisko tested the traditional belief that leaf crops are best sown during the waxing Moon, in contrast to root crops, which are best sown under the waning Moon. She concluded that all vegetables grow best when planted shortly before or close to the full Moon.[3]

According to Maria Thun, even the Moon's nodes influence plant growth. She warns against sowing when the Moon is crossing its nodes, becaise the *"streamings from the cosmos are not helpful to plant life."*[4]

Finally, it is important to note the observation of the lunar calendar for successful planting. Extensive research by Nick Kollerstrom over the years reveals conclusively that the planting calendar responds most favorably to the sidereal month, which relates to the actual location of the Moon against the background of the stars, rather than the

---

2 Thun and Thun, *The North American Biodynamic Sowing and Planting Calendar.* See also the annual calendar *Stella Natura.*

3 Kolisko, *The Moon and the Growth of Plants,* p. 86.

4 In Straker, *Astrosophy,* p. 34.

location of the Moon indicated in the tropical calendar commonly used by astrologers.

It is important to remember that we can understand the lunar month as the interval from one new Moon to the next. This is the *synodic* month of about 29 ½ days. The division of the zodiac occupied by the Moon is quite independent of the Moon's phase. There are typically three ways to define zodiacal division:

1. the equal-division *tropical sign* used in contemporary astrology;
2. the unequal-division *constellation* used in astronomy;
3. the equal-division *sidereal sign* used in ancient star wisdom by the Babylonians, Egyptians, Greeks, and Romans, and today by Hindu (Vedic) astrology.

Nick Kollerstrom's research shows that the results of planting seeds by the Moon using the first means are poor, good in the second case, and excellent when using the equal-division sidereal zodiac.[5] The third means determines the *Moon sign* by the Moon's apparent background of fixed stars. There are twelve *sidereal signs* through which the Moon passes in approximately 27 ⅓ days, the sidereal month. One lunar sidereal year (a period of 354.86 days) includes twelve lunar sidereal months. As Kollerstrom's findings indicate, the best results in planting by the Moon are obtained in conjunction with the sidereal month, using the passage of the Moon through the twelve equal-division sidereal signs. We use precisely this division into twelve equal 30° sidereal signs (the foundation of the astrological revolution) in the yearly *Journal for Star Wisdom*, which one may therefore use to "plant by the Moon" as practiced in biodynamic agriculture.

The following example may sound complicated, but it is actually easy to use the ephemeris pages of the *Journal for Star Wisdom* to plant by the Moon by following the Moon's passage through each sidereal sign every 2⅓ days through the year.

As an example of applying the yearly *Journal for Star Wisdom* to plant by the Moon, we see from the April 2007 ephemeris page under "Ingresses" that the Moon entered Virgo April 1 at 5:16 a.m. At midnight, April 1 to 2, the Moon was located at 9° 15' Virgo.

---

5 Kollerstrom, *Planting by the Moon*, pp. 37–53.

Under "Aspects," we see that the full Moon (at about 17½° Virgo) took place at 17:14 (5:14 p.m.) April 2. All times are in Universal Time (UT), which is identical to GMT. Therefore, those in California, for example, must subtract eight hours from these times, which is the amount by which Pacific Standard Time (PST) is behind GMT. (It would be seven hours for Daylight Savings Time—see note on Time below).

Expressed in PST, this means that the Moon entered Virgo at 21:16 (9:16 p.m.) on March 31, that the Moon was located at 9° 15′ Virgo at 16:00 (4:00 p.m.) on April 1, and that the full Moon (at about 17½° Virgo) took place at 9:14 a.m. on April 2.

Looking again under "Ingresses," we see that at 18:07 (6:07 p.m. GMT)—corresponding to 10:07 a.m. PST—on April 3, the Moon left Virgo and entered Libra. For California, the Moon was in Virgo on April 1 and 2, and on the morning of April 3 until 10:07 a.m. Therefore, April 1 and 2 would be good days for planting root crops (potatoes, carrots, turnips), since Virgo is an earth sign. In California, as noted, the Moon entered Virgo at 9:16 p.m. March 31, but normally one would not choose to plant crops during the hours of darkness. Therefore, only April 1 and 2 are considered. We could also have considered the morning of April 3, until 10:07 a.m., but according to Kollerstrom's research, the maximum effect of planting by the Moon occurs when the Moon is located near the middle of the sidereal sign; therefore, April 1 and 2, 2007 were "prime times" for planting root crops.

According to Maria Thun, the phase of the Moon makes no difference. Only the Moon's sidereal background needs to be considered. However, according to the research of Lili Kolisko, especially because the Moon was full on April 2, this would have enhanced the growth of root crops planted at this time of the full Moon.

By applying a simple time conversion from GMT to our local time zone, we can easily use the ephemeris pages of the *Journal for Star Wisdom* to figure the best times for planting all kinds of crops according to the Moon's position in the sidereal signs of the zodiac.

As a resource for planting by the Moon, the *Journal for Star Wisdom* it is precise, since the exact times (hours and minutes) of the Moon's entry to a new sidereal sign are given throughout the whole year.

REGIONAL TIME ADJUSTMENTS: for those who live in North America or Hawaii, the conversion from London's Greenwich Mean Time (or Universal Time) is made by way of subtraction from GMT according to the local time zone:

TIME ZONE	STANDARD TIME	DAYLIGHT SAVING
Hawaii–Aleutian time	– 10 hours	– 9 hours
Alaska time	– 9 hours	– 8 hours
Pacific time	– 8 hours	– 7 hours
Mountain time	– 7 hours	– 6 hours
Central time	– 6 hours	– 5 hours
Eastern time	– 5 hours	– 4 hours
Atlantic time	– 4 hours	– 3 hours
Newfoundland time	– 3 ½ hours	– 2 ½ hours

Information gathered from the article entitled *"Lunar Calendar for Farmers and Gardeners"* by Robert Powell reported in the *Mercury Star Journal* (mid-summer 1977, vol. 3, no. 2). This appendix is excerpted from the chapter on the Moon in Lacquanna Paul and Robert Powell, *Cosmic Dances of the Planets*

BIBLIOGRAPHY

(Bibliographic data for cited articles
from periodicals are given in the relevant footnotes)

Allen, Richard Hinckley, *Star Names: Their Lore and Meaning* (New York: Dover Publications, 1963).

Andreev, Daniel, *The Rose of the World* (Great Barrington, MA: Lindisfarne Books, 1997).

Baigent, Michael, Richard Leigh, and Henry Lincoln, *The Holy Blood and the Holy Grail* (London: Corgi Books, 1983).

Besant, Annie, and Charles W. Leadbeater, *Lives of Alcyone* (2 vols.; Adyar, India: Theosophical Publishing House, 1924).

Blavatsky, H. P., *The Secret Doctrine: The Synthesis of Science, Religion, and Philosophy* (2 vols.; New York: Theosophical Publishing, 1888).

Brown, Dan, *The Da Vinci Code* (New York: Doubleday, 2003).

Bullinger, E. W., *The Witness of the Stars* (Grand Rapids, MI: Kregel Publications, 1967).

Campion, Nicholas, *An Introduction to the History of Astrology* (London: Institute for the Study of Cycles in World, 1982).

Cayce, Edgar, *14,306 Psychic Readings: Complete Edgar Cayce Readings* on CD-Rom (Virginia Beach: A.R.E. Press, 2003).

Culture and Cosmos: A Journal of the History of Astrology and Cultural Astronomy, Nicholas Campion, ed. (London: The Astrological Association, biannual).

Dorsan, Jacques, *The Clockwise House System* (Great Barrington, MA: Lindisfarne Books, 2011).

Dowling, Levi, *The Aquarian Gospel of Jesus the Christ: The Philosophic and Practical Basis of the Religion of the Aquarian Age of the World and of the Church Universal* (Camarillo, CA: DeVorss, 1982).

Eckert Willehad Paul, (ed., trans.), *Das Leben des heiligen Thomas von Aquino, erzählt von Wilhelm von Tocco* (Düsseldorf, 1965).

Evangelium Infantiae ("The Infant Gospel"), from volume I of the Codex Apocryphus Novi Testamenti edited by Ioannes Carolus Tbilo (Leipzig, 1832).

Gershom, Yonassan, *Beyond the Ashes: Cases of Reincarnation from the Holocaust* (Virginia Beach: A.R.E. Press, 1993).

Gleadow, Rupert, *Your Character in the Zodiac* (London: Dent and Sons, 1968).

Guinness, H. Grattan, *The Approaching End of the Age Viewed in the Light of History, Prophecy, and Science* (London: Hodder & Stoughton, 1878).

Gundel, Wilhelm and Hans Georg Gundel, *Astrologumena, die astrologische Literatur in der Antike und ihre Geschichte* (Wiesbaden: Sudhoffs Archiv, 1966).

Guthrie, Kenneth Sylvan (ed., trans.), *The Pythagorean Sourcebook and Library*, (Grand Rapids, MI: Phanes Press, 1987).

Hathaway, Michael R., *Complete Idiot's Guide to Past Life Regression* (New York: Penguin/Alpha Books, 2003).

Haug, Martin, *Essays on the Sacred Language, Writings, and Religion of the Parsis*, E. W. West, trans. (London: Trübner, 1878).

Hymers, John, *The Elements of the Theory of Astronomy* (Cambridge, UK: Deighton Bell, 1840).

Jung, C. G., *Aion: Researches into the Phenomenology of the Self* (Bollingen Series; Collected Works of C. G. Jung, Volume 9, Part II; Princeton, New Jersey: Princeton University Press, 1978).

———, *Flying Saucers: A Modern Myth of Things Seen in the Skies* (Princeton, NJ: Princeton University Press, 1991).

———, *Letters, Volume I, 1906–1950* (Princeton, NJ: Princeton University Press, 1992).

Kampherbeek, Jan, *Cirkels* (Amsterdam: Uitgeverij Schors, 1980).

Karlén, Barbro, *And the Wolves Howled: Fragments of Two Lifetimes* (London: Clairview Press, 2000).

Keller, Hans-Ulrich, *Kosmos Himmelsjahr 2000* (Stuttgart: Kosmos, 1999).

Kennedy, E. S., and David Pingree, *The Astrological History of Masha'allah* (Cambridge, MA: Harvard University Press, 1971).

King, Leonard William, trans., *The Seven Tablets of Creation: Or, the Babylonian and Assyrian Legends Concerning the Creation of the World and of Mankind* (London: Luzac, 1902).

Kirchner-Bockholt, Margarete, and Erich Kirchner-Bockholt, *Rudolf Steiner's Mission and Ita Wegman* (privately printed for members of the Anthroposophical Society; London: Rudolf Steiner Press, 1977).

Kolisko, Lili, *The Moon and the Growth of Plants* (London, 1938).

Kollerstrom, Nick, *Planting by the Moon: A Gardener's Calendar* (Totnes, UK: Prospect Books, 1998),

Le Cour, Paul, *L'ére de Verseau: Avènement de Ganimède,* (Paris: Atlantis, 1937).

Leo, Alan, *How to Judge a Nativity,* part II (London: L. N. Fowler, 1909).

Lewy, Hans, *Chaldaean Oracles and Theurgy: Mysticism, Magic, and Platonism in the Later Roman Empire* (Paris: Etudes augustiniennes, 1978).

MacLaine, Shirley, *Out on a Limb* (New York: Bantam Books, 1983).

Manilius, *Astronomica,* trans. G. P. Goold (Cambridge MA: Harvard University Press, 1977).

Maternus, Firmicus, *Mathesis* (Cumberland, MD: The Golden Hind Press, 2004).

Michelsen, Neil, *The American Sidereal Ephemeris,1976–2000* (San Diego: ACS, 1981).

———, *The American Sidereal Ephemeris, 2001–2025* (San Diego: ACS, 1981).

Neugebauer, Otto, and Richard A. Parker, *Egyptian Astronomical Texts,* volume III, Plates (Providence, RI: Brown University Press, 1969).

———, and H. P. van Hoesen, *Greek Horoscopes* (Philadelphia: The American Philosophical Society, 1959).

Novalis—Zeitschrift für spirituelles Denken (Schaffhausen, Switzerland: Novalis Verlag, monthly journal).

O'Callaghan, Joseph F., *The Learned King: The Reign of Alfonso X of Castile* (Philadelphia: University of Pennsylvania Press, 1993).

Paul, Lacquanna, and Robert Powell, *Cosmic Dances of the Planets* (San Rafael, CA: Sophia Foundation Press, 2007).

———, *Cosmic Dances of the Zodiac* (San Rafael, CA: Sophia Foundation Press, 2007).

Pingree, David, *The Thousands of Abu Ma'shar* (London: The Warburg Institute, 1968).

———, *The Yavanajataka of Sphujidhavaja*, 2 vols. (Cambridge, MA: Harvard University Press, 1978).

Powell, Robert, *The Christ Mystery: Reflections on the Second Coming* (Fair Oaks, CA: Rudolf Steiner College Press, 1999).

———, *Christian Hermetic Astrology: The Star of the Magi and the Life of Christ* (Great Barrington, MA: Steiner Books, 1998).

———, *Christian Star Calendar* (San Rafael, CA: Sophia Foundation Press, annual)— now published as *Journal for Star Wisdom* (Great Barrington, MA: Steiner-Books, yearly, from 2010).

———, *Chronicle of the Living Christ: The Life and Ministry of Jesus Christ: Foundations of Cosmic Christianity* (Great Barrington, MA: Steiner Books, 1996).

———, *Elijah Come Again: A Scientific Study of Reincarnation* (Great Barrington, MA: SteinerBooks, 2009).

———, *General Introduction to the Christian Star Calendar: A Key to Understanding* (Palo Alto: Sophia Foundation of North America, 2003).

———, *Hermetic Astrology*, volume I: Astrology and Reincarnation (San Rafael, CA: Sophia Foundation Press, 2007).

———, *Hermetic Astrology*, volume II: Astrological Biography (San Rafael, CA: Sophia Foundation Press, 2007).

———, *History of the Planets* (San Diego: ACS Publications, 1989).

———, *History of the Zodiac* (San Rafael, CA: Sophia Academic Press, 2007).

———(ed.), *Journal for Star Wisdom* (Great Barrington, MA: SteinerBooks, annual from 2010); see page 239 of this book.

———, and Kevin Dann, *Christ & the Maya Calendar: 2012 and the Coming of the Antichrist* (Gt. Barrington, MA: SteinerBooks, 2009).

———, and Peter Threadgold, *The Sidereal Zodiac* (Tempe, AZ: AFA Publications, 1985).

Ptolemy, Claudius, *Tetrabiblos*, F. E. Robbins, trans. (Cambridge, MA: Harvard University Press, 1940).

Rolleston, Frances, *Mazzaroth* (York Beach, ME: Weiser, 2001).

Samuel, Alan E., *Greek and Roman Chronology* (London: Taylor and Francis, 1972).

Schöffler, Heinz Herbert, *Rudolf Steiner und die Astrologie* (Dornach, Switzerland: Verlag am Goetheanum, 1996).

Seiss, Joseph A., *The Gospel in the Stars* (Grand Rapids, MI: Kregel, 1972).

Semkiw, Walter, *Return of the Revolutionaries: The Case for Reincarnation and Soul Groups Reunited* (Charlottesville, VA: Hampton Roads, 2003).

Smith, E. M., *The Zodia* (London: Elliot Stock, 1906).

Socrates and Sozomenus, *Ecclesiastical Histories*, Philip Schaff, trans. (New York: Christian Literature, 1886).

Steiner, Rudolf, *According to Matthew: The Gospel of Christ's Humanity* (Great Barrington, MA: SteinerBooks, 2003).

———, *Agriculture Course: The Birth of the Biodynamic Method* (London: Rudolf Steiner Press, 2005).

———, *Ancient Myths and the New Isis Mystery* (Great Barrington, MA: Anthroposophic Press, 1994).

———, *Background to the Gospel of St. Mark* (London: Rudolf Steiner Press, 1968).

———, *Bees* (Great Barrington, MA: Anthroposophic Press, 1998).

————, *Beiträge zur Rudolf Steiner Gesamtausgabe* ("Contributions to the Complete Works of Rudolf Steiner"; Dornach, Switzerland: Rudolf Steiner Verlag, annual publication).

————, *Calendar 1912–1913: Facsimile edition of the original book containing the calendar created by Rudolf Steiner for the year 1912–1913* (Great Barrington, MA: SteinerBooks, 2004).

————, *The Easter Festival in the Evolution of the Mysteries* (Hudson, NY: Anthroposophic Press, 1988).

————, *Education for Special Needs: The Curative Education Course* (London: Rudolf Steiner Press, 1998).

————, *Foundations of Esotericism* (London: Rudolf Steiner Press, 1983).

————, *From the History and Contents of the First Section of the Esoteric School 1904–1914: Letters, Documents, and Lectures* (Great Barrington, MA: SteinerBooks, 2010).

————, *The Karma of Untruthfulness: Secret Societies, the Media, and Preparations for the Great War*, vol. 2 (London: Rudolf Steiner Press, 2005).

————, *Karmic Relationships: Esoteric Studies*, vols. 1–8 (London: Rudolf Steiner Press, 1953–1972).

————, *Life between Death and Rebirth* (Great Barrington, MA: Anthroposophic Press, 1975).

————, *Man in the Light of Occultism, Theosophy, and Philosophy* (London: Rudolf Steiner Press, 1964).

————, *Materialism and the Task of Anthroposophy* (Hudson, NY; Anthroposophic Press, 1987).

————, *Mystery of the Universe: The Human Being, Model of Creation* (London: Rudolf Steiner Press, 2001).

————, *Occult History: Historical Personalities and Events in the Light of Spiritual Science* (London: Rudolf Steiner Press, 1982).

————, *The Occult Movement in the Nineteenth Century* (London: Rudolf Steiner Press, 1973).

————, *An Outline of Esoteric Science* (Great Barrington, MA: Anthroposophic Press, 1997).

————, *The Principle of Spiritual Economy: In Connection with Questions of Reincarnation* (Great Barrington, MA: Anthroposophic Press, 1986).

————, *The Reappearance of Christ in the Etheric: A Collection of Lectures on the Second Coming of Christ* (Great Barrington, MA: SteinerBooks, 2003).

————, *The Spiritual Beings in the Heavenly Bodies and in the Kingdoms of Nature* (Great Barrington, MA: Anthroposophic Press, 1992).

————, *Spiritual Guidance of the Individual and Humanity* (Great Barrington, MA: Anthroposophic Press, 1992).

————, *The Spiritual Hierarchies and the Physical World: Zodiac, Planets & Cosmos* (Great Barrington, MA: SteinerBooks, 2008).

————, *Spiritualism, Madame Blavatsky, and Theosophy: An Eyewitness Account of Occult History* (Great Barrington, MA: SteinerBooks, 2002).

————, *Verses & Meditations* (London: Rudolf Steiner Press, 2005).

————, *What Is Biodynamics? A Way to Heal and Revitalize the Earth* (Great Barrington, MA: SteinerBooks, 2005).

———, *World of the Senses and World of the Spirit* (North Vancouver, BC: Steiner Book Centre, 1979).

Straker, Hazel, *Astrosophy: Introduction to a Quest for a New Star Wisdom* (Weobley, UK: Anastasi, 2000).

Sucher, Willi, *Cosmic Christianity & The Changing Countenance of Cosmology: An Introduction to Astrosophy: A New Wisdom of the Stars* (Great Barrington, MA: SteinerBooks, 1993).

Surya-Siddhanta: A Text-Book of Hindu Astronomy, E. Burgess, trans. (New Haven, CN: American Oriental Society, 1860, 2005).

Sutphen, Richard, *You Were Born Again to Be Together: Documented Cases of Reincarnation that Prove Love Is Immortal* (New York: Simon & Schuster, 1976).

Taeger, Hans-Hinrich, *Internationales Horoskope-Lexikon*, vols. 1–4 (Freiburg, Germany: Verlag Hermann Bauer, 1991, 1992, 1992, 1998).

Tester, Jim, *A History of Western Astrology* (Suffolk, UK: Boydell Press, 1987).

Thacker Shelby, and José Escobar, trans., *Chronicle of Alfonso X* (Lexington, KY: University Press of Kentucky, 2002).

Thun, Maria and Matthias K. Thun, *The North American Biodynamic Sowing and Planting Calendar* (Edinburgh: Floris Books, annual).

Tidball, Charles, and Robert Powell, *Jesus, Lazarus, and the Messiah: Unveiling Three Christian Mysteries* (Great Barrington, MA: SteinerBooks, 2005).

Tomberg, Valentin, *Christ and Sophia: Anthroposophic Meditations on the Old Testament, New Testament, and Apocalypse* (Great Barrington, MA: SteinerBooks, 2006).

Tradowsky, Peter, *Kaspar Hauser: The Struggle for the Spirit* (London: Temple Lodge, 1997).

Tresemer, David, and Robert Schiappacasse, *Star Wisdom & Rudolf Steiner: A Life Seen through the Oracle of the Solar Cross* (Great Barrington, MA: SteinerBooks, 2007).

van der Waerden, B. L., *Science Awakening*, 2 vols., Arnold Dresden, trans. (New York, Oxford University Press, 1961).

Vetter, Suso, *Das Geburtshoroskop der Welt: Ägyptische Geburstskonstellation der Welt und die Kulturepochen* ("The Birth Horoscope of the World: The Egyptian Birth Constellation of the World and the Cultural Epochs") (Dornach, Switzerland: Verlag am Goetheanum, 1993).

Voltmer, Ulrike, *Wie frei ist der Mensch? Über Möglichkeiten und Grenzen der Astrologie* (Stuttgart: Verlag Urachhaus, 1999).

von Eschenbach, Wolfram, *Parzival*, H. Mustard and C. Passage, trans. (New York: Vintage, 1961).

Vreede, Elisabeth, *Astronomy and Spiritual Science: The Astronomical Letters of Elizabeth Vreede* (Great Barrington, MA: SteinerBooks, 2001).

Wachsmuth, Günther, *Kosmische Aspekte von Geburt und Tod: Beiträge zur Karma-Forschung* ("Cosmic Aspects of Birth and Death: Contributions to Karma Research"; Dornach, Switzerland: Verlag am Goetheanum, 1990).

Weidner, Ernst, *Gestirn-Darstellungen auf babylonischen Tontafeln* (Vienna, 1967).

West, Edward William, ed. *The Book of the Mainyo-i-khard: the Pazand and Sanskrit Texts, as Arranged by Neriosengh Dhaval in the Fifteenth Century* (London: Trübner, 1871).

Wildfeuer, Sherry (ed.), *Stella Natura: Working with Cosmic Rhythms: Inspiration & Practical Advice for Home Gardeners & Professional Growers* (Kimberton Hills, PA: Camphill Village Kimberton Hills, annual).

Wüstenfeld, Ferdinand, *Vergleichungstabellen zur muslimischen und iranischen Zeitrechnung* (Wiesbaden, 1961).

Zend Avesta II (Sacred Books of the East, vol. 23), James Darmesteter, trans. (London, 1883).

COMPUTER PROGRAM

Astrofire was designed by Peter Treadgold and is distributed by the Sophia Foundation of North America, San Francisco, California. *Astrofire* has a comprehensive research module for data storage and comparison charts, a star catalog with more than 4,000 stars, and a database of birth and death charts of historical personalities. It is capable of printing out geocentric and heliocentric/hermetic sidereal charts and ephemerides throughout history. With this program:

- compute birth charts in a large variety of systems (tropical, sidereal, geocentric, heliocentric, hermetic);
- calculate conception charts using the hermetic rule, in turn applying it for correction of the birth time;
- produce charts for the period between conception and birth;
- print out an "astrological biography" for the whole of life with the geocentric and heliocentric planetary systems;
- work with the sidereal zodiac according to the definition of your choice (Babylonian sidereal, Indian sidereal, unequal-division astronomical, etc.);
- work with planetary aspects with orbs of your choice.

The software includes eight house systems and a variety of chart formats, as well as an ephemeris program with search function. *Astrofire* runs on Microsoft (Windows 2000, XP, Vista, or Windows 7). Retail price: $285.00 USD (upgrade $175). To purchase *Astrofire*, email sophia@sophiafoundation.org. You may also contact by regular mail:

Sophia Foundation of North America
525 Gough St #103
San Francisco, CA 94102
Phone: (415) 522-1150.

JOURNAL FOR STAR WISDOM 2011
EDITOR AND AUTHOR ROBERT POWELL

Contributors: Daniel Andreev, William R. Bento, Kevin Dann,
Wain Farrants, Brian Gray, Claudia McLaren Lainson,
Sally Nurney, and David Tresemer

The *Journal for Star Wisdom 2011* includes articles of interest concerning star wisdom (Astrosophy), as well as a guide to the correspondences between stellar configurations during the life of Christ and those of today. This guide comprises a complete sidereal ephemeris and aspectarian, geocentric and heliocentric, for each day throughout the year. Published yearly, new editions are available beginning in November for the coming new year.

According to Rudolf Steiner, every step taken by Christ during his ministry between the baptism in the Jordan and the resurrection was in harmony with—and an expression of—the cosmos. The *Journal for Star Wisdom* is concerned with these heavenly correspondences during the life of Christ. It is intended to help provide a foundation for cosmic Christianity, the cosmic dimension of Christianity. It is this dimension that has been missing from Christianity in its two-thousand-year history.

The 2011 *Journal for Star Wisdom* focuses on the significant year of 2012, with 2011 as a stepping stone to this pivotal year in the history of humanity and the Earth. Apart from articles by David Tresemer and Robert Powell more directly concerning 2012, William Bento's article offers important perspectives on the theme of prophecy—its meaning and significance for modern human beings. Kevin Dann's article highlights the Christ rhythm of 33 ⅓ years in the biography of Henry David Thoreau and in the history of the United States. Brian Gray's article looks at the Moon Node rhythm of 18 years 7 months in Rudolf Steiner's life, especially in relation to Steiner's artistic activity, which, according to Brian's interpretation, is indicated in Steiner's horoscope of birth. David Tresemer's second article offers deep insights into the qualities of certain degrees of the zodiacal signs. Wain Farrants' article reviews the clockwise house system pioneered by Jacques Dorsan. The monthly commentaries by Claudia McLaren Lainson and David Tresemer are supported by monthly astronomical previews provided by Sally Nurney and offer profound insights into the meaning of stellar configurations during the year 2011.

PAPERBACK • STEINERBOOKS • ISBN: 9780880107280
$20.00 • 8¼ X 11 INCHES • 100 PAGES

ABOUT THE AUTHORS:

 Robert Powell, PhD is an internationally known lecturer, author, eurythmist, and movement therapist. He is founder of the Choreocosmos School of Cosmic and Sacred Dance, and cofounder of the Sophia Foundation of North America. He received his doctorate for his thesis on the History of the Zodiac, now available as a book from Sophia Academic Press, and he is on the adjunct faculty of Wisdom University. His published works include *The Sophia Teachings*, a six-tape series (Sounds True Recordings), as well as the following books: *Christ & the Maya Calendar* (2009, with Kevin Dann); *Elijah Come Again* (2009); *The Mystery, Biography, and Destiny of Mary Magdalene* (2008); *The Sophia Teachings* (2007); *The Sign of the Son of Man in the Heavens* (2007); *History of the Zodiac* (2006); *The Most Holy Trinosophia and the New Revelation of the Divine Feminine* (2000); *Chronicle of the Living Christ* (1996); *Divine Sophia, Holy Wisdom* (1995); *Christian Hermetic Astrology* (1991); as well as others. Robert is also editor of the annual *Journal for Star Wisdom* (formerly *Christian Star Calendar*) and other works published by Sophia Foundation Press. He translated the spiritual classic *Meditations on the Tarot* and co-translated Valentin Tomberg's *Lazarus, Come Forth!* He is coauthor (with Lacquanna Paul) of *Cosmic Dances of the Zodiac* and *Cosmic Dances of the Planets*. He teaches a gentle form of healing movement: the sacred dance of eurythmy (from the Greek, meaning "harmonious movement") as well as the cosmic dances of the planets and signs of the zodiac. Through the Sophia Grail Circle he facilitates sacred celebrations dedicated to the Divine Feminine. Robert offers workshops in Europe, Australia, and North America and, with Karen Rivers, cofounder of the Sophia Foundation, leads pilgrimages to the world's sacred sites (1996, Turkey; 1997, Holy Land; 1998, France; 2000, Britain; 2002, Italy; 2004, Greece; 2006, Egypt; 2008, India; 2010, Grand Canyon). Websites: www.sophiafoundation.org and www.astrogeographia.org.

Kevin Dann has taught history at SUNY Plattsburgh, the University of Vermont, and Rutgers University. His books include: *Christ & the Maya Calendar: 2012 & the Coming of the Antichrist* (2009, with Robert Powell); *Lewis Creek Lost and Found* (2001); *Across the Great Border Fault: The Naturalist Myth in America* (2000); and *Bright Colors Falsely Seen: Synaesthesia and the Search for Transcendental Knowledge* (1998). Visit Kevin's unique and informative website: beyondmainstreet.blogspot.com.

Breinigsville, PA USA
04 November 2010
248682BV00003BA/1/P

9 781584 200833